The Survival Resource Book

Edited by
M. A. Henderson

ST. MARTIN'S PRESS
NEW YORK

Contents

The Ultimate Survivalist: The True Story of Wild Bill Moreland

3
City Survival

The Ten Most Dangerous Areas of The United States in a Nuclear Attack

Urban Survival

4
Building & Alternative Energy

Preparing the Survival Home: How to Remodel a Home for Self-sufficiency

5
Survival Vehicles

Survival Vehicles

6
The Retreat

The Ten Safest Areas of the United States in a Nuclear Attack

Survival Guns

Introduction

Robert Himber

Fingers intertwined, the gentle fiftyish couple reclined easily in their stormbound, late model sedan. The exhausted state trooper waded through a snowdrift that engulfed the car. He asked a quick question as he gently squeezed the woman's shoulder. It was like granite. The people had frozen to death hours ago. Later, the car's fuel tank was found to be one-quarter full.

Similar stories have been repeated all too often—stories of panicked people drowning in three or four feet of water, tales of experienced winter campers succumbing to hypothermia (exposure) and perishing with packs containing food and stoves, and incidents of light-plane pilots leaving survival kits in their wrecked planes and attempting to walk out to safety. But rather than dwell on this needless waste of human life, let us explore alternatives to a passive or premature death.

Throughout this book, you will learn invaluable tips and techniques for survival in environments ranging from urban to wilderness. Books will be suggested, and a wide range of survival equipment will be discussed. This information is essential to a survivalist, lest he become a victim through ignorance.

A thorough knowledge of survival methods for varying terrain, climate, and socio-economic conditions affords the possessor well-earned self-confidence. Whether survival is only a mild interest or is mandatory because of one's occupation or locale, this book will be illuminating. However, if you think that this or any other publication will fully prepare you for all contingencies, you are mistaken. Just as amassing vast quantities of knowledge will not necessarily lead to wisdom, neither will compiling survival information necessarily make one a survivor. Other factors equal or surpass knowledge in importance.

Our materialistically oriented culture often misleads us. We may infer that one who owns hundreds of modern firearms is a superb shot, or that the owner of a herd of thoroughbreds is a fine rider. But acquisition does not mean mastery. Just as important is the fact that while a person is usually a fine swimmer, under stress that same person might drown. Regardless of the survival tools that one has stored away, two attributes cannot be learned or purchased—mental and physical toughness.

Mental toughness is usually formed during adolescence. It can be strengthened through rigorous conditioning and life experiences, or it can be weakened by self-indulgence and a decadent lifestyle. The choice is yours to make. If you have triumphed in a life-threatening situation, you know the power of the will to live. It, like love, is difficult to explain unless it has been experienced.

The book *Alive* by Piers Paul Read comes close to communicating the power of the will to live. In this fascinating account, a planeload of soccer players crashes high in the Andes of South America. Routine searches fail to reveal the wreckage, and the crash survivors, with no hope of rescue and with only those items on board, maintain the best possible existence. Through ingenuity, organization, and strong religious conviction, they attend to the injured, make clothes, construct shelters, survive an avalanche, and finally walk out of some of the most rugged mountains in the world. But the thrust of this modern epic is that these people had no formal survival skills and no survival equipment. Even if they had had both, their story would be only slightly less compelling. The lesson is that they carried with them all that was necessary to save their lives—mental and physical toughness.

Opposite: Photo by Devon Christensen

Living on the eastern slope of the Rocky Mountains, I encounter numerous so-called survivalists. They own the latest and most sophisticated gear: cross-country skis, mountaineering and technical rock-climbing hardware, avalanche beacons, rescue strobes, expensive weaponry, and other gear. Yet some of them are not fit enough to run around their homes. What good are the fruits of technology if the owner is too weak to carry them? And what good is a survival cache if you are not likely to be near it when the balloon goes up? ("When" was chosen over "if.")

The Walter Mittys of the world will relate myriad survival scenarios, all of which share a common theme. That is, Walter will always be in perfect health, well fed, in fine weather, on familiar turf, carrying a pack (or, more likely, driving a van) stocked with everything but the opposite sex. Yet logic dictates that survival situations occur by happenstance. Otherwise they would not be true survival conditions. Thus, even a slight dependence on equipment or on others may put you at a psychological disadvantage because you may be that much more off balance when encountering a novel situation. Factual accounts demonstrate that most survivors have only the clothes on their back, if that. Therefore, mind and body should be your best maintained implements.

Make no mistake—the fact that you can run or swim a given distance does not necessarily mean that you are mentally and physically tough. Do not confuse stamina with determination. It is the ability to continue after exceeding your limits that determines toughness. Many people go through life not knowing their limits, and that is a tragedy.

Another important facet of survival is avoidance. As a pilot and friend once told me, "I don't care how good a bush pilot you are, the weather will ultimately win. It's learning to recognize a bad situation in advance that's important, not being savvy enough to fly out of it." And that cannot be overstressed. Avoiding a life-threatening situation is always preferable to surviving it.

I began this introduction with an incident describing submission to circumstances. I will end it with a happier case history. It is the story of two friends of mine who did their best when fate dealt them a potentially losing hand.

Gary Neptune smiles a lot. He doesn't look his thirty-four years. Born in Tulsa, Oklahoma, and raised all over the world, Gary has been rock climbing since he graduated from high school. His wife, Ronnie (Veronica Dempsey at the time), also shatters the mid-thirties stereotype. At thirty-seven, she has been an Outward Bound instructor in Colorado and is an accomplished climber and runner.

They and a couple of friends, Mike Munger and Scott Johnston, decided to climb the 'Y' couloir (ice gully) on Mount Ypsilon in Rocky Mountain National Park.

Mid-November of 1976 was about average for Colorado. It was cool but not cold. The four felt ready for the next day's climb after having spent the night about five miles from Horseshoe Park trail head. They had camped without a tent at about 10,500 feet and had noticed that there was not much snow.

After breakfast they broke camp and started trudging toward their goal at 8 A.M. By 9 A.M. they had reached the base of the climb. They roped up and began assailing the 1,000 feet of ice. By 11 A.M. they had reached the halfway point. But things did not feel right. Nobody was climbing up to par, so they decided to abort. They began descending and had moved only a few hundred feet when, out of the corner of her eye, Ronnie saw snow moving. She did not even have time to react. She recalls, "I was being thrown like a rag doll down rocks and ice."

Gary remembered, "I heard a muted thump and knew instantly that it was an avalanche. I saw sky, snow, rocks, all spinning. Then, as I clawed at the rocks, I felt the rope to Ronnie tighten, and I knew I was going to be yanked. I was jerked out of the snow, flew about fifty feet, and landed on my feet on a ledge about the size of a sofa. I heard my leg snap when I hit. I stood up and put in an anchor [a metal wedge for securing ropes] and tried to pull the rope up to tie in. But there was no slack. I looked over the edge, and the rope hung free to the bergschrund [crevasse] 130 feet below.

"I called for Ronnie and after a few tries got an answer. I asked if she was okay, and she answered, 'I don't know.' Then I called to Mike and Scott and told them I needed another rope to get to Ronnie. Mike went down to Ronnie. I went down on another rope and saw that the crampon [two rows of points strapped to a boot for climbing ice] on my good foot was dangling. The one on my broken foot had the frame and four prongs bent.

"We reached Ronnie and talked with her. She was in shock and was disoriented. Her back hurt. I decided to send Mike and Scott back for help, while I stayed with Ronnie. The three of us moved Ronnie very carefully onto a pad and traversed in the bergschrund about twenty feet. I kept the sleeping bags and other warm gear for us, and we bivouacked on our sides, face-to-face, for twenty-four hours on the ice. Water splashed us, but we reassured each other."

Ronnie had some bad moments. She related, "I thought, what if nobody comes? But Gary was there. He was the perfect person to be with—no whining, no complaining, no negativity, but also no pretending."

The couple barely slept. The sun cheered their spirits, but twenty-four hours seemed an eternity in those conditions. Gary continued, "Then the rescue crew came bursting through the ice to us. They were all friends, and I felt elated. Then we were lowered in litters. They were very gentle with Ronnie, not so gentle with me. It took them six hours to get us down the steep snow and ice. We made it down to Ypsilon Lake to a helicopter."

Thus did two determined people survive an ordeal. Their key strength lay in their attitude—one of the few factors over which they had any control. Weather and terrain could not be changed, and the injuries they had sustained could not be adequately treated where they were. But they did have each other, and they kept up their spirits under disastrous conditions.

Ronnie had sustained a compression fracture to her twelfth thoracic vertebra and processes and had a broken rib. The two vertebrae above and the two below the fracture had to be fused. Gary had broken his ankle but was otherwise all right.

What are the Neptunes doing now? After giving his foot several months to heal, Gary entered a charity marathon and ran thirty miles. After retiring her brace, Ronnie recently finished her second marathon. They still climb and ski and share a deeper understanding of each other than most couples.

Vietnam veteran Robert Himber has instructed at Outward Bound School, Mount Kilimanjaro, Kenya, and has taught technical rock climbing for the University of Colorado at Denver. He has taught technical rock climbing to elements of the army's elite 10th Special Forces Group. He holds a master's degree from California State University, Humboldt, and has traveled throughout East Africa, Southeast Asia, India, and Europe. Himber plans to climb Ama Dablam, a Himalayan peak, in the near future. He is a bachelor and lives in Boulder, Colorado.

LABOR.
Mural Painting in the Congressional Library, Washington.
By C. S. Pearce.

Useful Arts

The Useful Arts is a generic term which embraces all the manifold products and processes relating to our daily sustenance, clothing, shelter, transport, and enjoyment; in short, our necessaries, conveniences, comforts, and luxuries. The evolution of the useful arts coincides with the march of civilization. The history of invention is the story of mankind. The beginnings of what is broadly styled "culture" are shrouded in the mists of antiquity; but relics have come down to us from the ages when written or graven records were unknown, and from these remains of primeval arts alone, we piece together our knowledge of their users and designers. By a comparative study of the arts of primitive races, we realize that the growth of these arts is subject to well defined laws of evolution. We perceive that a race either advances or retrogrades according to its power of invention, and its adaptability to environment. And this formative process is going on in our own time, so that we may read the past in the clearer light of the present.

Invention is stimulated by human needs, and the order and development of the useful arts would naturally be dependent on the primal wants of the race. Briefly stated the most important stimuli are: —

(1) Food, its nature and preparation.
(2) Needs of defense and offense.
(3) Shelter and clothing.
(4) Needs of transportation–communication.

I. Food. — Human needs may be divided into two classes: viz., those that act from within the individual, and those that affect him from without. Hunger is undoubtedly the chief of the subjective stimuli, and the need of providing and storing food must have given rise to the first inventions. Food getting would lead to the development of varied activities, and call into use all available manual aids. It would obviously lead to the multiplication and specialization of utensils, thus opening the way for advancement in the shaping arts and the evolution of culture. The food problem has ever been paramount even among the primitive races of the world. There are four great phases through which the civilized nations of the temperate zone have passed — hunting and fishing, sheep and cattle raising, agriculture, and industry; and these are but a succession of improvements in the means of raising food.

Whatsoever man's habitat, his food resources were restricted to the products of animal and vegetable life around him, and it is easy to understand that tools and weapons of some kind would soon become necessary. Man is described as a tool-making animal. Certain it is that this trait distinguishes him from the brutes. His first implements and weapons were made of wood, bone, or stone; each innovation marking a distinct era, and a higher order of intelligence.

The use of fire is another distinguishing feature of the human race. It is presumable that the preservation of fire produced by natural forces preceded its artificial production. Motion and chemical affinity are the two chief productive forces of fire. The former is employed in three different ways: (1) friction, as the rubbing together of two pieces of wood; (2) concussion, the striking together of two mineral substances; and (3) pneumatic compression. Producing fire by friction stimulated primitive inventiveness, and three distinct methods were applied: (a) simple rubbing, which usually takes the form of rubbing a small stick of hard wood against a log of soft wood until incandescent particles are produced; (b) the sawing method, which consists in sawing one piece of bamboo with the cutting edge of another piece until the heated sawdust sets fire to the tinder placed beneath; (c) the rotatory method, that is, twirling the end of a stick set upright upon a piece of wood until a hole is hollowed and the pulverized wood becomes incandescent.

Cooking. — The knowledge of fire begat methods of cooking. At first heated stones were used with which to cook meat and vegetables. Pottery, no doubt, followed close upon the discovery of fire, for there is no trace of unbaked pottery.

The evolution of the potter's wheel grew out of the three special methods of manufacturing primitive pottery: (a) modeling by hand; (b) molding to a bark or wicker mold which burns away afterwards in the process; (c) coiling in clay. With the knowledge of wheels and levers came the perfecting of the modern potter's wheel.

The grinding of wheat led to further development of the useful arts. The North American tribes used generally to combine the threshing, winnowing, and roasting in one operation. The grain after being triturated in the hands is thrown into a receptacle containing red-hot stones; these burn off the husk, and at the same time roast the grain. The crushing of a grain of wheat between two stones — possibly accidental — led to the discovery of flour. Three ways of preparing flour were developed; (a) pounding in a mortar; (b) trituration on a flat surface; (c) grinding by means of a mill turned by hand or other motive power.

Hunting and Fishing. — The inventive faculty was called into play to devise means for capturing birds, beasts, and fishes. Traps, snares, and pitfalls, as well as a diversity of weapons, were fashioned by primitive man.

II. Weapons. — In the early stages of culture manufactured objects were not confined to particular uses; the weapon of today frequently became the tool of tomorrow. Neither is the distinction between defensive and offensive weapons clearly marked, but most weapons would serve both purposes equally well.

Offensive weapons consist of those held firmly in the hand, such as the various kinds of clubs, and missile weapons. A sharp-ended club such as is met with in the New Hebrides developed into pointed weapons, of which the assagai,

--Spear throwers. *a.* Supposed to possess strong magic properties (South-East Australia). (After Howitt.) *b.* Decorated spear-thrower (Central Australia).

lance, spear, and fork are familiar examples. With the exception of the ax, cutting weapons are invariably piercing weapons as well. A knife, made either of flint, bronze, or iron, is the simplest example. From the knife is evolved the saber, while from the flint poignard is derived the steel sword. Missile weapons grew out of the necessity of throwing a stone, stick, or other object with greater accuracy and force than is possible with the human hand. The next step was to construct some apparatus for hurling the missiles. These contrivances may be divided into three classes according to the force employed: (a) muscular force of man, e.g., the *amentum* of antiquity, the throwing

stick, the sling; (b) elasticity of certain solid bodies, e.g., the various kinds of bows and arrows; (c) pressure of gases.

Defensive weapons embrace, for example, the various forms of shields. A shield is merely an exaggerated kind of club. The evolution of protective armor (breastplate, helmets, coats of mail, etc.) is easy to understand. The red Indians used breastplates of buffalo hide, while various materials, such as bone, ivory, wood, lacquer, and metals, are used either singly or compositely by different peoples to serve the purpose of protective armor.

III. Shelter and Clothing. — *The Hut.* — The prototype of the fixed habitation was doubtless derived from the screen made of branches and so arranged as to shelter the precious fire as well as to protect primitive man from the elements. The primeval hut was thus virtually an inclosed hearth.

The roof was strengthened and made more weather-proof by the use of straw, and so the thatched hut was evolved. The quadrangular huts developed into such dwellings as are met with in the French Congo and the coast of Guinea. Sometimes these quadrangular huts are erected on poles in marshy countries or where inundations are frequent. Such elevated houses may be seen to-day in Ceylon, while among the Indians of the Northwest, as well as in Madagascar and New Zealand, such houses may be seen raised on poles even when no water is near.

To give greater solidity to the walls of reed or twig, recourse was had to mud plastering. In dry countries it was discovered that lumps of clay formed suitable material for walls, and this led to the making of sun-dried bricks, which were in use among the ancient Babylonians and Egyptians, just as they are to-day in the Sudan and Mexico.

Movable Habitations. — So far we have traced the evolution of the fixed habitation, that is, any hut however primitive and frail it may be, which has not been built with a view to being moved. For such dwellings materials of vegetable origin were the first to be utilized. But for movable habitations materials derived from animals were more adapted for constant removal. When the prehistoric hunter stretched the skin of a wild beast on two or three poles and fell asleep

An Indian Village at the Roanoke Settlement.

their being despoiled by wild beasts. Primitive ladders, made by notching a tree trunk, were employed in order to gain access to these raised structures. Straw huts built on trees were made for emergencies as well as for observation, and these were the prototypes of the later watchtowers.

Heating and Lighting.—A fire in the center of the hut is the most primitive form of heating, the smoke issuing through the roof and doorway. The chimney is a comparatively recent idea, and dates only from the eleventh century. The mantelpiece over the hearth seems to have been a European invention, and really preceded the introduction of the real chimney.

Among the dwellers in tropical climes the cocoanut supplied all the requirements of a lamp. The divided shell formed the receptacle for the cocoanut oil, and the fibers covering the fruit provided the wick. Among primitive tribes resinous torches or large pine knots are burned for lighting purposes. Before the invention of the candle, torches were extensively used in Europe. It is possible that in western Europe a vessel improvised from the leaf of some suitable plant served as a model for the so-called Roman lamp with wicks.

Furniture.—Among primitive races domestic needs and conveniences are easily supplied. Some skins, straw, or dry grass to lie down upon is all the furniture required. Mats are a mark of a more advanced civilization: carpets, seats, and beds come still later. Chests and other receptacles for linen, plate, etc., are comparatively modern inventions.

Dress and Ornament.—Nudity is not necessarily synonymous with savagery. While many savage tribes know nothing of dress, there are others more advanced in civilization, like the Nyam-Nyams, who are ignorant of its uses. Dress is a question of climate and convention. In cold latitudes man was driven to protect himself from the cold and damp, but no such motive inspired the inhabitants of a hot country. Vanity alone was the primal cause.

It is a well established fact in ethnography that dress was preceded by ornament. Among primitive races the first ideas of ornament took the form of daubing some

pigment upon the body. Next ornaments were attached to the body itself, and, as there were no garments on which to hang the objects of adornment, the ear, nose, lips, or other member was pierced.

The second stage in the evolution of ornament was the attachment of objects to the body without mutilation. Strips of hide, plaited fibers, and the like were fastened around the neck, wrists, waist, and ankles. To these garlands, collars, belts, and bracelets, secondary ornaments were attached, such as shells, beads of bone or colored stone, teeth and claws of animals, feathers, and strips of fur. And so dress itself began to be evolved. The beast's skin hanging from the collar foreshadowed the mantle; the appendages of the girdle developed into the skirt.

At first skins of various animals were used in their natural state. In warm climates the next step was to strip off the hair, and soak the skin in water to which cinders or other alkaline matter had been added. A large variety of plants has been utilized to provide materials for garments.

The art of weaving was known in

Egyptian palanquin.

the earliest times, for specimens have been found in the pyramids of Egypt. Plaiting no doubt preceded actual weaving. In its most primitive form spinning consists simply in rolling some suitable fibers between the palms of the hands, or with one hand on the thigh. Dyeing is known to all peoples familiar with weaving. Prehistoric tribes severed their hides or other materials with flint knives, and sewed the pieces together after the manner of a shoemaker. They bored holes with a bone or horn awl, while the thread they used consisted of the sinews of some animal or of woven fiber, etc.

beneath it his device foreshadowed the tent. Skins long remained the best material, until the invention of plaited or woven fabrics. Like the hut, the tent took its shape from the original framework; it is conical among the North American Indians, dome-shaped among the Kaffirs, and quadrangular, in the form of a prismatic roof, among the Tibetans and the Gypsies.

Granaries and storehouses were afterwards constructed, and these were usually built on wooden piles, as among the Ainus and Malays, or on a clay stand, in order to prevent

Primitive Vehicles.—The needs of transport and communication were fertile sources of invention.

The cart was gradually evolved from the two trailing branches attached to the sides of a horse. The sledge represents the middle stage. Rollers were next placed under the framework of the sledge, and step by step wheels began to be formed, as ease of traction became better

Persian litter.

understood. The wheels at first were solid, and in appearance were

something like a grindstone.

More important changes have taken place in water transport. It is a far cry from the air-filled leather bottles used by the Assyrians for crossing rivers, and which still serve the same purpose in Turkestan, to the modern sailing yacht; or from the reed raft of the ancient Egyptians to the magnificent liners which traverse every sea.

8

Homesteading 1

Introduction

Since the 1960s, the United States has been witnessing a transition from urban to rural life as thousands of city dwellers pack up and move to the farm. Tired of crowding, polluted air and water, crime, and the relentless rise in food prices, many of us yearn for a simpler way of life and the independence that can be achieved by raising our own food.

While life on the farm may be simpler, however, it is not easier than city life. Cows have to be milked, even in a blizzard, fences must be mended, crops need to be planted at the proper times and then religiously tended, and on and on—but you get the idea. Self-sufficiency is possible for the small homesteader, but only as the result of hard work. Many learn to their dismay that the peaceful country silence, broken only by bird song and the lowing of cows, the endless chores, and the disastrous vagaries of weather, are not, after all, what they had in mind.

Fortunately, it is not necessary to give up everything urban in order to enjoy some of the benefits of country living. You need not, in fact, live in the country. Even a small plot of ground can produce enough vegetables for a large family when intensive gardening methods are used. The part-time farmer can keep a city job and still make strides toward self-reliance.

Then, too, rural land and the knowledge gained by learning to work it can be an investment for the future. During the Depression, farm families who owned their land often fared much better than did their relatives in the city. "We didn't have much spending money," one such woman said, "but we always had plenty of good food to eat. We kids never knew we were poor."

This chapter has been compiled both for the self-sufficient homesteader and the weekend gardener who wants to stave off the supermarket food bill. Find a little of everything in the following pages, from books on beekeeping, livestock, canning and preserving, and companion planting to catalogs for veterinary supplies, seeds and composters, magazines to help the farmer and gardener—and a lot more. We have not tested all of the methods proposed in the books included here, nor have we been able to try all of the products advertised in the catalogs, but all have been recommended by reliable sources. We will be more than glad to receive any complaints, compliments, or other comments that you may have. You might even be quoted in future editions of this catalog. But we cannot be held accountable for the efficacy or the quality of the books and products that follow.

Some of the listings are followed by comments or brief reviews; this is not intended as a slight to or judgment on those not annotated. One final note: if government information sources appear to be over-emphasized, this does not reflect a zealous dependence on Big Brother, but our realization that Department of Agriculture and other government research has been thorough over the years. In addition, the publications are reasonably priced.

Access

Government Sources

Soil Conservation Service (SCS)

This service works through the local soil and water conservation district and will supply information on your land and water resources. SCS staff can also tell you how to make improvements which should result in higher crop yields, increased wildlife, and a greater supply of good water, all of which can help you make more money from your land.

SCS is usually listed in the phone book under U.S. Government, Department of Agriculture. Or write: U.S. Department of Agriculture, Soil Conservation Service, P.O. Box 2890, Washington, D.C. 20013.

Farmers' Home Administration (FHA)

Low and moderate income families can get loans for restoring old houses to adequate condition through this office. Loans are made for well installation, plumbing, waste disposal facilities, and home insulation, but not for such improvements as landscaping, gardening on a noncommercial scale, or work on land which is not a part of the actual homesite.

The FHA should be listed in the directory by itself, alphabetically, or write: Farmers' Home Administration, U.S. Department of Agriculture, Washington, D.C. 20250.

Agricultural Stabilization and Conservation Service (ASCS)

Turn to the ASCS in case of disaster; they can supply emergency feed and aid in restoration of farmland. They also make indemnity payments for pesticide losses to beekeepers and answer questions about federal farm programs, costsharing assistance for soil and water conservation practices, or loans for farm storage facilities. If you participate in a federal farm program, ASCS will see that you are paid for crop losses. This service is listed in the phone book either alphabetically by itself or under the U.S. Government or your county heading.

County Extension Office

Look in the phone book under your county government heading. If it is not there, try under the name of the land-grant college in your area. This helpful governmental branch is variously listed as County Agent or Agricultural or Cooperative Extension Service.

The office in your area can furnish you with information on crops, livestock, pesticide regulations, and so on, based on local factors, The County Extension Office is also equipped to test your soil and supply you with relevant USDA pamphlets.

State Extension Office

State Agricultural Extension directors are affiliated with the state land-grant colleges listed below. These people will answer questions about farming and gardening.

Alabama: Auburn U., Auburn 36830
Alaska: U. of Alaska, Fairbanks 99701
Arizona: U. of Arizona; Tucson 85721
Arkansas: Box 391, Little Rock 72203
California: U. of CA, 2200 University Ave., Berkeley 94720
Colorado: CO State U., Fort Collins 80521
Connecticut: U. of CT, Storrs 06268
Delaware: U. of Delaware, Newark 19711
District of Columbia: Federal City College, 1424 K St., NW 20005
Florida: U. of FL, Gainesville 32601
Georgia: U. of GA, Athens 30601
Hawaii: U. of Hawaii, Honolulu 96822
Idaho: U. of ID, Moscow 83843
Illinois: U. of IL, Urbana 61801
Indiana: Purdue U., Lafayette 47907
Iowa: Iowa State U., Ames 50010

Kansas: Kansas State U., Manhattan 66502
Kentucky: U. of Kentucky, Lexington, 40506
Louisiana: LA State U., Baton Rouge 70803
Maine: U. of Maine, Orono 04473
Maryland: U. of Maryland, College Park 20742
Massachusetts: U. of MA, Amherst 01002
Michigan: MI State U., East Lansing 48823
Minnesota: U. of Minn., St. Paul 55101
Mississippi: Miss. State U., Miss. State 39762
Missouri: U. of Missouri, Columbia 65201
Montana: Montana State U., Bozeman 59715
Nebraska: U. of Neb., Lincoln 68503
Nevada: U. of Nev., Reno 89507
New Hampshire: U. of NH, Durham 03824
New Jersey: Rutgers U., New Brunswick 08903
New Mexico: N.M. State U., Las Cruces 88001
New York: N.Y. State College of Agric., Ithaca 14850
North Carolina: N.C. State U., Raleigh 27607
North Dakota: N.D. State U., Fargo 51802
Ohio: OH State U., 2120 Fyffe Rd., Columbus 43210
Oklahoma: OK State U., Stillwater 74074
Oregon: Oregon State U., Corvallis 97331
Pennsylvania: Penn. State U., University Park 16802
Rhode Island: U. of RI, Kingston 02881
South Carolina: Clemson U., Clemson 29631
South Dakota: SD State U., Brookings 57006
Tennessee: U. of Tenn., Box 1071, Knoxville 37901
Texas: Texas A&M U., College Station, 77843
Utah: Utah State U., Logan 84321
Vermont: U. of Vermont, Burlington 05401
Virginia: Va. Poly Inst., Blacksburg 24061
Washington: Washington State U., Pullman 99163
West Virginia: W. Va. U., 294 Coliseum, Morgantown 26506
Wisconsin: U. of Wisconsin, 432 N. Lake St., Madison 53706
Wyoming: U. of Wyoming, Box 3354, Univ. Station, Laramie 82070

Your State Land-Grant College

Call or write your state-supported land-grant college for a catalog of publications. These schools specialize in agricultural research conducted according to the weather, soil, and geographical conditions of the areas in which they reside.

Sources of Publications and Audio-Visual Materials

B H DATA
P.O. Box 726
Pleasantville, NJ 08232

Reference guide, $2.00. Thousands of free or inexpensive publications and audio-visual materials dealing with gardening and farming.

Garden Way Publishers
Charlotte, VT 05445

Bulletins, books, and plans on gardening, farming, nutrition, energy, etc.
Free catalog.

The Stephen Greene Press
109 Fessenden Rd.
Brattleboro, VT 05301

Reprints and new titles on various aspects of country living; some informative, some mainly for entertainment.
Free catalog.

Mother's Bookshelf
Mother Earth News
P.O. Box 70
Hendersonville, NC 28739

Excellent selection of books by various publishers on ecological, self-sufficient living. Gardening, farming, alternative energy, building, textiles, food preservation, etc. Good reading in itself (annotations are informative and entertaining), the catalog presents some of the best books on the market.
Catalog, $1.00.

Pomona Book Exchange
33 Beaucourt Rd.
Toronto, Ontario
M8Y 3GI

Books on every aspect of horticulture. Rare, out-of-print, and new books available; will conduct book searches.
Free catalog.

Rodale Press, Inc.
Book Division
33 East Minor St.
Emmaus, PA 18049

Books dealing with farming, gardening, nutrition, building, and energy efficiency.
Free catalog.

Yankee Books
Box AL8, Depot Square
Peterborough, NH 03458

New England and country books from the publishers of *The Old Farmer's Almanac*.
Free catalog.

Buying Land

Ask your local FHA office for information on buying repossessed land. When the FHA repossesses a piece of property, the property can be bought for the remainder of the mortgage. Weather bureaus can supply data on average growing conditions of specific areas; county officials will give you the facts on tax levels, zoning restrictions, and building requirements, and real estate brokers can tell you about property values and proposed land use changes or restrictions.

Books

Finding and Buying Your Place in the Country
Les Scher. 1974.
$6.95, paper.
Collier Books
Order Dept.
Front & Brown Sts.
Riverside, NJ 08075

The author, a lawyer, details the legal "ins" and "outs" of purchasing rural properties.

Living on a Few Acres
The Yearbook of Agriculture, 1978.
"Part 2: Acquiring that Spot," pp. 38–52
U.S. Department of Agriculture
For sale by the Superintendent of Documents,
U.S. Government Printing Office, Washington,
D.C. 20204 $7.00, hardcover.

The yearbooks, which read like textbooks, are worth consulting. This one will take you through all the steps: deciding whether to move to the country, farming, raising various crops and livestock, and disposing of your property.

Old-Fashioned Recipe Book: An Encyclopedia of Country Living
Carla Emery. 1977.
$8.95, paper.
Bantam Books, Inc.
666 5th Ave.
New York, NY 10019

The author imparts some shrewd tips and insights on the subject of buying land—ideas that would never occur to the inexperienced.

Settlement Costs
U.S. Department of Housing and Urban Development, Office of Consumer Affairs and Regulatory Functions, HUD-368-F(2), Aug. 1977. For sale by the Superintendent of Documents, U.S. Government Printing Office, Washington, D.C. 20402

Catalogs

United Farm Agency
612 W. 47th St.
Kansas City, MO 64112

Publishers of a large, biyearly catalog of rural property for sale. An excellent introduction to the rural real estate market in any part of the country. Write for current price.

General Information

Books

Almanac of Rural Living
Harvey C. Neese. 1976.
$6.95
N & N Resources
P.O. Box 332
Troy, ID 83871

How to manage a farm. Encyclopedia format.

Country Women: A Handbook for the New Farmer
Jeanne Tetrault and Sherry Thomas.
$6.95, paper.
Doubleday & Co.
245 Park Ave.
New York, NY 10017

Farming for Self-Sufficiency: Independence on a Five-Acre Farm
John and Sally Seymour. 1976.
$7.50.
Shocken Books
200 Madison Ave.
New York, NY 10016

Five Acres and Independence
M. G. Kains. 1973.
$3.50, paper.
Dover Publications, Inc.
180 Vanick St.
New York, NY 10014

How to manage the small farm.

Foxfire (five-book series)
Eliot Wiggington, ed.
Doubleday & Co.
245 Park Ave.
New York, NY 10017

Paper. Books 1 and 2 sell for $4.50 each; books 3 and 4 sell for $5.95 each. *Foxfire 5* is priced at $6.95.

A collection of folklore, folkways, and farming, building, crafts, beekeeping, and food preparation techniques of the Appalachian region, taken in part from *Foxfire Magazine*.
 They's a lot of this stuff that began to slip my mind until I started reading these here *Foxfire Papers*. But all that stuff is the truth. I bet they ain't a word in there from them old fellers what ain't the truth.
—Charlie Ross Hartley, *Foxfire 4*.

The Gardener's Almanac (rev.)
$4.45, paper.
Horticulture Magazine
Book Dept.
300 Massachusetts Ave.
Boston, MA 02115

Homesteading: How to Find New Independence on the Land
Gene Logsdon.
$8.95, hardcover.
Rodale Press, Inc.
Book Division
33 East Minor St.
Emmaus, PA 18049

Living off the Country for Fun and Profit
John L. Parker. 1978.
$5.95, paper.
Bookworm Publishing Co.
Box 3037
Ontario, CA 91761

Includes chapter on raising and training livestock guard dogs.

Living on a Few Acres
Yearbook of Agriculture, 1978.
$7.00, hardcover.
U.S. Department of Agriculture
Stock No. 001-000-03809-5
For sale by the Superintendent of Documents,
U.S. Government Printing Office, Washington,
D.C. 20204

Mother Earth News Almanac
$2.50, paper.
Bantam Books, Inc.
666 5th Ave.
New York, NY 10019

The Manual of Practical Homesteading
John Vivian. 1977.
$5.95, paper.
Rodale Press, Inc.
Book Division
33 East Minor St.
Emmaus, PA 18049

Guide to farming self-sufficiency. Gardening, livestock care, canning and preserving, etc.

Old-Fashioned Recipe Book
Carla Emery. 1977.
$8.95, paper.
Bantam Books, Inc.
666 5th Ave.
New York, NY 10019

Real homestead pioneering, written from experience. Just about everything anyone would need to know about food preservation, poultry, dairy, home industries, and much more.

Courtesy Colorado Historical Society

The Old Farmer's Almanac
Annual, $1.00, paper.
Yankee Books
Dublin, NH 03444

The ubiquitous little yellow paperback that has been sold in newsstands and markets longer than anyone can remember. "Published every year since 1792 . . . Weather Forecasts for 16 Regions of the United States . . . Planting Tables, Zodiac Secrets, Recipes . . . Astronomical Tables, Tides, Holidays, Eclipses, etc."

Simple Living: An Illustrated Workbook for the New Farm and Home
Jacques Massacrier. 1975.
$7.95.
Music Sales Corp.
Quick Fox Distributor
33 W. 60th St.
New York, NY 10023

Successful Small-Scale Farming
Karl Schwenke.
$8.95, paper.
Garden Way Publishing
Charlotte, VT 05445

Practical, in-depth discussions of soils and soil improvement, plants for farm crops, farm machinery for the small farm, health farm practices, livestock, farm water, and much more.

Wintering in Snow Country
William E. Osgood.
$4.95 paper; $8.95 hardcover.
The Stephen Greene Press
109 Fessenden Rd.
Brattleboro, VT 05301

"How to save heat, energy and money—and be mobile and happy in the cold five months of your life! New ways to dress, eat, keep your car unfroze and enjoy yourself in winter."

Spinning-wheel.

Gardening and Farming

Books

A to Z Hints for the Vegetable Gardener
$3.95, paper.
Garden Way Publishing
Charlotte, VT 05445

Amaranth, From the Past—For the Future
John N. Cole.
$8.95, hardcover.
Rodale Press, Inc.
Book Division
33 East Minor St.
Emmaus, PA 18049

History, growing instructions, recipes, and current research on an ancient grain. "May resolve the world hunger crisis."

Better Vegetable Gardens the Chinese Way
Peter Chan with Spencer Gill. 1977.
$4.95, paper.
Graphic Arts Center Publishing Co.
2000 NW Wilson
Portland, OR 97209

15

Country Wisdom Bulletins
Garden Way Publishing Co.
Charlotte, VT 05445

$1.00 each; if order is under $4.00, add 50¢
postage and handling.
Bulletins are illustrated, 32 pages. 80¢ if you buy
5 or more.

A-1 Grow the Best Strawberries
A-2 The Amazing Wide-Row Planting Technique
A-4 Growing the Best-Ever Potatoes, Irish and
Sweet
A-5 Cover-Crop Gardening
A-9 All the Onions and How to Grow Them
A-17 Hens and Chicks with a Minimum of Feed
A-18 Raising Ducks and Geese on the Small
Place
A-19 Build your Own Pond
A-20 Soil Improvement for Successful Gardening
A-21 What Every Gardener Should Know about
Earthworms
A-22 Building and Using a Root Cellar
A-27 Growing the Best-Ever Tomatoes
A-33 Berries, Rasp- and Black

Encyclopedia of Organic Gardening (rev. edition)
By the Staff of *Organic Gardening Magazine.*
Book Division
Rodale Press, Inc.
33 East Minor St.
Emmaus, PA 18049

The *Encyclopedia* gives in-depth treatment of the
basic elements of organic husbandry: composting,
mulching, natural soil fertility, and control of
disease and insect pests. Innovations and
improvements in this revised edition reflect new
developments in the fields of entomology,
agronomy, nutrition, and microbiology. The 1,236-
page hardcover is attractive, well-illustrated, well-
organized, and readable. Some examples of
subjects covered: companion planting; greenhouses; beekeeping; canning, drying, and freezing
of foods; herbs; and livestock.

Forest Farming
J. Sholto Douglas and Robert A. de J. Hart.
$8.95, hardcover.
Rodale Press, Inc.
Book Division
33 East Minor St.
Emmaus, PA 18049

Growing trees by a system midway between
forestry and agriculture for food and other
purposes.

Gardening for Food and Fun
Yearbook of Agriculture, 1977.
$6.50, hardcover.
U.S. Department of Agriculture.
For sale by the Superintendent of Documents,
U.S. Government Printing Office, Washington,
D.C. 20402

The Gardener's Catalogue
Tom Riker and Harvey Rottenburg, 1974.
$6.95, paper.
William Morrow & Co., Inc.
105 Madison Ave.
New York, NY 10016

"*The Gardener's Catalogue* is a profusely illustrated compendium of sources and information
for indoor and outdoor gardening."

The Gardener's Guide to Better Soil
Gene Logsdon.
Rodale Press, Inc.
Book Division.
33 East Minor St.
Emmaus, PA 18049
$4.95, paper.

Courtesy Colorado Historical Society

Grow It
Richard W. Langer, 1973.
$4.95, paper.
Avon Books
250 W. 55th St., 8th Floor
New York, NY 10019

Growing Berries and Grapes at Home
J. Harold Clarke
$7.50.
Peter Smith Publisher, Inc.
6 Lexington Ave.
Magnolia, MA 01930

How to Grow Vegetables and Fruits by the Organic Method
J. J. Rodale and Staff.
$13.95, hardcover.
Rodale Press, Inc.
Book Division
33 East Minor St.
Emmaus, PA 18049

How to Grow Your Own Groceries for $1 a Year
Clifford Ridley. 1974.
$2.95, paper.
Hawkes Publishing, Inc.
3775 S. 500 W.
Box 15711
Salt Lake City, UT 84115

How to Have a Green Thumb Without an Aching Back
Ruth Stout. 1968.
$1.95, paper.
Cornerstone Press
P.O. Box 28048
St. Louis, MO 63119

Improve Your Garden with Backyard Research
Lois Levitan.
$5.95, paper.
Rodale Press
Book Division
33 East Minor St.
Emmaus, PA 18049

Making the Weather Work for You: A Practical Guide for Gardener and Farmer
James J. Rahn.
$7.95, paper.
Garden Way Publishing
Charlotte, VT 05445

Mulches
$1.75, paper.
Brooklyn Botanic Garden
Brooklyn, NY 11225

Natural Gardening
Handbook #77
$1.75, paper.
Brooklyn Botanic Garden
Brooklyn, NY 11225

Organic Way to Mulching
By the editors of *Organic Gardening Magazine.*
$8.95, hardcover.
Rodale Press, Inc.
Book Division
33 East Minor St.
Emmaus, PA 18049

The Original Victory Garden
(Original title: *Food Gardens for Defense*)
M. G. Kains.
$3.95, paper.
Stein & Day Publishers
Scarborough House
Briarcliff Manor, NY 10510

Pruning Simplified: A Complete Guide to Pruning Trees, Shrubs, Bushes, Hedges, Vines, Etc.
Lewis Hill.
Rodale Press, Inc.
Book Division
33 East Minor St.
Emmaus, PA 18049

Rodale Guide to Composting
Jerry Minnich, M. Hunt, and the editors of *Organic Gardening Magazine.*
$12.95, hardcover.
Rodale Press, Inc.
Book Division
33 East Minor St.
Emmaus, PA 18049

The Rodale Herb Book: How to Use, Grow and Buy Nature's Miracle Plants
William H. Hylton, ed.
$12.95, hardcover; $14.95, hardcover deluxe.
Rodale Press, Inc.
Book Division
33 East Minor St.
Emmaus, PA 18049

Secrets of Companion Planting
Louise Riotte.
$5.95, paper; $8.95, hardcover.
Garden Way Publishing
Charlotte, VT 05445

Success with Small Food Gardens Using Special Intensive Methods
Louise Riotte and Walter Hard. 1977.
$5.95, paper; $8.95, hardcover.
Garden Way Publishing
Charlotte, VT 05445

300 of the Most Asked Questions about Organic Gardening
By the editors of *Organic Gardening Magazine.*
$7.95, hardcover.
Rodale Press, Inc.
Book Division
33 East Minor St.
Emmaus, PA 18049

Sure-Shot Method of Poisoning Gophers in Their Dens

With this little tool, you can get poisoned bait into gophers' runways without disturbing the soil

If you have been unsuccessful in poisoning gophers in their dens or runways, the trouble was probably due to not getting the poisoned bait properly located. With this tool, which is made from a length of ½-in. pipe and an iron rod, you can get the bait into the runway without disturbing the latter and without covering the bait with dirt. The rod is just long enough for the pointed end to project from the lower end of the pipe. In use, the assembly is pushed into the ground until the lower end breaks through the roof of the runway. The rod is removed and the bait poured through the pipe.

Insect Pest Control

For chemical pesticides, consult the county cooperative extension agent in your area. Local soil, water, and climatic conditions and state law and local ordinances must all be taken into consideration when pesticides are used. Biologic or "organic" methods of insect and plant disease control are listed here.

Books

Biological Control of Plant Pests
Handbook #34
$1.75, paper.
Brooklyn Botanic Garden
Brooklyn, NY 11225

The Bug Book: Harmless Insect Controls
Helen and John Philbrick. 1974.
$3.95, paper.
Garden Way Publishing
Charlotte, VT 05445

The authors explain how to identify, control, and—believe it or not—*appreciate* your garden marauders.

Color Handbook of Garden Insects
Anna Carr.
$12.95, hardcover.
Garden Way Publishing
Charlotte, VT

"The only full-color photographic identification guide devoted specifically to garden insects. . . . Over 200 pollinating, pestiferous and predatory insects."

A Field Guide to the Insects
(The Peterson Field Guide series)
Donald J. Borror and Richard E. White. 1970.
$4.95, paper.
Houghton Mifflin Co.
1 Beacon Street
Boston, MA 02107

Organic Plant Protection
Roger B. Yepsen, Jr., ed.
$14.95, hardcover.
Rodale Books, Inc.
Book Division
33 East Minor St.
Emmaus, PA 18049

Bio-Control Co.
10180 Ladybird Dr.
Auburn, CA 95603

Live lady bugs and praying mantis egg cases.
Free brochure.

Cothard, Inc.
P.O. Box 370
Canutillo, TX 79835

Cothard offers a biological insect control program.
Free brochure.

Organic Controls, Inc.
P.O. Box 25382
Los Angeles, CA 90025

How to control such pests as aphids, cabbage-loopers, caterpillars, etc.
Free catalog.

Nurseries and Seed Companies

Note: Before making heavy investments in mail-order plants and seeds, it would be a good idea to talk with your neighbors and feed and seed store merchants to find out what crops are suited to your region. Varieties that yield well in one area may not be hardy in another locale.

Catalogs

Alexander's Blueberry Nurseries
RFD 4
Middleboro, MA 02346

Send S.A.S.E. for price list.

W. F. Allen Co.
Salisbury, MD 21801

Berry plants since 1885. "World's finest selection of strawberry plants."
Free catalog.

Bountiful Ridge Nurseries, Inc.
Princess Anne, MD 21853

Specializes in fruit trees and plants. Grape vines, nut trees, etc. Since 1907.
Free catalog.

Brittingham Plant Farms
Salisbury, MD 21801

Berries, grapes, asparagus.
Free planting guide.
Free catalog.

Buntings Nurseries
Selbyville, DL 19975

Specify retail or wholesale catalog.
Free catalogs.

Burpee Seed Co.
1009 Burpee Bldg.
Warminster, PA 18974
or
Clinton, IA 52732
or
Riverside, CA 92502

One of America's largest and most reputable seed companies. Vegetables, some fruits and trees. Excellent hybrids for the home gardener. Free catalog.

D.V. Burrell Seed Growers Co.
P.O. Box 150
Rockyford, CO 81067

A major outlet for commercial growing. Large selection of seeds; catalog contains growing instructions. "Since the turn of the century." Free catalog.

California Nursery Co.
Box 2278
Fremont, CA 94536

Since 1865. Fruit and nut trees, grapevines. Free price list.

Caprilands Herb Farm
534 Silver St.
Coventry, CT 06238

Complete outfitting for the herb gardener. Free brochure.

Connor Co., Inc.
P.O. Box 534
Augusta, AR 72006

Strawberry plants. Cannot ship to Colorado or California. Free catalog.

De Giorgi Co., Inc.
P.O. Box 413
Council Bluffs, IA 51501

"Since 1905." Seed catalog, 60¢.

Emlong Nurseries, Inc.
Stevensville, MI 49127

Red raspberries, trees, etc. Since 1916. Free catalog.

Evans Plant Co.
P.O. Box 1649
Tifton, GA 31794

Field-grown vegetable plants. Free catalog.

Farmer Seed & Nursery Co.
Fairbault, MN 55021

Since 1888. "Minnesota's leading mail-order seed house." Good selection of plants, seeds, trees, and supplies.

Henry Field Seed & Nursery Co.
5586 Oak St.
Shenandoah, IA 51602

Complete line of nursery products. Free catalog.

Finch Blueberry Nursery
Rt. #1
Bailey, NC 27807

Grace's Gardens
39-M Ave. C
Bayonne, NJ 07002

"Rare, gigantic and Oriental vegetables . . . World's most unusual seed catalog." Free catalog.

Gurney Seed & Nursery Co.
3112 Page St.
Yankton, SD 57079

In business for 113 years. Seeds, nursery stock, supplies. Free catalog.

Hickin's
RFD 1
Brattleboro, VT 05301

Asparagus, berries, potatoes, etc. Free brochure.

Interstate Nurseries, Inc.
Hamburg, IA 51644

"America's largest direct-to-you nurseries." Trees, fruits, seeds, etc. Free catalog.

Johnson Orchard and Nursery
Rt. 5, Box 325
Ellijay, GA 30540

Catalog, $1.00, refundable with order.

J. W. Jung Seed Co.
P.O. Box 201
Randolph, WI 53956

Since 1907. Vegetables, fruit trees, etc.
Free catalog.

Kelly Bros. Nursery
311 Maple St.
Dansville, NY 14437

Strawberries, trees, nursery stock, etc. In business
for over 90 years.
Free catalog.

Kester's Wild Game Food Nurseries, Inc.
P.O. Box V
Omro, WI 54963

"Specializing in wildlife plantings for better
hunting and fishing areas and improvement of
our environment. More than 75 years experience."
Free catalog.

May Nursery Co.
P.O. Box 1312
Yakima, WA 98907

Since 1909. Trees—fruit, shade, etc.
Free catalog.

Mellinger's, Inc.
2380 V Range
North Lima, OH 44452

Plants, seeds, and supplies, including rye seed for
cover crops and green manure, milky spore bac-
teria for eliminating Japanese beetles.
Free catalog.

J. E. Miller Nurseries, Inc.
5060 West Lake Rd.
Canandaiqua, NY 14424

Berries, fruit trees, nut trees, supplies, etc.
Free catalog.

Mushroompeople
12783 Sir Francis Drake Blvd.
P.O. Box 607
Inverness, CA 94937

Free catalog lists mushroom books and culti-
vation supplies.

Nichols Garden Nursery
1190 Pacific
Albany, OR 97321

Includes over 80 different herb seeds and plants.
Free catalog.

Old-Fashioned Herb Co.
Box 1000
Springville, UT 84663

"Mail order herbs direct."
Catalog 25¢.

Old South Orchard
Marion, AL 36756

Special apple varieties for southern climates and old-fashioned, hard-to-find varieties.
Free list.

Omaha Plant Farms
Box 787
Omaha, TX 75571

Onion and cabbage plants.
Catalog 25¢.

George W. Park Seed Co., Inc.
37 Cokesbury Rd.
Greenwood, SC 29647

Seeds, plants, bulbs, vegetables. Gardening information.
Free catalog.

Pike's Peak Nurseries
Box 670
Indiana, PA 15701

Evergreens for Christmas tree plantations and reforestation. General nursery stock.
Free catalog.

Rayner Bros.
Box 348
Salisbury, MD 21801

Berries, fruit and nut trees.
Free catalog.

Savage Farm Nursery
P.O. Box 125
McMinnville, TN 37110

Nut trees, fruits, berries, etc.
Free catalog.

R. H. Shumway Seedsman
P.O. Box 777
Rockford, IL 61101

Seeds, plants, etc. Since 1870.
Free catalog.

Stark Bros. Nurseries & Orchards Co.
Box 12178
Louisiana, MO 63353

Nut trees, fruit trees, berries, and other nursery stock for the home gardener. "The famous Luther Burbank selected Stark Brothers to continue his important experiments. We pass the results of his research on to you through the superior varieties we offer."
Since 1816; U.S. patented varieties.
Free catalog.

Thompson & Morgan
P.O. Box 100
Farmingdale, NJ 07727

Vegetables, herbs, trees, and more.
Free catalog.

Vermont Bean Seed Co.
1 Garden Lane
Bomoseen, VT 05732

"Largest bean, pea and corn seed selection in the world. . . . Shelling, freezing, canning and drying varieties. Pea seeds of every variety for every climate."
Catalog, 25¢.

Waynesboro Nurseries
Waynesboro, VA 22980

Fruit and nut trees, berry plants, grapevines, etc. Free catalog, planting guide.

Bob Wells Nursery
Box 606
Lindale, TX 75771

Berry plants—all varieties. Fruit, nut, and shade trees.

Western Maine Forest Nursery Co.
P.O. Box 98
Fryeburg, ME 04037

Evergreen trees.
Free catalog.

Wildlife Nurseries
P.O. Box 2724
Oshkosh, WI 54901

Seed for living plants for habitat modification—to attract ducks, birds, and deer to your property.

Dave Wilson Nursery
Box 60
Hughson, CA 95326

"Our 1980 catalog is accompanied by a climate zone map of your section and a chart which indexes each of our fruit, nut and grape varieties for fruiting ability in your zone. These localized variety recommendations provide more than a simple guide to plant hardiness: they indicate the likelihood of each variety bearing fruit in your area, under reasonable care."
Free catalog.

Orchards

Books and pamphlets by the U.S. Department of Agriculture, for sale by the Superintendent of Documents, U.S. Government Printing Office, Washington, D.C. 20402

Establishing and Managing Young Apple Orchards
Farmers' Bul. No. 1897. 1976. 35¢.

Growing Apricots for Home Use
H & G Bul. No. 204. 1973. 70¢

Growing Cherries East of the Rocky Mountains
Farmers' Bul. No. 2185. 1977. 70¢

Growing Nectarines
Agric. Info. Bul. No. 379. 1975. 40¢

High-Density Apple Orchards: Planning, Training and Pruning
Agric. Handbook 458. 1975. 85¢

Greenhouses

See also the greenhouse section in Chapter 4, *Building and Alternative Energy.*

Catalogs

Barrington Industries
P.O. Box 133
Barrington, IL 60010

Over 1,200 greenhouses and garden supply items.

English Greenhouse Products Corp.
11th & Linden Sts.
Camden, NJ 08102

Free brochure and name of nearest dealer.

Four Seasons Greenhouses
672 Sunrise Hwy.
W. Babylon, NY 11704

Solar-heated greenhouse. For $3.00, Four Seasons
will send a sample window, assembly manual,
and heating guide.
Free catalog.

Greenhouse Specialties
9849 Kinker Lane
St. Louis, MO 63127

Plans, wholesale prices, equipment list, $1.00.

McGregor Greenhouses
Box 36
Santa Cruz, CA 95063

"Double-layer design greenhouse cuts energy
costs—handles wind and snow storms with ease.
Redwood and clear acrylic fiberglass."
Free brochure.

Peter Reimuller—the Greenhouseman
980 17th Ave.
Santa Cruz, CA 95062

"Freestanding and lean-to and dome models and
accessories. Pre-cut and pre-drilled." Shatterproof
fiberglass, redwood frame.
Free catalog.

Turner Greenhouses
Highway 117 South
Goldsboro, NC 27530

Free catalog.

Vegetable Factory Greenhouses
P.O. Box 2235
Grand Central Station
New York, NY 10017

Solar panel greenhouse "uses 60% less heat."
Free brochure.

Tillers, Tools, and Miscellanea

Books

Country Woodcraft
Drew Langsner.
$12.95, hardcover.
Rodale Press, Inc.
Book Division
33 East Minor St.
Emmaus, PA 18049

"The woodworker's guide to traditional wood-
crafting techniques—from harvesting trees to the
finished product . . . simple mallets to . . . working
tools, agricultural implements . . . kitchenware,
furniture."

Edge of the Anvil
Jack Andrews.
$9.95, hardcover.
Rodale Press, Inc.
Book Division
33 East Minor St.
Emmaus, PA 18049

A beginning blacksmithing guide that shows how
to work metal into tools, hinges, hand-wrought
fences, and other useful items; how to set up a
forge and shop; how to temper steel; and more.

Tan Your Hide: Home-Tanning Furs and Leathers
Phyllis Hobson.
$4.95, paper.
Garden Way Publishing
Charlotte, VT 05445

Hand Jack Exerts Powerful Lift to Pull Large Fence Posts

This jack makes short work of the tedious job of pulling old fence posts. It consists of three hardwood parts; a handle, a movable or lifting member and a stationary member. The last two are cut to the same length and an equal number of holes are bored in each one. Two pieces of flat iron are bolted to the handle and holes are drilled in these for heavy bolts which pass through the holes in the stationary and lifting members. A short length of chain, run through an eye bolt at the top of the lifting member, is looped about the post.—George Janser, Rockford, Ill.

Tractor and Small Engine Maintenance
Arlen D. Brown and Ivan Gregg Morrison.
4th ed., 1973.
$10.00
Interstate
19-27 N. Jackson St.
Danville, IL 61832

Catalogs

Amerind MacKissic, Inc.
Box 111
Parker Ford, PA 19457

Shredder-chippers for composting, tillers, sprayers, log-splitters.
Free catalog.

Ariens Company
805 W. Ryan St.
Brillion, WI 54110

Rear-tine tiller.
Free information.

Earthmaker
Gardening Naturally
1109 Industrial Park
Stockbridge, MA 01262

Revolving drum composter.
Free catalog.

Edison Kitchen Composter Co., Inc.
Box 21
Rumson, NJ 07760

Turns kitchen scraps to compost.
Free catalog, gardening-composting guide.

Global Services, Inc.
Box 297
Lewisburg, PA 17837

Compost tumbler—turns lawn, kitchen, and garden wastes to compost.
Free details.

A. M. Leonard, Inc.
Piqua, OH 45356
Horticultural tools and supplies for the nursery, greenhouse, gardener. Since 1885.
Free catalog.

Nasco
901 Janesville Ave.
Fort Atkinson, WI 53538
        or
Nasco West
1524 Princeton Ave.
Modesto, CA 95352

Farm and ranch catalog contains all kinds of homestead items, including weather equipment, electric fence chargers, spray equipment, veterinary supplies, and a power failure alarm.

Precision Valley Mfg. Co.
Box 1300
Springfield, VT 05156

Yellowbird rear-end tiller for home gardening.
Free brochure.

Rotocrop
93 Aero Park
Doylestown, PA 18901

Compost bins—"Make a ton in one season."
Free catalog.

Smith and Hawken
68 Homer
Palo Alto, CA 94301

"Hand-crafted English garden tools for the professional and skilled gardener."
Catalog, $1.00.

Sudbury Laboratories, Inc.
572 Dutton Rd.
Sudbury, MA 01776

Accessories, animal repellents, garden-growing
aids, soil test kits, and water soluble fertilizers.
Free brochure.

Troy-Bilt Roto Tillers
Garden Way Manufacturing Co., Inc.
102nd St. & 9th Ave.
Troy, NY 12180

Troy-Bilt Roto Tillers have their blades in the
rear, enabling the gardener to till and compost
more easily. "... Easily chops up and mixes into
the soil organic matter of all kinds ... And so
easy to handle, you guide it with just one hand!"
Free catalog is 112-page booklet, *The Joy of Gardening the Troy-Bilt Way*, containing gardening
information.

W-W Grinder, Inc.
2957B N. Market
P.O. Box 4029
Wichita, KS 67204

Shredder-grinder for composting.
Free catalog.

Livestock — General

Books

Draft Horse Primer: A Guide to the Care and Use of Work Horses and Mules
Maurice Telleen.
$10.95, hardcover.
Rodale Press, Inc.
Book Division
33 East Minor St.
Emmaus, PA 18049

The Family Cow
Dirk Van Loon.
$5.95, paper.
Garden Way Publishing
Charlotte, VT 05445

Homesteader's Handbook to Raising Small Livestock
Jerome D. Belanger. 1974.
$3.95, paper.
Rodale Press, Inc.
Book Division
33 East Minor St.
Emmaus, PA 18049

Lameness in Horses
O. R. Adams, 1974.
$22.50, text edition.
Lea & Febiger
600 Washington Square
Philadelphia, PA 19106

A Practical Guide to Small-Scale Goatkeeping
Billie Luisi.
$8.95, hardcover.
Rodale Press, Inc.
Book Division
33 East Minor St.
Emmaus, PA 18049

Raising a Calf for Beef
Phyllis Hobson.
$4.95, paper.
Garden Way Publishing
Charlotte, VT 05445

Contains complete butchering instructions.

SECTION OF BULLOCK.

1. Cheek.
2. Neck or Sticking Piece.
3. Clod.
4. Shin.
5. Shoulder or Leg of Mutton Piece.
6. Chuck Ribs.
7. Middle Ribs.
8. Fore Ribs.
9. Brisket.
10. Surloin.
11. Thin Flank.
12. Rump.
13. Aitch-bone.
14. Round or Buttock.
15. Mouse Bullock.
16. Veiny Piece.
17. Thick Flank.
18. Leg.

Raising Poultry the Modern Way
Leonard Mercia. 1975.
$5.95.
Garden Way Publishing
Charlotte, VT 05445

Raising Rabbits
Ann Kanable.
$8.95, hardcover.
Rodale Press, Inc.
Book Division
33 East Minor St.
Emmaus, PA 18049

Raising the Homestead Hog
Jerome D. Belanger
Rodale Press, Inc.
Book Division
33 East Minor St.
Emmaus, PA 18049

The Shepherd's Guidebook
Margaret Bradbury
$7.95, hardcover.
Rodale Press, Inc.
Book Division
33 East Minor St.
Emmaus, PA 18049

Small Scale Pig Raising
Dirk Van Loon. 1977.
$5.95, paper.
Rodale Press, Inc.
Book Division
33 East Minor St.
Emmaus, PA 18049

Starting Right with Turkeys
G. T. Klein
$3.50, paper.
Garden Way Publishing
Charlotte, VT 05445

SECTIONS OF SHEEP, OR LAMB.

1. Leg.
2. Shoulder.
3. Breast.
4. Scrag end of neck.
5. Best end of loin.
6. Best end of neck.
7. Chump end of loin.
8. Head.

Livestock—Poultry

Note: Before buying poultry, take the time to find out about the different varieties. Chickens bred for the table may not be good layers; some chickens bred for egg production will not bother with sitting on the eggs.

Catalogs

Country Hatchery
P.O. Box 747
Wewoka, OK 74884

Wide selection of chickens, ducks, turkeys, keets, peafowl; also breeding equipment and supplies.
Free brochure.

Grain Belt Hatchery
P.O. Box 125
Windsor, MO 65360

Chickens, all breeds.
Free catalog.

Vegetables Fed to Chickens in Spring-Coil Holders

When carrots, turnips, beets, etc., are fed to poultry, coils from an old bedspring, fastened to a post, stake or wall, are just the thing for holding the vegetables to avoid waste. Stretch the coils a little so that the birds can get at the feed easily.
—A. S. Wurz, Jr., Rockyford, Alta., Can.

Chickens will consume raw vegetables without waste if these food holders are used

Heart of Missouri Hatchery
P.O. Box 954
Columbus, MO 65201

Chicks, young ducks, geese, etc.
Brochure, 50¢.

Marti Poultry Farm
Box 27-18
Windsor, MO 65360

Araucana chickens: they lay blue, olive, green, and pink eggs.
Free catalog.

Northwest Farms, Inc.
P.O. Box 3003
Portland, OR 97208

Commercial poultry, game birds, hatching eggs, etc.
Catalog, $1.50.

Ronson Farms
Box 12565
Columbus, OH 43212

Pheasants, quail, waterfowl, more. Also, equipment, incubators, and books.
Catalog, $1.00.

Livestock—Supplies

Catalogs

Hoegger Supply Co.
College Park, GA 30349

Goat-keeping supplies, milking pails, milking machines, other equipment.
Catalog, $1.00.

Jones Mfg. Co.
P.O. Box 123
Ramona, CA 92065

Cages in which to raise rabbits, other supplies and equipment.
Catalog, 50¢.

Keipper Cooping Co.
3235 W. Burnham St.
P.O. Box 15138
Milwaukee, WI 53215

Collapsible, all-wire animal coops.
Free brochure.

Kennel-Aire Mfg. Co.
725 N. Snelling Ave.
St. Paul, MN 55104

Enclosures for animals; accessories.
Free catalog.

UPCO
St. Joseph, MO 64504

"Buy pet and livestock supplies wholesale! Specify pet or livestock catalog."
Free catalogs.

These sanitary nests can be removed for washing at regular intervals

Veterinarian Guides

Keeping Livestock Healthy: A Veterinary Guide
N. Bruce Haynes, DVM.
$9.95, field guide edition.
Garden Way Publishing
Charlotte, VT 05445

Veterinary Guide for Animal Owners
C. E. Spaulding, DVM.
$9.95, hardcover.
Rodale Press, Inc.
Book Division
33 East Minor St.
Emmaus, PA 18049

Veterinarian Supplies

Catalogs

Amerex Laboratories
P.O. Box 32827
San Antonio, TX 78216

Horse nutrition supplement, 'Liquid 747."
Free information

Eastern States Serum Co., Inc.
1727 Harden St.
Columbia, SC 29240

Pharmaceuticals, medications, etc.
Free catalog.

Kansas City Vaccine Co.
Stock Yards
1611 Genesee Sts.
Kansas City, MO 64102

Veterinary supplies, instruments for livestock, poultry, pets.
Free catalog.

UPCO of California
8693 La Mesa Blvd.
La Mesa, CA 92041

Medications, supplies, and grooming aids.
Free catalog.

Vet Vax, Inc.
P.O. Box 11304
Edwardsville Station
Kansas City, KS 66113

Vaccines and medications.
Free catalog.

Wholesale Veterinary Supply, Inc.
P.O. Box 2256
Rockford, IL 61131
Medications, supplies, grooming aids. Specify:
1. Small animal and horse
2. Large animal
3. Sheep
Free catalogs.

Beekeeping

Books

First Lessons in Beekeeping (rev. edition)
C. P. Dadant. 1976.
$1.00, paper.
Dadant & Sons, Inc.
Hamilton, IL 62341

Guide to Bees and Honey
Ted Hooper.
$10.95, hardcover.
Rodale Press, Inc.
Book Division
33 East Minor St.
Emmaus, PA 18049

Practical Beekeeping
Roger Griffith and Enoch Tompkins. 1977.
$5.95, paper.
Garden Way Publishing
Charlotte, VT 05445

Queen Rearing
H. H. Laidlaw, Jr. and J. E. Eckert. 1962 (2nd ed.)
$7.95.
University of California
2223 Fulton
Berkeley, CA 94720

Selecting and Operating Beekeeping Equipment
U.S. Department of Agriculture
Agricultural Research Office
Farmers' Bul. No. 2204. 1969.
For sale by the Superintendent of Documents
U.S. Government Printing Office
Washington, D.C. 20402

Catalogs

Dadant & Sons, Inc.
Hamilton, IL 62341
Free catalog.

Diamond International Corp.
Apiary Dept.
Chico, CA 95926
Free catalog.

Forbes and Johnson
P.O. Box 212
Homersville, GA 31634

Cypress bee supplies and equipment.
List, $1.25.

Los Angeles Honey Co.
1559 Fishburn Ave.
Los Angeles, CA 90063
Free catalog.

A. I. Root Co.
Medina, OH 44256
Free catalog.

Sunstream Bee Supply Co.
P.O. Box 484
Pittsburgh, PA 15230
Catalog, 50¢.

Food Preservation

Safe storage methods for food vary from region to region. You might want to contact your county cooperative extension agent for information on methods and conditions of storing products in your geographic area.

Books, Pamphlets

The ABC's of Home Food Dehydration
Barbara Densley. 1975.
$3.95, paper.
Horizon Publishers and Distributors
P.O. Box 490, 50 South, 500 West
Bountiful, Utah 84010

A wide variety of drying methods is covered in this timely book, which describes how to preserve fruits, herbs, meat, fish, and vegetables. Includes many hints; recipes.

Ball Blue Book
$2.00, paper.
Box 2005
Muncie, IN 47302

Beef Slaughtering, Cutting, Preserving and Cooking on the Farm
U.S. Department of Agriculture
Farmers' Bul. No. 2263. 1977.
$2.00, paper.
For sale by the Superintendent of Documents
U.S. Government Printing Office
Washington, D.C. 20402

Canning, Freezing, Curing and Smoking of Meat, Fish and Game
Wilbur F. Eastman, Jr. 1975.
$11.95, hardcover; $5.95, paper.
Garden Way Publishing
Charlotte, VT 05445

This book has been designed to provide basic and safe information to help the home owner process meat, fish, and game. By processing is meant the procedures for canning, freezing, curing, and smoking; in other words, storing meat for future use. Even if you should decide not to do your own processing, the book can still provide you with an understanding of what has happened to the meat products that you see in the markets and which you may ultimately purchase for household needs.

Home Canning of Fruits and Vegetables
Home Canning of Meat and Poultry (2 pamphlets)
U.S. Department of Agriculture.
15¢ each.
For sale by the Superintendent of Documents
U.S. Government Printing Office
Washington, D.C. 20402

The Joy of Cooking
Irma S. Rombauer.
$10.95, hardcover; $20.00, deluxe.
The Bobbs-Merrill Co., Inc.
4300 W. 62nd St.
Indianapolis, IN 46268

A favorite and much relied-upon source book. Rightly so, because the recipes are tested and easy to follow, sage advice is generously dispensed, and the book contains a store of infor-

A. Rump.
B. Mouse Buttock.
C. Leg or Hock.
D. Buttock or Round.
E. Aitch-bone or Top.
F. Surloin.
G. Fore Ribs.
H. Middle Ribs.

I. Chuck Rib.
J. Neck, Clod, or Sticking Piece.
K. Shin.
L. Shoulder or Leg of Mutton Piece.
M. Brisket.
N. Thin Flank.
O. Thick Flank.
P. Veiny Piece.

mation not to be found in any other single book. For food preservation, consult the following sections: "The Foods We Keep"; "Canning, Salting, Smoking and Drying"; "Freezing"; "Jellies and Preserves"; and "Pickles and Relishes."

Just in Case. A Manual of Home Preparedness
Barbara G. Salsbury.
$5.50, paper.
Bookcraft Publishers
1848 West, 2300 South
Salt Lake City, UT 84120

Ruling out mere existence as a goal, the author indicates the way to maintain good health under all conditions as she outlines the knowledge and skills that will prepare a family for almost any eventuality. Here is detail on preserving food by canning, drying, freezing, brining; on storing food in basements, apartments, root cellars; on growing food in home gardens, even in containers. To enhance preparedness by current usage, facts and know-how are supplied on standard foods like wheat and other grains, legumes, milk, and eggs, as well as some of the newer foods and food processes. Thirty tables put a host of summarized facts at the reader's fingertips. The picture is completed with an abundance of preparedness information in the nonfood area.

Keeping the Harvest: Home Storage of Fruits and Vegetables
Nancy Thurber and Gretchen Mead. 1976.
$5.95, trade paper; $6.95, spiral; $12.95, hardcover.
Garden Way Publishing
Charlotte, VT 05445

Canning–Freezing–Bottling–Curing–Pickling–Storing:
—Over 200 step-by-step photos

—Planting and harvest information for proper quantities and quality
—Special diet canning, new garden varieties
—Frank advice about unorthodox methods like commercial jar substitutions, open-kettle canning, pickling, "shortcuts"
—Over 200 family-tested recipes
—Bulk grain storage, building a root cellar and drier.

Kerr Home Canning Book
$1.00, paper.
Kerr Glass Mfg. Co.
Sand Springs, OK 74063

Lamb Slaughtering, Cutting, Preserving and Cooking on the Farm
Farmers' Bull. No. 2264. 1977.
$1.40, paper.
For sale by the Superintendent of Documents
U.S. Government Printing Office
Washington, D.C. 20402

*Making the Best of the Basics: Family
Preparedness Handbook*
James Talmage Stevens.
$5.95, paper.
Peton Corp.
P.O. Box 11925
Salt Lake City, UT 84111

Preserving, storing, and using foods; recipes;
instructions for storing fuel and water; yard gardening; soap-making; basic medical supplies; and
other useful information. Attractive and easy to
follow, this book appears to be an excellent buy
for the money.

*Root Cellaring: The Simple, No-Processing Way to
Store Fruits and Vegetables*
Mike and Nancy Bubel.
$11.95, hardcover.
Rodale Press, Inc.
Book Division
33 East Minor St.
Emmaus, PA 18049

*Stocking Up: How to Preserve the Foods You
Grow Naturally*
By the editors of *Organic Gardening Magazine*
(rev. edition)
$13.95, hardcover; $15.95, deluxe.
Rodale Press, Inc.
Book Division
33 East Minor St.
Emmaus, PA 18049

Stocking Up takes the reader through every step
of food preservation, including choosing fruit and
vegetable varieties best suited for storing; preserving; instructions for underground storage; and
recipes for the preparation of stored foods.
Canning foods in high-altitude areas, how to
make soft and hard cheese, freezing, canning,
curing, smoking and storing meat, poultry and
fish—this book probably contains all the information you will need.

Storing Vegetables and Fruits in Basements,
Cellars, Outbuildings and Pits
Home and Garden Bul. No. 119
Pamphlet, 40¢.
For sale by the Superintendent of Documents
U.S. Government Printing Office
Washington, D.C. 20402

Catalogs

Barth's of Long Island
Valley Stream, NY 11582

Grain-mill, juicer, yogurt-maker, and seed
sprouter, as well as vitamin and mineral supplements and natural foods.
Free catalog.

B&J Industries
514 State St.
Marysville, WA 98270

The Equi-Flow food dehydrator and a full line of
other food preservation items.
Free catalog.

Country Catalog
265 Petaluma Ave.
Sebastapol, CA 95472

"Complete sections on food preparation, books,
old-time items, farm needs. Lowest prices—best
savings."
Catalog, $2.95; $2.50 refund with first $20 order.

Countryside General Store
Highway 19 East SU
Waterloo, WI 53594

Kitchen and homestead products, books, and
tools for livestock.
Catalog, $1.00.

Cumberland General Store
Route 3, Box 470
Crossville, TN 38555
Catalog, $3.00.

Excalibur Products
6083 Power Inn Rd.
Sacramento, CA 95824

"We offer you the best quality grain-mill on the
market at the most reasonable price."
Free information.

Garden Way Country Kitchen Catalog
Garden Way Catalog Dept.
90461–1300 Ethan Allen Ave.
Winooski, VT 05404

"The most complete selection anywhere! Dehydrators, pea and bean shellers, jelly strainers,
sausagemakers, etc. More than 500 hard-to-find
items for home canners and folks who preserve
food at home."
Free catalog; 25¢ postage.

Garden Way Press for Cider
Garden Way Research
Charlotte, VT 05445

Available in kits.
Free information.

Glen-bel's Country Store
Rt. 5, Box 390
Crossville, TN 38555

"300-page catalog, 3,000 items, wood-stoves . . .
farrier's tools, grain mills, corn shellers, butter
moulds."
Catalog, $4.00, refundable with order.

Good Nature Products
P.O. Box 233
East Aurora, NY 14052

Hydraulic cider press, etc.
Catalog, $1.00, refundable with order.

Potato Gun

A potato gun is great fun. Get a piece of thin walled tubing as at Fig. 7. The kind used for a combination pen and pencil or a glass drinking tube will do. File one end sharp so it will cut the potato easily. Make a handle of a round piece of wood as at Fig. 8. Drive a nail through the handle so the end cannot be pushed all the way through the tube. It should stop about ¾″ from the end, Fig. 9. Slice a potato as at Fig. 10 about ⅛″ thick. Plug the end of the tube by forcing it through the slice of potato which should be placed flat on a piece of board. Plug the other end, and with the plunger push one plug through the tube. The other will fly out making a loud report.

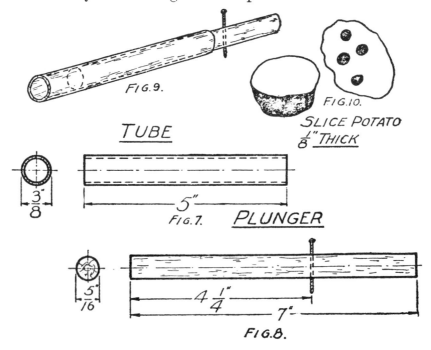

FIG. 9.
FIG. 10.
SLICE POTATO
1/8″ THICK
TUBE
3/8″
5″
FIG. 7.
PLUNGER
5/16″
4 1/4″
7″
FIG. 8.

The Grover Company
211 S. Industrial Park Ave.
Tempe, AZ 58282

Marathon electric flour mill: "The only mill that grinds *all* grains, even soybeans and peas.
Free information.

Happy Valley Ranch
P.O. Box 9153
Yakima, WA 98909

Assembled or kit cider press: "will grind a bushel of apples in less than five minutes."
Catalog, 50¢.

Mother's General Store
Box 506
Flat Rock, NC 28731

Homestead items, cast-iron cookware, food-processing devices.

New England Cheese-Making Supply Co.
Ashfield, MA 01330

Cheese-making supplies: rennet, moulds, starter culture, presses, and more.
Catalog, $1.00.

Nutri-Flow, Inc.
5201 SW Westgate Dr.
Portland, OR 97221

Food dehydrators. "Exterior thermo control. One year warranty."
Free catalog and recipes.

R & R Mill Company
Corona Dept.
Smithfield, UT 84335

Convertible mill—stones for grains, metal plates to grind nuts, and other useful items.
Free catalog.

Reliance Products
1900 Olympic Blvd.
Walnut Creek, CA 94596
Reliance Supplies General Catalog.

Bulk food storage containers, home grain mills, food dehydrators, books, as well as fireplace paraphernalia to increase energy efficiency, books, much more. A reputable company, quality merchandise.
Free catalog.

Sears, Roebuck & Co.
925 S. Homan Ave.
Chicago, IL 60607

Free suburban, farm, and ranch catalog. Canning and freezing equipment, grain mills, cider presses, more. (Also in Sears' free general catalog.)

Farm Buildings and Repair

[See also Chapter 4, *Building and Alternative Energy*.]

Books and Pamphlets

Barns, Sheds and Outbuildings: Placement, Design and Construction
Byron D. Halstead, ed. 1977.
(Reproduction of 1881 edition.)
$6.95.
The Stephen Greene Press
109 Fessenden Rd.
Brattletoro, VT 05301

"Basic time-tested help on building or re-modelling everything from a dairy barn to a tool shed to a bird house. 257 illustrations."

Building with Adobe and Stabilized Earth Blocks
U.S. Department of Agriculture
Leaflet 535
35¢.
For sale by the Superintendent of Documents
U.S. Government Printing Office
Washington, D.C. 20402

Country Comforts: Designs for the Homestead
Christian Bruyere and Robert Inwood. 1975.
$6.95, paper.
Drake Publications, Inc.
801 2nd Ave.
New York, NY 10017

How to build fireplaces, root cellars, wood-burning water heater, etc.

Fences, Gates and Bridges: A Practical Manual
George A. Martin
$6.95.
The Stephen Greene Press
109 Fessenden Rd.
Brattleboro, VT 05301

"From old-time sources, the best, easiest, cheapest ways to build all types of fences, gates, bridges, stiles, culverts, etc."

House Construction: How to Reduce Costs
U.S. Department of Agriculture
Farmers' Bul. No. 2227
Pamphlet, 35¢.
For sale by the Superintendent of Documents
U.S. Government Printing Office
Washington, D.C. 20402

In Harmony with Nature: Creative Country
Construction
Christian Bruyere and Robert Inwood. 1975.
$6.95, paper.
Drake Publications, Inc.
801 2nd Ave.
New York, NY 10017

Building with logs.

The Owner-Built Homestead
Ken Kern. 1974.
Owner-Built Publications
Box 550
Oakhurst, CA 93644

Roofing Farm Buildings
Farmers' Bul. No. 2170
Pamphlet, 45¢.
For sale by the Superintendent of Documents
U.S. Government Printing Office
Washington, D.C. 20402

Successful Small Farms: Building Plans and
Methods
Herbert T. Leavy. 1978.
$14.00, hardcover; $5.95, paper.
Structures Publications Co.
P.O. Box 423
Farmington, MI 48024

A BIRD-HOUSE

This is how the old tin can looks when transformed into a bird home and swung
into a tree.

Tools for Homesteaders, Gardeners and Small-Scale Farmers
$12.95, paper.
Rodale Press, Inc.
Book Division
33 East Minor St.
Emmaus, PA 18049

Catalogs

Hammond Barns
P.O. Box 584
New Castle, IN 47362
Brochure, 25¢.

Midwest Plan Service
Agricultural Engineering
Iowa State University

A catalog of inexpensive handbooks and plans for barns, storage buildings, and livestock housing. Free catalog.

Water

Books and Pamphlets

Planning for an Individual Water System
American Association for Vocational Instructional Materials. 1973.
$6.95.
Engineering Center
Athens, GA 30602

Treating Farmstead and Rural Home Water Systems
Farmers' Bul. No. 2248
35¢.
U.S. Department of Agriculture
For sale by the Superintendent of Documents
U.S. Government Printing Office
Washington, D.C. 20402

Water Supply Sources for the Farm and Rural Home
U.S. Department of Agriculture
Farmers' Bul. No. 2237
For sale by the Superintendent of Documents
U.S. Government Printing Office
Washington, D.C. 20402

Farming and Gardening Magazines

Backyard Poultry
Waterloo, WI 53594
Free information; sample copy, $1.00; monthly, $7.00 year.

One-Piece Cover on Water Tank Raised by Twisting Ropes

This One-Piece Cover Allows Stock to Drink from All Sides of the Tank

Instead of protecting your stock-watering tank in winter with a cover hinged in several sections for easy removal, make it in one piece and suspend it with two ropes from a pipe frame over the tank, crossing them as shown. To raise the cover, it is rotated by means of handles provided, causing the ropes to shorten in twisting. At the proper height, a bolt is inserted through one of the pipe standards and through screw eyes in the cover to hold it in place when it is raised.

Country Journal
205 Main Street
Brattleboro, VT 05301
$15 for one year; 12 issues

Countryside
Rt. 1
Waterloo, WI 53594

"A unique old-fashioned magazine for today's homesteaders . . . all aspects of practical self-sufficiency and small farming." Since 1917. (Recommended by the USDA Yearbook, 1978 to those interested in raising goats.)
Free information; $8.95 for 9 months; $15.75 for 18 months.

Dairy Goat Journal
Box 19080
Scottsdale, AZ 85252
$9.00 year. "Write for complete book list."

For anyone interested in the back-to-the-land movement, this should prove a helpful and entertaining tool. Sturdily bound for future reference; covers alternative energy news, gardening techniques, livestock, food preservation and recipes, low-cost building construction, etc.
2 issues/month; $12.00/year; $23 for 2 years; $33.00 for 3 years.

Index to Mother Earth News
Mother's Indexers
P.O. Box 203
Boulder, CO 80302

If you want to know what *Mother Earth News* has to say on any particular subject, get down to the public library and ask the reference librarian where to find this index. It is not done by the same people who publish the magazine, but by a self-proclaimed bunch of amateur indexers; still, they do a competent job. And if you do not use the index, you will have to leaf through all the back issues yourself.

The New Farm
Robert Rodale, ed.
Rodale Press, Inc.
33 East Minor St.
Emmaus, PA 18049

Edited by the originator of the famous *Organic Gardening Magazine, The New Farm* has more detailed "how to do it" articles and even delves into pesticide use.
7 issues/year, $10.00.

North American Pomona
North American Fruit Explorers
1848 Jennings Dr.
Madisonville, KY 42431

Find out about the new varieties of fruits and nuts and the good old varieties.
Quarterly, $5.00/year.

Fruit Varieties Journal
American Pomological Society
103 Tyson Bldg.
University Park, PA 16802
Quarterly; $8.00 year.

Hortscience
American Society for Horticultural Science
7931 East Blvd.
Alexandria, VA 22308

An excellent magazine for those who want to keep up with scientific and technical aspects of agriculture.
$25.00/year.

Mother Earth News
P.O. Box 70
Hendersonville, NC 28739

Organic Gardening
Rodale Press, Inc.
33 East Minor St.
Emmaus, PA 18049

Good articles on every aspect of gardening, farming, and usable alternative energy from the standpoint of self-reliance. Combines a feeling of old-time practicality and ingenuity with modern techniques and scientific research. Easy for beginners to understand and follow. The December issue includes an index of the previous year's articles by subject.

Monthly; $9.00 for 1 year; 2 years, $16.50; 3 years, $23.00. Canada: $2.00 extra per year for postage.

Rabbits
Waterloo, WI 53594

''The ideal livestock for the small place and self-sufficiency.''
Free information; sample copy, $1.00; $7.00/year.

Finding GOLD in SILT and SAND

By George H. Eckhardt

PRIMARILY intended as a simple but effective help for the prospector whose chief object is to find where the gold lies, rather than to mine it on a large paying scale, the simple gold-recovery apparatus described in this article can be cheaply made by anyone, is collapsible and light in weight, and does not require skillful handling to make it work efficiently. It was designed by Samuel Gordon, associate curator of mineralogy at the Academy of Natural Sciences in Philadelphia, to meet actual field conditions, and in connection with its use, Mr. Gordon also gives some valuable information usually not available outside of mining engineering circles.

The apparatus extracts gold from silt, fine sand, clay, and sludge. The whole arrangement consists of a funnel mounted on a tripod, a length of metal tubing connecting the funnel to a U-shaped glass tube, two short lengths of rubber hose giving the required flexibility to this part of the outfit. The U-shaped glass tube is filled with mercury, the mercury column extending well up both arms of the "U." A riffle, made of boards with strips across the bottom, somewhat resembling a washboard, is placed under the open end of the glass tube to catch and hold any globules

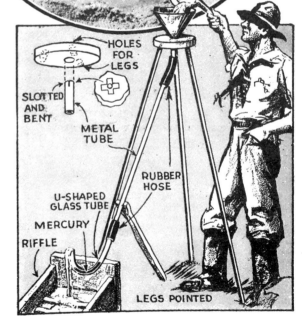

When a gold-bearing sludge is poured through this simple apparatus, the gold amalgamates with mercury contained in a U-shaped glass tube

water until it is brought to an easy-pouring consistency. This sludge is then poured through the apparatus, steadily and not too rapidly, adding water if necessary. As the sludge passes slowly through the tube and out into the riffle, the gold amalgamates with the mercury.

It's easy to separate the gold from the mercury and recover the latter for use again and again. The mercury-gold amalgam is removed from the glass tube and squeezed in a chamois, or several thicknesses of linen handkerchiefs, to remove the dirt. It is then placed in an iron pan or spade and a large potato is cut in half and the center hollowed out to form a "tent" over the puddle of amalgam. The pan is then held over a fire. The heat volatilizes the mercury, causing the release of its gold content, the latter collecting in a tiny "button" on the bottom of the pan. At the same time the mercury is condensed as globules in the potato where it can be recovered by mashing the latter in a kettle of water. A brass, copper or zinc pan must not be used with mercury, nor should these metals be used in making any part of the apparatus because of the reaction of mercury with these metals.

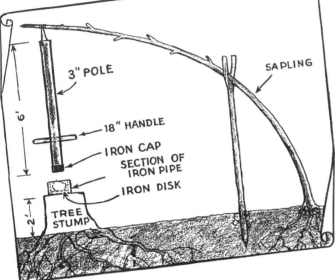

Utilizing a sapling, a stump and pieces of iron pipe, the prospector can make a miniature "stamp mill" for crushing small quantities of ore so that it may be run through the gold-recovering apparatus

of mercury which may be forced out of the tube. The bottom of the riffle is inclined to carry away the water and sludge, but should be sealed tightly at the sides and along the strips so that any mercury escaping from the tube will be retained. The "U" need not necessarily be of glass tubing—it may be iron or steel—but glass is preferable because the operation can be better observed.

Now, before ore or sand carrying gold can be poured through the apparatus it must be crushed very fine. This can be done in a dolly which is easily made by utilizing a sapling, a stump, and a few pieces of iron pipe as in one of the illustrations. The arrangement makes a very effective crusher for small quantities of ore. The fine material that comes from the crusher is thoroughly worked up with

Strangely enough gold is quite widely distributed among the rocks of the earth's crust, and can often be found in unsuspected places. Scientists have calculated that five-ten-millionths of one per cent of the earth's crust is made up of gold. This may seem an almost microscopic percentage, but it should be remembered that gold is a precious metal. For instance, no one would expect to find gold in the clay excavated for a subway in Philadelphia, yet this was found to contain one part of gold in one million parts of clay, and each cubic foot carried about three cents worth of gold. The Delaware river near Philadelphia has never been famous as a gold-carrying stream, yet workmen have netted as high as sixty cents per day panning gold along its banks. Every county in California contains gold, in fact it is mined in two-thirds of the counties of this state. Yet before 1824 most of the gold brought to the United States mint came from Georgia, Alabama, North and South Carolina, and Virginia. At present, an iron mine at Cornwall, Pa., yields $13,000 worth of gold a year as a by-product.

Mr. Gordon says that there are two modes of occurrence of gold which interest the prospector. Everyone is familiar with the fact that gold occurs in veins of quartz. Quartz, however, is the most common of all minerals, and it is obvious that veins of it carrying gold in paying quantity are exceedingly rare on the face of the earth. More often they contain "fool's gold" or pyrite. This is very hard, it cannot be scratched with a penknife, whereas gold is soft and malleable, and forms fernlike crystals rather than the beautiful symmetrical cubes and octahedra of pyrite. Of course, both pyrite and gold may occur in the same quartz vein and this has been a help to the prospector. At the outcrop of a quartz vein pyrite "rusts" or weathers, forming limonite, a yellowish brown porous material which gives the vein a rusty appearance. This weathering of the vein, and leaching away of the more soluble constituents, causes some concentration of the gold in the outcrop, where it can be detected with a hand glass by the prospector. Where this concentration has occurred through the ages, by disintegration of quartz veins in mineralized areas, placer deposits may be formed in the beds of creeks or rivers. Rains and snows wash silt, dirt, clay, and gold down the hills and mountain sides. The lighter materials are carried on to the sea, while there is a tendency for the heavy gold particles to be concentrated in riffles in the stream beds along with magnetite and other heavy minerals. Nature has thus concentrated for the prospector small accumulations of gold. The richest hoards, however, have been found in ancient water courses, that is in "fossil" rivers and creeks, channels where water once flowed, but now filled with sand, silt, and gravel. Perhaps the stream was diverted to another channel, or the district became arid. At any rate, some of the richest finds in Australia and the Klondike have been made in such ancient "gutters."

❡Cover sharp corners of workshop machinery with adhesive tape to avoid tearing the clothing.

Recovering both the gold and the mercury is easy. Heat volatilizes the latter which condenses as globules in half of a potato and leaves the gold in the bottom of the container. Mashing the potato in a pan of water releases the mercury

2
Wilderness Survival

Introduction

Over the past few years, an increasing number of Americans have shown signs of discontent with sedentary living and push-button conveniences. Motivated, perhaps, by an intuition that times are going to get harder, people all over the country are trying to toughen up—or "get in shape," as the popular expression goes. Physical fitness is in vogue, along with its spiritual counterpart, appreciation of nature. With the current interest in "body image" and "getting in shape" comes the realization that human beings are a part of nature, part of the whole. This sounds obvious, but for many years emphasis was placed upon rational conquest of nature, as if man were somehow above the natural order of the universe. This was pragmatic thinking for building up industry; but now industry shows signs of failing. Poisoned by our own chemical and radioactive wastes and fearful of the consequences of petroleum shortages, we as a nation are trying to get back on good terms with the Earth.

As a result of this new interest in physical fitness and the out-of-doors, hiking, backpacking, camping, and skiing have become stylish. Droves of vacationers take off for the wilderness, eager to commune with Mother Nature. Many of these enthusiasts, unfortunately, know her only from margarine commercials or from postcards and calendars. And Mother Nature does make a pretty calendar girl.

Snowladen pines in a mountain setting so breathlessly undisturbed, one would think no gale ever rocked their branches. The desert in bloom after a spring rain. Lush woodland scenes complete with deer peacefully abrowse amongst the wild flowers. And always beneath bright blue skies or technicolor sunsets. One tends to forget that Mother Nature has her dark side, difficult to capture on film. Her mood swings can be dangerous; and blizzards, avalanches, parching heat, or unremitting cold are not likely to strike the unprepared wilderness sojourner as especially pretty.

The materials listed in this chapter have been selected with a view to preparedness, both physical and mental. Some of the clothing and equipment offered in the catalogs is pretty basic, not advertised as survival gear. We include these sources with the old adage, "prevention is better than cure." The person who is appropriately dressed and properly outfitted may never encounter an emergency situation.

Not everyone, of course, who gets into trouble with the elements planned to get back to nature at all. A plane is forced down in the Rocky Mountains, and the passengers, who had confidently expected to land in Denver, are faced with a crisis. A family takes an air-conditioned auto cruise through the desert, only to encounter engine trouble miles from help. Even travelling the Interstate in winter can be hazardous. In these situations, knowledge and attitude can be as important as kits and equipment. Many of the books listed in this chapter provide survival information that will come in handy in any emergency, no matter how unexpected.

Camping Out: Tips from the Nineteenth Century

From *The Successful Housekeeper,* 1886.

The man who is to plunge into the woods and really forget his worn-out self, should be sure not to forget his worn-out clothes. See that your trowsers are easy, neatly mended, strong as to buttons, and not too dark, nor yet too light, lest your sense of the value of cleanliness make intimacies with mud too unpleasantly noticeable. Try to imagine that you are getting nearer to Mother Nature and are another Thoreau, always excepting his egotism, which Heaven forbid should ever fall upon the brain of another mortal.

For six people, the following kitchen articles are required: A camp-kettle with cover, for hot water; a three-quart coffee-kettle and a two-quart tea pot; two bake-pans, one frying pan, one water-pail, two cooking-forks and two cooking spoons of tinned iron; and, if the party be very fastidious, a gridiron will be a boon. To broil a bird or a fish, a pointed stick is the woodman's chief joy.

A large box of pulverized charcoal for filtering water after a rain is a real luxury, and will add safety, as well as satisfaction, to drinking water. Matches should be kept in corked bottles, and there should be rubber-cloth sheets for use during a storm that refuses to keep out of the tents while one is making the most of a sleeping season. Spread upon the ground, when one desires to lie prone upon one's back and enjoy long intervals of dreaminess, with eyes wide open and turned upward to the blue which flickers through the foliage of the trees, a rubber sheet is a great comfort.

Of course, it is not against the law to take a serving woman, but such feminines are liable to demand more conveniences and languish with more vehement discontent in the absence of civilization than the mistress herself. Indeed, domestic appendages of this description not infrequently revolt determinedly or disappear altogether from the most fascinating of game and trout dinners served a la hemlock plank and from couches of aromatic pine needles and blankets.

Western Historical Collection, University of Colorado Libraries.

Access

Outdoor Equipment and Clothing

Catalogs

ACR Electronics, Inc.
3901 N. 29th Ave.
Hollywood, FL 33020

Emergency transmitters, 5-year flashlights and anchor and marker, water-activated and strobe lights, beam guns, transceivers.
Free catalog.

racquettes Aigle Noir (Black Eagle Snowshoes, Inc.)
251 Boule. La Riviere, CP 250
Loretteville, P.Q.
Canada G2A 1H2

A variety of snowshoes for different terrains, pursuits. White ash and leather. Repair kit. Free brochure in French and English.

Allison Forge Corp.
P.O. Box 404
Belmont, MA 01178

"Life Tool" survival tool: screwdriver, can opener, file, knife, compass, signal mirror, and wire-stripper, all in one.
Free catalog.

Antelope Camping Equipment
21740 Granada
Cupertino, CA 95014

Pack outfits in many styles, price ranges.
Catalog, 25¢.

Eddie Bauer
3rd & Virginia
P.O. Box 3700
Seattle, WA 98124

Clothing, tents, sleeping bags. Knives by Case, Buck, Gerber, including the Gerber Mark I Survival Knife. Kel-Lite heavy-duty flashlights. Excellent line of down products. Fine quality and expensive.
Free catalog.

L. L. Bean
Freeport, ME 04032

L. L. Bean has long been known for good quality and a certain New England style. The catalog makes good reading even if you decide not to order anything—but if you do order, you will not regret it.
Free catalog.

Beck Outdoor Projects
Box 1038
Crescent City, CA 95531
Free catalog.

Beckel Canvas Products
P.O. Box 20491
Portland, OR 97220

Tents and camping equipment. Note: cabin tent designed to accommodate a wood stove.

Brigade Quartermasters
P.O. Box 108
Powder Springs, GA 30073

Clothes, knives, military goods, outdoor gear, camping equipment. Air Force–issue survival knife, rescue lights, flashlights, survival and first aid kits.
Catalog, $2.00.

Cabela's, Inc.
812 13th Ave.
Sidney, NB 69162

The *Complete Hunter's Catalog* cites Cabela's, along with Herter and L. L. Bean, as the catalog offering "the best quality merchandise at the most reasonable cost." Complete line for the explorer, hunter, and fisherman. "Space blanket" is worthy of note: it is light, easily stored, and warm, as it reflects back your own body heat.
Free catalog.

Charter Oak Distributors, Inc.
50 Walnut St.
Middletown, CT 06457

Outdoor gear, including reloading and muzzle-loading equipment, fishing, and hunting gear. Supplies, books.
Free catalog.

Co-op Wilderness Supply
1607 Shattuck Ave.
Berkeley, CA 94709

Cold weather clothing, tents: Eureka, Jansport,
Snow Lion, Caribou; packs, sleeping bags, Mountain House foods, Silva barometer/altimeter and
compasses, Swift binoculars, more.
Free catalog.

Doan Machinery and Equipment Co.
P.O. Box 21334
South Euclid, OH 44121

Note Doan's magnesium fire starter.
Free brochure.

Eastern Mountain Sports, Inc.
Vose Farm Rd.
Peterborough, NH 03458

Equipment for climbing, snowshoeing, skiing,
packing; clothes, boots, books. First aid,
climate/topographical instruments, trail foods,
inflatable boats.
Free catalog.

Arthur Ellis & Co., Ltd.
Private Bag
Dunedin, New Zealand

Ellis specializes in down. Prices and merchandise
look tempting in the catalog, but we have no
firsthand experience. The catalog is, in fact, so
attractive that you may want to gamble.
Free catalog.

Emge Aviation/Marine Products, Inc.
Aviation and Marine Survival Equipment
Wood Lane, Woodbourne Industrial Air Park
P.O. Box 157
Langhorne, PA 19047

Safety, survival, and air crew personal equipment.
Examples: antiexposure suits, communication
equipment, oxygen equipment, parachutes,
survival kits, survival accessories, diesel engines,
personal armor. "A commercial sales approach is
difficult as most items are expensive due to con-
formity with government specs, and sales leaflets,
catalogs and established price lists with descriptions are not available. We make specific quotations against definite requirements."
Free product list.

Eureka Tent and Awning Co., Inc.
Box 966
Binghampton, NY 13902

All kinds of tents, plus fourteen different kinds of
tent and awning material sold by the yard at
reasonable prices. Some of Eureka's tents are
excellent, others not as good. You might want to
check *Backpacking Equipment Buyer's Guide* for
evaluations.
Free catalog.

Fabiano Shoe Co.
850 Summer St.
S. Boston, MA 02127

Ski and cold weather boots.
Free brochure.

Filson Outdoor Clothes
C. C. Filson Co.
205 Maritime Bldg.
Seattle, WA 98104

Fine quality, sturdy outdoor work clothes, wool
and cotton.
Free catalog.

F&L Packing Corp.
681 Main St.
Belleville, NJ 07109

"Outdoorstuff" catalog featuring first aid kits, survival knife (U.S. Coast Guard), water purification tablets, and other useful items. "Serving you since the 1940s."
Free catalog.

Fly Fisherman's Bookcase and Tackle Service
3890 Stewart Rd.
Eugene, OR 97402

Outdoor sportsman's supplies.
Free catalog.

Forrest Mountaineering, Ltd.
1517 Platte St.
Denver, CO 80202

Mountain climber's gear.

Frostline Kits
Frostline Circle
Denver, CO 80241

Source of sew-it-yourself mountaineering clothing, tents, packs, etc.

Frostline Outdoor Equipment
452 Burbank
Broomfield, CO 80020

Clothing and gear.
Free catalog.

Gander Mountain, Inc.
P.O. Box 248
Wilmot, WI 53192

Camouflage clothing, flotation vests, rubber rafts, tents, sleeping bags, reloading equipment, portable toilets, telescopic rifle sights, portable CB radios, more.
Free catalog.

Gerry
5450 Valley Hwy.
Denver, CO 80216

Known for the quality of their clothing, packs.
Free catalog.

Gibbs Products
854 Padley St.
Salt Lake City, UT 84108

Mountain climbing and hiking gear.
Free brochure.

Great Pacific Iron Works
P.O. Box 150
Ventura, CA 93001

Fine technical rock and ice climbing hardware, clothes, and books.
Catalog, $1.00.

Great World
Box 250
West Simsbury, CT 06092

Ski touring gear, clothing, knives, etc.
Free catalog.

Herter's
R.R. 2
Mitchell, SD 57301

A huge catalog with everything for the outdoorsman. Gear, clothing, food, etc. An established, dependable outfit; highly recommended by the *Hunter's Catalog*.
Catalog, $1.00.

High Lonesome (used to be the Colorado Tent and Awning Co.)
3333 E. 52nd Ave.
Denver, CO 80216

Good equipment, specializing in tents, packing (horses), kayaks, and trail expedition merchandise. Offers a 50% discount if no dealer is located in your area.
Free catalog.

Holubar
Box 7
Boulder, CO 80306

Quality tents, packs, clothing, etc. for cold weather; Tekna and Mag-Lite professional flashlights. Svea stove and Waterpik Portable Instapure water decontamination kit.
Free catalog.

Laake & Joy's
1432 N. Water St.
Milwaukee, WI 53202

Outdoor and marine equipment and supplies; lightweight food.
Free catalog.

Peter Limmer and Sons, Inc.
Intervale, NH 03845

Boots and clothing. Good packs and tents. Rich-Moor low-moisture foods.
Free catalog.

Kalem Glove Mfg. Co.
Phyllis A. Kalem
2557 N. Dubonnet Ave.
Rosemead, CA 91770

Equipment for the falconer: cow- and goathide gloves, leash, bells, leather falconer's bag, swivels, jesses, and other necessary items.
Free brochure.

Moor and Mountain
63 Park St.
Andover, MA 01810

Backpacking equipment, kayaks, canoes, cross-country skis, lightweight foods, books. All kinds of accessories, including first aid kits, signal mirror, space and rescue blankets.
Free catalog.

Mountain High Enterprises (Berghaus)
RD 2, Box 229
Shelbourne, VT 05482

Gear and clothing.
Free catalog.

Mountain Safety Research
631 S. 96th St.
Seattle, WA 98108

Mountain and cold weather gear. Note: avalanche probe.
Free information.

Netcraft Fishing Tackle
The Netcraft Co.
2800 Tremainsville Rd.
Toledo, OH 43613
Free catalog.

The North Face
Box 2399, Station A
Berkeley, CA 94702

Tents, packs, gear, clothing.
Free catalog.

Northwoods
P.O. Box 609
Menomonee Falls, WI 53051

Tackle, clothing, and equipment.
Catalog, $1.25.

Orvis
The Orvis Co., Inc.
Manchester, VT 05254

Hunting and fishing catalogs. Good but expensive merchandise.
Free catalogs.

P&S Sales
P.O. Box 45095
Tulsa, OK 74145

Fishing and hunting gear, binoculars, gun racks, slingshots, pilot survival knife, lightweight polyethylene tarp, tents, more.
Free catalog.

Recreational Equipment, Inc.
1525 11th Ave.
P.O. Box 88125
Seattle, WA 98122

Wide selection of climbing, backpacking, and camping gear.
Free catalog.

Revere Survival Products
605 W. 29th St.
New York, NY 10001

Revere has the best prices around on high-quality survival equipment. Emphasis on marine necessities.
Free catalog.

Rothco, Morris Rothenberg & Son, Inc.
25 Ranick Rd.
Smithtown, NY 11787

Rothco offers such items as Vietnam jungle boots, canteens, and flashlights.
Free catalog.

HOW TO MAKE A SKATE SAIL

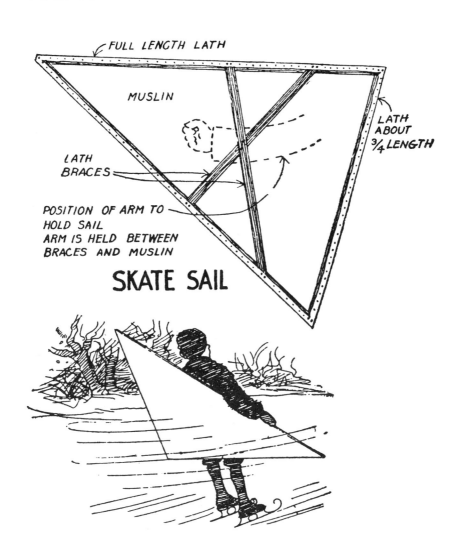

FULL LENGTH LATH

MUSLIN

LATH ABOUT ¾ LENGTH

LATH BRACES

POSITION OF ARM TO HOLD SAIL
ARM IS HELD BETWEEN BRACES AND MUSLIN

SKATE SAIL

Ruvel Company
3037 N. Clark St.
Chicago, IL 60657

Army/Navy surplus by mail. Outdoor clothing, camouflage clothes, duffel bags, gas cans, dehydrated food, tents, inflatable boats.

Seattle Tent & Fabric
900 N. 137th St.
P.O. Box 33576
Seattle, WA 98133

Family-size tents.

SI Outdoor Food and Equipment
P.O. Box 12930
Oakland, CA 94604

"An access for equipment and food for the outdoors and other independent living." All kinds of great survival products.
Catalog, $1.00.

Sierra Designs/Kelty Pack
P.O. Box 12930
Oakland, CA 94604

Tents, cold weather gear. Kelty packs have become famous for quality.
Free catalog.

Ski Hut
1615 University Ave.
Berkeley, CA 94703

Down products, packs, clothing, and accessories, all dependable. Climbing stock: Chouinard, Peck Bonaiti, Salewa, etc. Boots by Galibier, Pivetta, Vasque. Survival book offered.

SKIING OUTFIT

STAFF

TWO WIRE NAILS HAMMERED INTO EACH SIDE OF POLE TO KEEP POLE FROM SLIDING THROUGH BLOCK

POLE OR BROOM STICK
HOLE LARGE ENOUGH TO ALLOW STRONG CORD TO PASS THROUGH 'ITH FREEDOM

STAPLE

BLOCK ABOUT 1" THICK BY 4" TO 6" SQUARE
HOLE ½" LARGER THAN POLE

WHITTLED TO POINT

BARREL STAVES

SNOW SHOE AND SKI COMBINED

LEATHER OR CLOTH BAND LARGE ENOUGH FOR SHOE TO FIT SNUGLY, NAILED OR TACKED ABOUT ONE-THIRD THE LENGTH OF STAVE FROM FRONT END

SHOWING HOW MUSLIN IS FOLDED OVER AND TACKED TO LATH

MUSLIN LATH TACKS

Snocraft
Oak Hill Plaza
Box 487
Scarboro, ME 04074

Oldest of the snowshoe companies, Snocraft is known for excellence. It even offers several folding sleds for transporting provisions or gear by snowshoe, ski, or snowmobile power.

Stephenson
Box 398
Gilford, NH 03246

Warmlite bags, tents, some clothing, packs and frames. Reasonable to high prices. Stephenson's Gold X tent, with its waterproof, windspilling, reflective, and very fragile surface may be the lightest on the market, weighing in at a mere two pounds, three ounces.
Free catalog.

Strand Surplus Center
2202 Strand
Galveston, TX 77550

Army surplus and other bargains.
Free catalog.

Synergy Works
255 4th St.
Suite 2B
Oakland, CA 94607

Clothing, waterproof gear, packs. Expensive, but if you have the money to spend it will pay off in the long run.
Catalog, $1.00.

Todd's
5 S. Wabash Ave.
Chicago, IL 60603

Boots, clothes, packs. Note: Todd's Chippewa hiking boots, insulated boots, and snake boots.
Free brochure.

Vermont Tubbs
18 Elm St.
Wallingford, VT 05773

One of the oldest names in snowshoes. Variety of styles and sizes in white ash and rawhide or neoprene. Ready-made and kits.
Free brochure.

West Fork, Inc.
Lakefield, MN 56150

Outdoor and camping equipment, accessories.
Free catalog.

Wilderness Experience
20120 Plummer St.
Chatsworth, CA 91311

Clothing and gear. Fine packs at reasonable prices. Detailed and beautiful catalog.
Free catalog.

Tools

Catalogs

Forestry Suppliers
205 W. Rankin St.
P.O. Box 8397
Jackson, MI 39204

Complete line of logging and woods tools and equipment. Everything most people could think of, including a combination combustible gas/oxygen detector.

Snow & Neally Co.
155 Perry Rd.
Bangor, ME 04401

Good steel timber tools.
Free catalog.

Ax Handle Protected by Rubber When Splitting Wood

Screwed to an ax handle as shown, a piece of rubber cut from an old auto casing will protect the handle against excessive wear when splitting wood. Also, the rubber will cushion the shock to the shoulders if the user over-reaches the work.

TSI Co.
P.O. Box 151
Flanders, NJ 07836

Lumbering and woods tools, measuring instruments, clothing, etc. geared to the professional rather than the weekend outdoorsman. Huge selection and dependable quality.

Angle-Iron Footrest on Spade

Riveted horizontally across the top of a spade, a piece of angle iron affords a wide surface for the shoe when pushing the spade into the ground, thus reducing strain on the foot. If the shape of the spade handle permits, the angle iron can be notched to fit around it. Or, two short pieces may be used.

Lightweight and Freeze-Dried Foods

Catalogs

If you prefer to dry your own trail foods, see the section on food preservation in Chapter 1, *Homesteading.*

Alia, Inc.
Box 8411
Asheville, NC 28004

Chuck Wagon Foods
11333 Atlantic
Lynnwood, CA 90262

Dri-Lite Foods
11333 Atlantic
Lynnwood, CA 90262

Recommended by the *Explorer's Ltd. Source Book.*

Freeze-Dry Foods, Ltd.
201 Savings Bank Bldg.
Ithaca, NY 14850

Kamp Pak Foods
Select Food Products, Ltd.
120 Sunrise Ave.
Toronto 16
Ontario, Canada

Moor & Mountain
63 Park St.
Andover, MA 01850

Moor and Mountain carries low-moisture Rich-Moor foods, reputedly very good.

National Packaged Trail Foods — Seidel
632 East 185th St.
Cleveland, OH 44119
Free price list.

Oregon Freeze-Dry Foods, Inc.
P.O. Box 666
Albany, OR 97321

Permapak
40 East 2430 South
Salt Lake City, UT 84155

Large variety of high-quality foods; relatively inexpensive. Two-day "crisis kits" to year's supply, practical packaging. Or you can put together a kit to suit your own needs.
Free price lists.

Reliance Products
1900 Olympic Blvd.
Walnut Creek, CA 94596

Reliance offers grain mills, vitamins, and all kinds
of products and books of interest to the survivalist as well as portable foods. Endorsed by Ruff of
Ruff Times, who ought to know.

Stow-A-Way
166 Cushing Highway
Cohasset, MA 02025

Knives

Catalogs

Atlanta Cutlery Corp.
Box 839
Conyers, GA 30207

Survivor belts, Air Force survival knife, supplies
for knife makers, and a fine selection of knives
for many purposes.
Catalog, $1.00.

Bowen Knife Co.
Rt. 3, Box 3245
Blackshear, GA 31516

Survival knife in belt.

Morris Lawing
1020 Central Ave.
Charlotte, NC 28204

Hunting and fishing knives.
Free brochure.

Randall Made Knives
P.O. Box 1988
Orlando, FL 32802

Note Randalls' attack survival knife.
Free catalog.

SLS Cutlery Distributors
(Eye Brand Cutlery)
Box 391
Pearl City, HI 96782

Hollow-handled survival knife holds matches,
hooks, water purification tablets, scalpel blade,
etc.
Catalog, $1.00; free brochure on survival knife.

57

Maps

National Cartographic Information Center
507 National Center
Reston, VA 22092

"NCIC's mission is to provide information on maps, aerial photographs, survey and related cartographic data available from government and private sources." NCIC will send you a free brochure, "Types of Maps Published by Government Agencies," which includes aeronautical charts, climatic maps, and weather and historical maps. This brochure will give you the names and addresses of governmental agencies that distribute the information you want; you then write to those agencies. An inexpensive way to buy maps, but it takes time. NCIC will also send you, free upon request, indexes showing published topological maps in each state. You select from the index, then send for your maps. Government map distributors will also send topological map indexes for each state.

Indexes of areas east of the Mississippi River, including Minnesota, Puerto Rico, and the Virgin Islands are distributed by:
Branch of Distribution
U.S. Geological Survey
1200 S. Eads St.
Arlington, VA 22202

Areas west of the Mississippi River, including Hawaii, Louisiana, Guam, and American Samoa:
Branch of Distribution
U.S. Geological Survey
Box 25286, Federal Center
Denver, CO 80225

Residents of Alaska may order directly from:
Distribution Center
U.S. Geological Survey
Federal Building, Box 12
101 12th Ave.
Fairbanks, AK 99701

"These indexes indicate the area covered by each quadrangle map, its name, scale and the year of the survey. They also contain lists of special maps and addresses of local map dealers and federal map distribution centers. An order blank is included with each index."

Maps of state and county highways are available from state highway departments, located in the state capitols.

U.S. Forest Service
Dept. of Agriculture
Bureau of Land Management, Building E
Rosslyn Plaza
Rosslyn, VA 22209

Write for ordering information on inexpensive, less detailed maps of forest areas.

Wilderness Press/Trail Maps
2440 Bancroft Way
Berkeley, CA 94704

Extremely accurate topographical maps of the High Sierras. More up-to-date than U.S. Geological Survey maps. Catalog includes trail guides, books on hiking and canoeing, and more.

Hunting

Books

All about Deer Hunting in America
Robert Elman, ed.
$12.95.
Winchester Press
205 E. 42nd St.
New York, NY 10017

Firearms and equipment; finding, shooting, carrying out, butchering, and preparing the game.

Archery World's Complete Guide to Bow Hunting
Glen Helgeland, ed.
$8.95.
Prentice-Hall, Inc.
Englewood Cliffs, NJ 07632

The Complete Fisherman's Catalog
Harmon Henkin.
Paper, $7.95.
J. B. Lippincott Co.
E. Washington Sq.
Philadelphia, PA 19105

A guide to products, with articles by major outdoor sportswriters.

The Complete Hunter's Catalog
Norman Strung.
Paper, $8.95.
J. B. Lippincott Co.
E. Washington Sq.
Philadelphia, PA 19105

"Where and how to find the best buys on equipment for the shooting sports: big game, upland

and waterfowl hunting, target and varmint, black powder, archery and more." True to its name, this book is complete. Pick up the *Hunter's Catalog,* open it to any page, and read its articles, product descriptions, and quotations for enjoyment, or refer to the index if you need specific information.

Guns Annual Book of Hunting
$3.95.
Guns Magazine.
591 Camino de la Reina
Suite 200
San Diego, CA 92108

The Hunting Rifle
Jack O'Connor.
Paper, $5.95.
Stoeger Publishing Co.
55 Ruta Court
South Hackensack, NJ 07606

The Modern Rifle
Jim Carmichael.
$12.95.
Winchester Press
205 E. 42 St.
New York, NY 10017

Survival Poaching
Ragnar Benson. 1980.
Hardcover, $12.95.
Paladin Enterprises
P.O. Box 1307
Boulder, CO 80306

With this book you can live off the land, even if you are a city dweller. In this one-of-a-kind text, Benson tells how to get a deer any time you go after one (well, alright, you do have to leave the urban center for this); provides plans for traps; gives lessons on woodcraft and scouting; and imparts information on necessary equipment, firearms, and much more.

Turkey Hunter's Guide
National Rifle Association Book Service. 1979.
Paper, $4.95; NRA member price, $4.45.
1600 Rhode Island Ave. NW
Washington, DC 20036

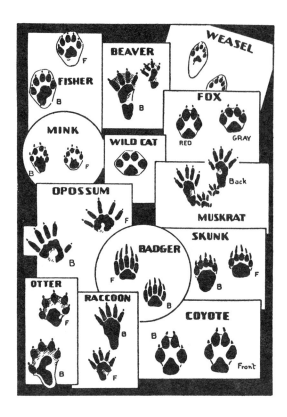

Catalogs

Air Rifle Headquarters
247 Court St. (Box 327)
Grantsville, WV 26147

Anderson Archery Corp.
Grand Ledge, MI 48837

Archery equipment.
Free catalog.

Armalite, Inc.
118 E. 16th St.
Costa Mesa, CA 92627.

Free information on
firearms and related equipment.

Bill Bassett
P.O. Box 315
Dripping Springs, TX 78620

Manufacturer of .50 caliber rifles; also makes a side mount for adapting telescopic sights to the Mini-14.

Ed Bauer Fur Co.
Smithboro, IL 62284

Hunting and trapping supplies.
Free catalog.

Bear Archery
RR 1
Grayling, MI 49738
Free catalog.

Beeman's Precision Airguns, Inc.
47 Paul Dr.
San Rafael, CA 94903

Sophisticated (expensive) airguns. Every accessory for indoor shooting or silent hunting. Catalog is a textbook on airgun use.

Brownell's, Inc.
Rt. 2, Box 1
Montezuma, IA 50171

Gun accessories.
Catalog, $2.50.

Browning (was Browning Arms)
Browning Consumer Sales Dept.
Rt. 1
Morgan, UT 84050

Quality guns, clothing, bows, arrows, knives; also, kennel and gun accessories, fishing tackle.
Free catalog.

Bushnell Optical Co.
2828 E. Foothill Blvd.
Pasadena, CA 91107

Binoculars, riflescopes, spotting scopes, bore sighters.
Free catalog.

Walter Craig, Inc.
P.O. Box 927
Selma, AL 36701

Guns and bullets, bows and arrows.
Free catalog.

E. J. Dailey's
P.O. Box 38
Union Hill, NY 14563

Trapping supplies.
Catalog, 25¢.

Decoys Unlimited, Inc.
P.O. Box 69
Clinton, IA 52732

Do-it-yourself decoys.
Free catalog.

Dixie Gun Works, Inc.
Gunpowder Lane
Union City, TN 38261

Black powder guns, kits, accessories; replicas, parts for shotguns, Kentucky rifles, and other sport and hunting guns; knives, blades, knife-making equipment, and shooting and gunsmithing supplies. Black powder arms may have a limited survival value, but you can make your own ammo, which can be a plus. Besides, this catalog is a lot of fun to read. Definite down-home style, especially if home happens to be Tennessee.
Catalog, $2.00.

Havahart
P.O. Box 551
Ossining, NY 10562

Live-catch traps. Repeating bird traps hold up to twenty birds at a time.
Catalog, 50¢.

Daryl O. Hunter
P.O. Box 44
Lee's Creek, OH 45138

Hunting dog supplies and accessories.
Free list.

Ken Nolan, Inc.
16901 Milliken
P.O. Box C-19555
Irvine, CA 92713

Camouflage clothing, flare pistols, ".45 auto" air pistols.

Penguin Industries
Frank A. Hoppe Division
Airport Industrial Mall
Coatesville, PA 19320

Hoppe's is well-known for its gun care products, accessories, and shooting supplies.
Free catalog.

Safari Outfitters
1826 Main St.
Baker, OR 97814

Telescopic sights, binoculars, reloading equipment, Lee Loader kits, shotgun shell bandoliers, more.

Sears, Roebuck & Co.
(store near you)
Ask for the camping and recreational vehicle catalog. It features tents, camping gear, folding cots and bunks, portable toilets and supplies, 12-volt accessories, and water purifiers.
Free catalog.

Unity Buying Service Co.
Membership Dept.
Camarillo, CA 93010

Excellent service and the best discounts you are likely to find on a wide selection of CB and multiband radios, walkie-talkies, camping supplies, outdoor clothing, electric outboard motors, tents, cook stoves, binoculars, knives, air purifiers.

Firearm Catalogs

Charter Arms Co.
265 Asylum St.,
Bridgeport, CT 06610

Colt Firearms Industries,
Hartford, CT 06601

Heckler & Koch, Inc.
933 N. Kenmore,
Arlington, VA 22201

Ithaca Gun Co.
Ithaca, NY 14851

O. F. Mossberg
P.O. Box 497,
North Haven, CT 06473

Remington Arms Corp.
Bridgeport, CT 06601

Smith & Wesson Inc.
2100 Roosevelt Ave.,
Springfield, MA 01101

Sturm, Ruger, & Co.
Southport, CT 06490

Dan Wesson Arms
P.O. Box 357,
Monson, MA 01057

Winchester Repeating Arms Co.
275 Winchester Ave.,
New Haven, CT 06504

Survival Stories

Books

Alive
Piers P. Read. 1975.
Paper, $1.95.
Avon Books
250 W. 55th St.
8th floor
New York, NY 10019

Excellent true account of
survival cannibalism in the Andes.

Ascent of Denali
Hudson Stuck. 1977.
Paper, $6.95.
The Mountaineers
P.O. Box 122
Seattle, WA 98111

Historical account of the first ascent of Denali,
now Mount McKinley; gripping survival adventure
story, documented by journal accounts.

One Survived
Ed Fortier. 1979.
Paper, $1.95.
Alaska Northwest Publishing Co.
130 2nd Ave. South
Edmonds, WA 98020

True Arctic survival story with maps, photographs, illustrations. "One of the great survival
stories of our time."

Snow Leopard
Peter Matthiessen. 1978.
Hardcover, $10.00.
Viking Press
625 Madison Ave.
New York, NY 10022
Paper, $2.95.
Bantam Books
666 5th Ave.
New York, NY 10019

The story of a less than pleasant journey through
the Himalayas. Exciting.

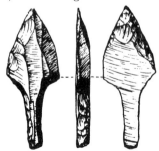

Signaling

One man, a group of men, or even an airplane, is
not too easy to spot from the air, especially when
visibility is limited. Your emergency signaling
equipment is designed to make you bigger and
easier to find.

Your airplane radio or emergency radio is your
best rescue aid. Try to make contact at once. Try to
get a fix; if the radio is serviceable, you can trans-
mit your position. When using the airplane radio,
save the battery; try to get an engine or auxiliary
generator to operate and charge the battery.

Use smoke by day, bright flame by night. Add
engine oil, rags soaked in oil, or pieces of rubber
(matting or electrical insulation) to make black
smoke; add green leaves, moss, or a little water to
send up billows of white smoke. Keep plenty of
spare fuel on hand.

Signaling aids, such as flares and smoke
grenades, must be kept dry. Use them only when
friendly airplanes are sighted or heard.

Practice signaling with the mirror in kit. A mirror
can be improvised from a ration tin by punching a
hole in the center of lid. Keep the mirror clean. On
hazy days, aircraft can see the flash of the mirror
before survivors can see the aircraft; so flash the
mirror in the direction of the plane when you hear
it, even when you cannot see it.

Signal with a flashlight or the blinker signaling
light of the emergency radio. If the airplane landing
lights are intact and you can get an engine to run,
remove the lights and extend them for signaling.
But do not waste the battery—save it for the radio.

Place or wave the yellow-and-blue cloth signal
panel in the open where it can be seen. Spread out
parachutes. Make a pattern of orange-colored Mae
Wests. Line up cowl panels from engine nacelles
upside down on airplane wings or ground; polish
the inside surfaces—they make good reflectors.
Arrange your ground signals in big geometric
patterns rather than at random—they will attract
more attention that way. The radio balloon or kite
makes a good signal.

Use the fluorescent dye available in the life raft
or Mae West kit for signaling on water or snow. Use
it carefully, for a little goes a long way; use it only
downwind for the fine dye will penetrate clothing
or food. On rivers, throw it out into the current for
a quick spread.

If you can climb a tall tree, hoist a large white or
colored improvised flag on a pole lashed to the top.

Do everything you can to disturb the "natural" look of the ground. If you are down in grass and scrub lands, cut giant markers—an 8-12 foot wide circular path, 60-75 feet in diameter, is easily seen from the air. A trampled or burned grass pattern will show from the air.

Arctic

Keep snow and frost off airplane surfaces to make a sharp contrast with the surroundings. Build your fire on a platform so it will not sink into snow. A standing spruce tree near timber line burns readily even when green. Build a "bird nest" of quickly inflammable material in the branches to insure a quick start.

Tramp out signals in snow. Fill them in with boughs, sod, moss, or fluorescent dye water.

In brush country, cut conspicuous patterns in vegetation.

In tundra, dig trenches, turn sod upside down at side of trench to widen signal.

A parachute tepee stands out in the forest or on the tundra in summer, especially at night with a fire inside.

REMEMBER: Sound does not carry well through snow. If your entire party is in snow cave or igloo, you may not hear rescue aircraft. Keep someone on guard as spotter. Build the spotter a windbreak but don't roof it.

Desert

You can make a good improvised flare from a tin can filled with sand and soaked with gasoline. Light it with care. Add oil and pieces of rubber to make dense smoke for daytime signal. Burn gasoline or use other bright flame at night.

Dig trenches to form signals or line up rocks to throw shadow.

If there is any brush in the area, gather it in piles and have it ready to light.

Smoke fires and smoke grenades are best for use in daytime. Flares and bright flames are hard to see.

The mirror is a very good desert signal; practice using it.

Tropics

Set up your fires and other signals in natural clearings and along edges of streams, or make a clearing. Signals under dense jungle growth won't be seen.

From Survival; AFM-64-5 (Paladin Press)

Wilderness Survival: Woods, Mountains, Desert, and Tropics

Books

Alive in the Desert: The Complete Guide for Desert Recreation and Survival
Joe Kraus. 1978.
Paper, $7.00.
Paladin Enterprises
P.O. Box 1307
Boulder, CO 80306

If you are planning a desert sojourn or are just passing through in your air-conditioned automobile, you should have a copy of this book—and read it.

Bending the Blade of a Hand Ax to Make It "Hug" Work

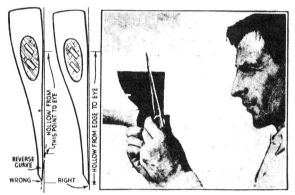

If your hand ax is beveled slightly on the flat side, it will do better work if the bevel is removed

The Art of Survival
Cord C. Troebst.
$5.95.
Doubleday & Co.
277 Park Ave.
New York, NY 10019

Poses and attempts to answer that burning question—just what *is* a survivor, and why? From the experiences of people who have won in life-or-death situations.

Basic Cold Weather Manual FM31-7
U.S. Army.
Paper, $8.00.
Paladin Enterprises
P.O. Box 1307
Boulder, CO 80306

How to use clothing and shelter to enable you to withstand very low temperatures; war in the snow; more.

Be Expert with Map and Compass
Bjorn Kjellstrom. 1976.
Paper, $6.95.
Charles Scribner's Sons
597 Fifth Ave.
New York, NY 10017

Bushcraft: A Serious Guide to Survival and Camping
Richard Graves. 1978.
Paper, $2.75.
Warner Books, Inc.
315 Park Ave. South
New York, NY 10010

Finding food and shelter, building shelters, how to determine time and direction, and other information you should have.

Equipment Lists, CG-190.
Commandant (CMC)
U.S. Coast Guard
Washington, D.C. 20591

U.S. Coast Guard–approved products, complete with manufacturers and their addresses. *"Semper paratus."*
Free.

Indian Scout Craft and Lore
Charles A. Eastman.
Paper, $4.00.
Dover Publications, Inc.
180 Varick St.
New York, NY 10014

Reprint. Describes the author's education as a young Sioux in the 1870s and 1880s. Physical training, hunting, etc.

The Master Backwoodsman
Bradford Angier. 1978.
$9.95.
Stackpole Books
Cameron & Kelker Sts.
Box 1831
Harrisburg, PA 17105

Outdoor Survival Skills
Larry D. Olsen. 1967.
$4.95.
Brigham Young University Press
Provo, UT 84601

How to survive in the wild without benefit of survival kit, waterproof matches, freeze-dried trail food, or other civilized trappings.

The Outdoorsman's Emergency Manual
Anthony J. Acerrano.
$10.00.
Winchester Press
205 E. 42nd St.
New York, NY 10017

Tested, practical advice with emphasis on common sense rather than heroics.

Outdoorsman's Fix-It Book
Monte Burch. 1971.
Harper & Row
Keystone Industrial Park
Scranton, PA 18512

Maintenance and basic repair to do at home so that you will not run into trouble far from the beaten path. How to fix tackle, chain saws, outboard motors, axes, knives, saws.

Fɪɢ. 97.—Bone awl. (After R. Brough Smith.)

Fɪɢ. 98.—Bone pins. (After R. Brough Smith.)

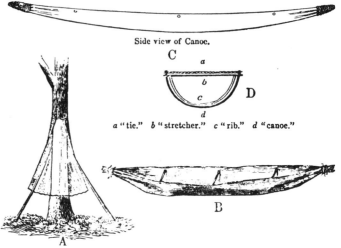

Side view of Canoe.

a "tie." *b* "stretcher." *c* "rib." *d* "canoe."

The bark-boat. *A*, to show how the bark is removed in one piece from the Eucalyptus tree ; *B*, the finished boat ; *C*, a slightly different form of bark boat, with ties and ribs as well as struts, as shown in the transverse section *D*. (After R. Brough Smith.)

Packrat Papers, Books 1 & 2
Paper, $3.95.
Signpost Books
8912 192nd St.
Edmonds, WA 98020

The experience of many backpackers makes these two volumes valuable reading for old hands (feet?) alike. Tips on food and equipment and lots of lore.

Survival!
U.S. Air Force Manual 64-5
Paper, $6.00.
Paladin Enterprises
P.O. Box 1307
Boulder, CO 80306

Sound advice for staying alive and well in all types of climate and terrain, from land to sea ice. Includes first aid, navigation, food, signalling, and fire making.

Survival Handbook
Bill Merrill. 1974.
Paper, $1.95.
Arc Books, Inc.
219 Park Ave. South
New York, NY 10003

How to avoid and survive wilderness emergencies.

Survival in the Outdoors
Byron Dalrymple. 1972.
$7.95.
E. P. Dutton and Elsevier Book Operations
2 Park Ave.
New York, NY 10016

Survival with Style
Bradford Angier. 1974.
Paper, $3.95.
Random House, Inc.
201 E. 50th St.
New York, NY 10022

Survival techniques practical from the Arctic to the tropics.

Surviving the Unexpected Wilderness Emergency
Eugene Fear. 1974.
Paper, $3.95.
Survival Education Association
9035 Golden Givens Rd.
Tacoma, WA 98445

Fear explains how the body reacts to stress and tells how to remain in control of tense situations. Specs for survival and first aid kits: aircraft, auto, and personal. Bibliography, index.

Understanding Avalanches: A Handbook for Snow Travellers in the Sierra and Cascades
Barbara Diltz-Siler. 1978.
Paper, $2.95.
Signpost Books
8912 192nd St.
Edmonds, WA 98020

Accurate information; *see* chapter on accident response.

Wilderness Handbook
Paul Petzoldt. 1977.
Paper, $4.95.
W. W. Norton & Co., Inc.
500 Fifth Ave.
New York, NY 10036

Expert advice on winter mountaineering.

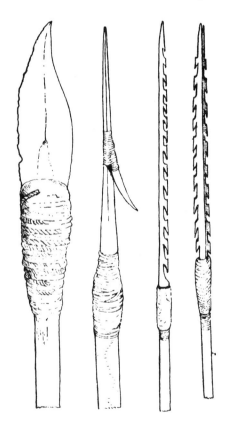

Health and Hazards

Keeping well is especially important when you are stranded on your own. Your physical condition will have a lot to do with your coming out safely. Protection against heat and cold and knowledge of how to find water and food are important to your health. But there are more rules you should follow:

Save your strength. Avoid fatigue. Get enough sleep. Even if you can't sleep at first, lie down, relax, loosen up. Stop worrying; learn to take it easy. If you are doing hard work or walking, rest for ten minutes each hour.

Take care of your feet. Your feet are important, especially if you are going to walk. If your feet hurt, stop and take care of them; it will save you trouble later on. Examine your feet when you first stop, to see if there are any red spots or blisters. Apply adhesive tape smoothly on your skin where shoes rub. If you have a blister, pierce through the thick skin at its base with a sterilized needle or pin and press out the fluid. Clean the skin thoroughly before puncturing the blister. Apply sterile bandage after drainage.

Guard against skin infection. Your skin is the first line of defense against infection. Use an antiseptic on even the smallest scratch, cut, or insect bite. Keep your fingernails cut short to prevent infection from scratching. Cuts and scratches are apt to get seriously infected, especially in the tropics. A bad infection may hurt your chance of coming out safely.

Guard against intestinal sickness. Diarrhea and other intestinal sicknesses may be caused by change of water and food, contaminated water or spoiled food, excess fatigue, over-eating in hot weather, or using dirty dishes. Purify all water used for drinking, either by purification tablets or by boiling for one minute. Cook the plants you eat, or wash them carefully with purified water. Make a habit of personal cleanliness; wash your hands with soap and water, if possible, before eating. If one member of your group gets diarrhea, take special care to enforce measures for proper disposal of human waste and to insure cleanliness in handling food and water. Field treatment of diarrhea is necessarily limited. Rest and fast—except for drinking water—for 24 hours; then take only liquid foods such as soup and tea, and avoid sugars and starches. Keep up a large intake of water, with salt tablets. Eat several meals instead of one or two large ones.

Don't worry about lack of bowel movement; this will take care of itself in a few days.

Keep your body and clothing clean. You will feel better and keep free from skin infections and body parasites. Examine each other for external parasites.

Keep your camp clean. Dump garbage in a pit or in a spot away from camp where it will not blow about. Dig a latrine or designate a latrine area away from the camp and water supply.

From Survival; AFM 64-5 (Paladin Press)

Field Guide to Edible Wild Plants
Bradford Angier. 1974.
$5.95.
Stackpole Books
Cameron & Kelker Sts.
Harrisburg, PA 17105

"A quick, all-in-color identifier of more than 100 edible wild foods growing free in the United States and Canada." Alphabetically listed plants, each with a clear illustration, Latin and folk names, and interesting, well-written information as to identification, distribution, and edibility.

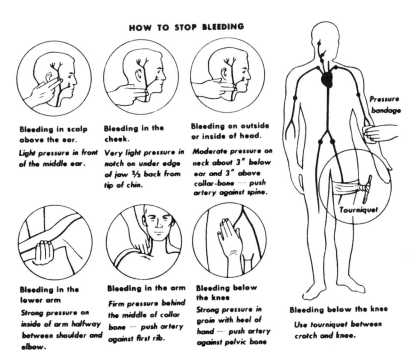

HOW TO STOP BLEEDING

Bleeding in scalp above the ear.
Light pressure in front of the middle ear.

Bleeding in the cheek.
Very light pressure in notch on under edge of jaw ⅔ back from tip of chin.

Bleeding on outside or inside of head.
Moderate pressure on neck about 3" below ear and 3" above collar-bone — push artery against spine.

Bleeding in the lower arm
Strong pressure on inside of arm halfway between shoulder and elbow.

Bleeding in the arm
Firm pressure behind the middle of collar bone — push artery against first rib.

Bleeding below the knee
Strong pressure in groin with heel of hand — push artery against pelvic bone

Bleeding below the knee
Use tourniquet between crotch and knee.

Pressure bandage

Tourniquet

Foraging

Books

Edible Native Plants of the Rocky Mountains
Paper, $6.95.
H. D. Harrington. 1974.
University of New Mexico Press
Albuquerque, NM 87106

Good for plant identification.

The Edible Wild
Berglund and Bolsby.
Paper, $3.45.
Charles Scribner's Sons
597 5th Ave.
New York, NY 10017

How to Know the Wild Fruits
Maude Gridley Peterson
Paper, $4.00.
Dover Publications, Inc.
180 Varick St.
New York, NY 10014

Over 200 berries, drupes, and pomes; 80 illustrations. Arranged by fruit color and family, with names, descriptions, edibility, and uses.

Huckleberry Country: Wild Food Plants of the Pacific Northwest
Mary and Steven Thompson.
Paper, $3.95.
Wilderness Press
2440 Bancroft Way
Berkeley, CA 94704

Edible plants from the Pacific shore to the Rockies (Oregon, Washington, Idaho, and western Montana). Descriptions of plants and their uses, with 70 drawings. ". . . the authors, wanting to communicate the actual experience of looking for wild plant foods as well as the botanical details, invite the reader along on walks where the plants grow. They discuss the plants and their uses as they come to them in their natural habitats."

The Mushroom Handbook
Louis C. C. Krieger.
Paper, $4.50.
Dover Publications, Inc.
180 Varick St.
New York, NY 10014

Thorough coverage of mushrooms in eastern and central United States. Thirty-two color plates and 126 other illustrations. Easy to use.

Since mushrooms have so little nutritive value, many knowledgeable outdoor folk deem it wise to eschew fungi altogether, even in a survival situation. To the untrained eye, one mushroom tends to look much like another, and even experienced foragers sometimes make fatal or highly discomforting mistakes. For those who persist in including these spore-spawned delicacies in their diet, a good handbook is a must.

Mushroom Hunter's Field Guide
Alex H. Smith. 1967.
Paper, $4.50.
University of Michigan Press
615 E. University
Ann Arbor, MI 48106

Have not seen this book, but the University of Michigan has a learned, diligent, and energetic crew of mushroom experts in the botanical department, and chances are this guide is well worth the money.

One Thousand American Fungi
Charles McIlvaine and Robert MacAdam.
Paper, $6.95.
Dover Publications, Inc.
180 Varick
New York, NY 10014

Identifying information for mushrooms in all parts of the United States. Special notes on the edibility of each species. Thirty-one plates, 182 illustrations.

Stalking the Blue-Eyed Scallop. 1964.
$3.95.
Stalking the Healthful Herbs. 1968.
$2.95.
Stalking the Wild Asparagus. 1962.
$2.95.
All by Euell Gibbons, all published by:
David McKay Co.
750 Third Ave.
New York, NY 10017

Wild Asparagus and *Healthful Herbs* are for the eastern and midwestern states; *Blue-Eyed Scallop* covers the west coast. These useful paperbacks have done much to popularize foraging.

Survival Handbook to Sierra Flora
Norman Weeden.
Paper, $6.95.
Wilderness Press
2440 Bancroft Way
Berkeley, CA 94704

A guide to edible and nonedible plants of the Sierras, with hundreds of drawings, glossary, and location map. The cover is resistant to moisture and tearing.

What You Don't Know Might Bite You: or, Take Me Along

Remember—if by some perverse twist of fate you happen to be bitten by a venomous snake, try to kill it. This may be easier said than done, because the *Ophidia* are notorious for their hit-and-run tactics. Then take its lifeless body with you to the hospital, if you can get to a hospital. This will help the doctors find the proper antivenin treatment for you. And a good snake identification book will save you the embarrassment of dragging in a common rat snake.

Books

Field Guide to Reptiles and Amphibians of the U.S. and Canada East of the 100th Meridian
(Peterson Field Guide Series)
Roger Conant. 2nd edition. 1975.
Paper, $4.95.
Houghton Mifflin Co.
1 Beacon St.
Boston, MA 02107

Field Guide to Western Reptiles and Amphibians
Robert C. Stebbins.
(Peterson Field Guide Series)
Paper, $4.95.
Houghton Mifflin Co.
1 Beacon St.
Boston, MA 02107

Snakebite First Aid
Thomas G. Glass, Jr., M.D.
$1.50.
Available from the author.
8711 Village Dr.
San Antonio, TX 78217

I cannot recall exactly how many species of poisonous snakes are in Texas, but there are plenty, and all of them are well represented. As a professor of surgery at University of Texas Medical School, Dr. Glass has treated many victims of snakebites, and he offers the benefit of his knowledge and experience herein.

What to Do about Bites and Stings of Venomous Animals
Arnold.
Paper, $1.95.
Collier/Macmillan, Inc.
866 Third Ave.
New York, NY 10022

Snakebite treatments are subject to controversy. The old method, with which most people are familiar, is to apply a tourniquet a few inches above the bite, make an incision across the bite mark with a knife or razor and suck out the poison. This should be continued for approximately an hour. The tourniquet must be loosened frequently. A big problem with this method is that inexperience or panic can cause gangrene or massive bleeding. A cloth soaked in a strong, hot solution of epsom salts should be applied to the cuts.

Another method of treating snakebites which has been accepted by many doctors in the past few years is the treatment known as cryotherapy. It was developed by the Poisonous Animals Research Laboratory at Arizona State University in Tempe, Arizona. Although this method is good if you are near civilization, it can pose problems in the wilderness for obvious reasons. Hold some ice on the bite while preparing a vessel of crushed ice and water. Immerse the leg or arm into the ice water up to well above the point of the bite, and keep it there for at least two hours. At all times, however, the victim must be kept warm. After these two hours an ice pack should be molded around the bitten area and left there for the next twenty-four hours. After this period the victim should be made uncomfortably warm and encouraged to drink a great deal of water.

In the field, a substitute for ice is bottled gas.

Although the newer method of treating snakebite has proven effective it is not recommended by the American Red Cross. The Red Cross' decision not to support the cold therapy treatment is based on a report made by the National Academy of Science/National Research Council in 1978. Because the report indicates that the cold therapy method still has flaws, the Red Cross continues to advocate the cut and suck method.

The Red Cross recommends that cuts be made no deeper than just through the skin, and that they be one half inch long, extending over the suspected venom deposit point. Because a snake strikes downward, the deposit point is usually lower than the fang marks. The cuts should not be made on the head, neck or trunk. Cross-cut incisions should not be made. The victim should not be given alcohol, sedatives or aspirin.

The usual hospital treatment for snake bite is antivenin. Since it is often difficult to get to a hospital quickly, it would be wise to buy antivenin to be kept in case of emergency. This medication can be purchased over the counter in most drug stores.

Produced by Wyeth Laboratories, the product available to the public is a starter system only and not as effective as the larger doses which might be administered in a hospital. As antivenin should be used within the first twelve hours after the victim has been bitten, it could be a valuable asset, even in the smaller dosage.

From Alive in the Desert
by Joe Kraus (Paladin Press).

First Aid

Books

Advanced First Aid and Emergency Care
American National Red Cross. 1973.
$3.95; paper, $2.50.
Doubleday & Co., Inc.
245 Park Ave.
New York, NY 10017

Red Cross advanced text.

Advanced First Aid for All Outdoors
P. F. Eastman. 1976.
Paper, $6.00.
Cornell Maritime Press, Inc.
Box 109
Cambridge, MD 21613

First Aid Principles and Procedures
P. B. doCarma and A. T. Patterson. 1976.
$5.95.
Prentice-Hall, Inc.
Englewood Cliffs, NJ 07632

One of the best first aid manuals. Clearly written; illustrated.

Medicine for Mountaineering
James Wilkerson, M.D. 1976.
$7.50.
The Mountaineers
P.O. Box 122
Seattle, WA 98111

"What to do after first aid and before the doctor comes—which may be a long period of time on expeditions."

Mountaineering First Aid: Guide to Accident Response and First Aid Care
Dick Mitchell. 2nd edition. 1975.
Paper, $2.95.
Backpackers Books
Bellows Falls, VT 05101

First Aid and Survival Kits

Amerex Laboratories
307 E. Nakome St.
San Antonio, TX 78216

Complete line, including "attractive, rugged, resealable, weather proof" snake bite freeze kit.
Free information.

E. D. Bullard Co.
2680 Bridgeway
Sausalito, CA 94965

"A wide choice of industrial first aid including UNI-PAC first aid kits, and industrial cabinet kits featuring color coding and the patented OSHA inspection form; Pocket First Aid Kits; products for the treatment of snake bite, burns and insect stings; and for the prevention and treatment of poison oak and ivy."
Free brochure.

Cutter Laboratories, Inc.
Berkeley, CA 94710

Insect repellants, snake bite kit, and compact first aid kits: Cutter pocket pack; trail pack; travel pack; camp pack; and marine pack.
Free brochure.

Dow Safety Products
Turner St.
Cleveland, MO 64734`

Note the Dow "Freeze-a-Bite" snake bite kit.
Free information.

Forestry Suppliers, Inc.
Box 8397
205 W. Rankin St.
Jackson, MI 39204

Resuscitation equipment, first aid, and snakebite kits at very reasonable prices.

Marion Health and Safety
9233 Ward Parkway
Kansas City, MO 64114

Color-coded first aid kits in sturdy, steel weather-proof cases. Also, snake bite kits (puncture type), hearing protection, salt tablets, and many emergency first aid products.
Free catalog.

Scott Aviation, Division of ATO
2225 Erie St.
Lancaster, NY 14086

First aid and survival kits; gas masks and respirators.
Free brochures.

Survival Equipment Co.
P.O. Box C-1
Oley, PA 19547

Kits: first aid and survival; signalling and navigation; hunting and fishing; defense; and custom.
Free brochure.

Survival Research Laboratories
17 Marland Rd.
Colorado Springs, CO 80906

Aviation survival kits.
Free catalog.

Tri-Med Surgical Supply
2 South St.
Garden City, NY 11530

All kinds of medical and first aid equipment.
Variety of first aid, trauma, and emergency kits,
poison antidotes.
Free catalog.

Game Cooking

Books

Game Cookbook
Geraldine Steindler. 1977.
Paper, $6.95.
Follett Publishing Co.
1010 W. Washington Blvd.
Chicago, IL 60607

"Hundreds of recipes for transforming foods from
forest, field, marsh, lake, stream, ocean—and
market—into gourmet dishes." This book covers
the whole field, with recipes suitable for campfire
cuisine or dinner parties back in town; everything
from game bird souffle to moose nose.

The Nitty Gritty of Smoke Cooking
Luhr Jenson.
Paper, 25¢.
P.O. Box 297
Hood River, OR 97031

A concise little booklet; lots of information in a
few pages.

Smoke Cooking
Jack Sleight and Raymond Hall
Paper, $6.95.
Stackpole Books
Cameron and Kelker Sts.
Box 1831
Harrisburg, PA 17105

Recipes, advice on proper woods for smoking
fish, fowl, and meat as well as brines, seasonings,
and complete instructions.

*The Venison Book: How to Dress, Cut Up, and
Cook Your Deer*
Audrey Ellen Gorton.
Paper, $3.95.
The Stephen Greene Press
Fessenden Rd.
Brattleboro, VT 05301

The author begins with tips on getting the deer in
the first place, then takes you through hog-
dressing, getting it home, butchering, freezing,
canning, salting, and smoking—and winds up with
recipes for venison and complementary side
dishes.

Wildlife Harvest Game Cookbook
John Mullin.
Paper, $3.50.
Arrowhead Hunting and Conservation Club
Goose Lake, IA 52750

How the experts prepare their game for the table.
Plenty of recipes for whatever you have bagged,
whether it is a dove or a wild boar.

Marine First Aid and Survival

Books

Advanced First Aid Afloat
P. F. Eastman. 1974.
Paper, $5.00.
Cornell Maritime Press, Inc.
Box 109
Cambridge, MD 21613

Clear, complete instructions for medical emergencies; what to do when you are days away
from shore and a hospital. Aimed at the reader
with some prior first aid experience.

Illustrating the crawl stroke.

Safety and Survival at Sea
Eric and Kenneth Lee. 1971.
$8.25.
W. W. Norton and Co.
500 Fifth Ave.
New York, NY 10036

Shipwreck, with its attendant physical and psychological effects, and how to survive it. Search and rescue, treatment to follow rescue, and suggestions for survival equipment.

Source of Nautical Information

Coevolution Quarterly
Winter, 1979 issue.
$3.00.
POINT
Box 428
Sausalito, CA 94965

CQ carries on the tradition and spirit of the *Whole Earth Catalog*. This issue devotes itself to boats and equipment for salts and freshwater sailors.

Marine Equipment

Catalogs

Berry
6059 W. Addison St.
Chicago, IL 60634

Scuba equipment, other marine gear.

Central Skindivers
2608 Merrick Rd.
Bellmore, NY 11710

Source of scuba tanks; pony tanks (small, compressed air bottles for emergencies); heavy-duty stainless knives; waterproof flashlights; rubber rafts; full-face airmasks; flotation equipment.

Emge Aviation/Marine Products, Inc.
Aviation and Marine Survival Equipment
Wood Lane, Woodbourne Industrial Air Park
P.O. Box 157
Langhorne, PA 19047

Land's End
2317 N. Elston Ave.
Chicago, IL 60614

Excellent rain suits, marine flashlights, signal flares, compasses, and other useful items. Yachting paraphernalia.

Mariner's Catalog: Vols. I-V
International Marine Publishing Co.
21 Elm St.
Camden, ME 04843
Vols. I and II, $4.95 each
Vol. III, $5.95
Vol. IV, $6.95
Vol. V, $7.95

The most thorough catalog for boats, canoes, kayaks, equipment—everything for the aquatically inclined.

KNOTS AND HOW TO TIE THEM

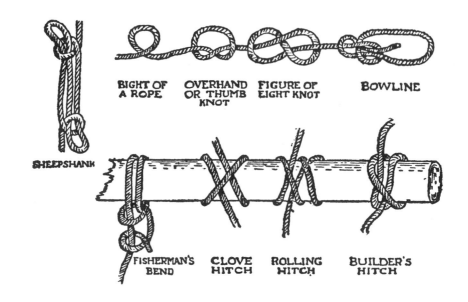

BIGHT OF A ROPE   OVERHAND OR THUMB KNOT   FIGURE OF EIGHT KNOT   BOWLINE

SHEEPSHANK

FISHERMAN'S BEND   CLOVE HITCH   ROLLING HITCH   BUILDER'S HITCH

Revere Survival Products
605 W. 29th St.
New York, NY 10001

U.S. Coast Guard Equipment Lists
Equipment Lists, CG-190.
Commandant (CMC)
U.S. Coast Guard·
Washington, D.C. 20591

Winslowe Company
P.O. Box 578
Osprey, Fla. 60614

Top-of-the-line enclosed life rafts.

The Ultimate Survivalist
The True Story of Wild Bill Moreland

Ragnar Benson

Who of us, having pulled a bucket of icy water out of a mountain stream, hasn't at one time or another thought about the early mountain men who, while checking their beaver traps regularly, waded these same waters in nothing more than buckskin boots.

Life for these hardy souls was tough and brutal. They had no rubber boots, or, for that matter, anything waterproof. Their guns were primitive, their axes were made of iron, the matches they used were soggy, their tents leaked, their sleeping bags consisted of a wool blanket, and even the traps they used were often nothing more than falling logs or a loop of brass wire. These were giants on the Earth then. Men like Jim Bridger, Liver Eatin' Johnson, Jed Smith, and Bill Sublett, who with a pound of powder, two pounds of lead, a sack of beans, and a side of bacon, began to open up our country.

But that was 200 years ago. No one in the United States today has to endure those kinds of conditions of duress and uncertainty. And perhaps no one could. Just maybe all of the giants have died.

Sleeping in a soaking wet bag in an open-ended tent with a minus twenty wind blowing is not fun. It is not romantic, it is not neat, and it is not an acceptable way of life, other than on the most temporary basis.

Grief and hardship is what they called it. The old mountain men could take all that Mother Nature could dish out, but, as John Dennis, a veteran of almost thirty years in Idaho's mountain wilderness said, "when it came to taking grief and hardship, Bill Moreland was in a class all by himself." All things considered, Bill Moreland's story is one of the most incredible ever to come out of the West.

For thirteen long, cold, starvation-producing years, he lived back in the Idaho snow country. By his own admission, he talked to humans only twice during all that time. As near as any man ever has, Moreland lived like an animal of the forest. He made his home in hollow logs, under bark-and-cedar-slab lean-tos called wickiups, in backwoods Forest Service shelters, and in open-ended canvas tents. Never during the entire thirteen years did he

build a permanent shelter or plant a garden. Not until eleven years had passed did the man even acquire a firearm, and then it was only a small .22 caliber rifle that he picked up in a Forest Service cabin.

Bill Moreland became a creature of the forest. But most remarkable of all, he did it voluntarily in relatively recent times—far beyond the time when people seriously thought about mountain men, true long-term survival, or similar matters. Residents of Idaho who lived on the fringes of Bill Moreland's home range (nobody lives permanently in that country) tend to feel that his story may be a hoax.

"It's impossible," they say, "for anyone to exist in that rugged mountainous terrain alone." But the record is good. In early fall of 1932, Bill Moreland left civilization, not to return again until February 11, 1945, when he was finally tracked down and brought out under quasi-arrest by Forest Service personnel.

Bill Moreland's home during those thirteen years was the central Idaho mountains comprising four national forests and no less than five major rivers, covering a minimum of 9,000 square miles! Annual precipitation in this area totals from thirty to forty inches. Most occurs in the winter as snow, when depths of five to eight feet are common. Even in the warmer, low valleys, thirty inches of snow will accumulate. Deer and elk often have to wade in snow chest-deep to forage for browse.

Mountains in the area are in the 7,000-foot range. They remain impassable until July each year. Twenty-foot depths of snow reaching as deep as fifty feet are typical. Even today, most of this country is not seen from the ground any more often than once or twice every five years. Some may never have been explored on foot at any time. Only God knows for sure. Indians, for instance, never lived in this country and did not even hunt it except infrequently.

Bill Moreland is one of perhaps twenty men who have ever seen parts of the St. Joe and Clearwater national forests during the winter. Idaho County alone comprised just a part of Moreland's territory. The county is bigger than several states. The entire

9,000-square-mile area over which he regularly roamed is larger than Connecticut, Delaware, Hawaii, Massachusetts, New Jersey, or Rhode Island.

Evidence pieced together later, based on petty break-ins, equipment thefts, and other acts of vandalism, indicates that the wild man regularly traveled a 200-mile loop and that he often went as far as 400 miles in his journeys through the wilderness.

During August 1979, approximately forty square miles of this type of country were devastated by forest fires. A veteran bush pilot contemplating the vastness of the area in which the burn occurred remarked that he could fly that country for the rest of his life and never see the scorched mountain. Forty square miles is just too small an area to notice relative to the surrounding country, he maintained.

Even in summer, this real estate is hostile. Lewis and Clark almost starved to death coming down the Lolo Trail out of Montana in late spring of 1804. Later, General Howard described the Lolo Trail as the worst trail through some of the most rugged mountains in North America. During the Nez Percé Indian War in 1877, Howard took 600 troopers and a pack string of mules through this steep, rocky country and almost met the same fate as Lewis and Clark.

Bill Moreland had two somewhat similar versions of how he came to the mountains of north Idaho. The tales differ principally in magnitude. His official statement to the courts in Orofino, where he was tried for breaking into Forest Service cabins, was as follows:

I was born October 1, 1900, in Wolf County near Landsaw, Kentucky. I believe my father's name was W. L. Moreland, and my mother's name was Emmie Moreland. Her maiden name was Emmie Stone. My mother is dead, and I have not heard from my father in over twenty years. I had a sister whom I believe was named Stella, and the last I know of her she was living in Morgan County. I have no other sisters or brothers.

My parents separated when I was small, and my father took my sister and my mother took me. When I was about nine years old I went with my grandmother Stone to live in Indiana and later moved across the river to Covington, Kentucky.

I went to school to about the fifth grade.

Photo by Ragnar Benson

Soon after going to Covington, my grandmother became sick, and I was taken by some other people and lived with them until I was twelve years old. About this time they put me in the reform school for running away from home. I stayed about one month and ran away and was soon picked up by the railroad police and put in another one. I believe I was in reform schools in Lancaster, Ohio, in Michigan, Wisconsin, and also Texas. This kept up until I was about sixteen years old, when I went to work for the Steven Lumber Company in Wells, Michigan, or Northland, Michigan.

I then went to Sault Ste. Marie and worked on an ore boat and finally reached Pennsylvania, where I stowed away on a McCormick Steamship Company boat which took to sea, and I was not discovered until somewhere off the New Jersey coast and they put me to work washing dishes. I don't know where we went, but about three months later I landed in Seattle.

I worked in Seattle at dishwashing and various other jobs and also worked on a Coast Guard vessel for about one week. I stayed around Seattle for about a year, then caught a freight train and was picked up in St. Paul.

I hit the freight trains again and went to Tacoma. My work in Tacoma was hauling fuel, putting wood in basements, and mowing lawns. I lived between two bridges near a sawmill. I think this was about the time Hoover was president. Times were tough, and I could only get twenty-five cents for unloading a full truckload of wood.

When I left I went to Vancouver, then on to a place called Wishram, where I stayed about a week, then to Bend, Oregon, where I bummed around town eight or ten days, then to Klamath Falls, then on to another place, I don't remember the name, then back to Wishram, then to Pendleton, probably to Pasco, next to Umatilla and Lewiston, Idaho, but there was very little work anywhere. I drifted like this for about four years.

I hired out in Lewiston, I think, to a sheepman who took me to a place on the Snake River near Mountain Home. This was about the time Roosevelt was being elected. I stayed at this place for about forty-two days.

When I left the sheep ranch near Mountain Home, I went to a mining town (probably Atlanta), bought tobacco, and went up to a lookout and started traveling in the mountains. I already had maps that I took near Avery and saw this cabin and the man was washing his clothes. When he left I went into the cabin, ate some food, picked up some maps and a shirt off the line, and left.

I believe it was the last of August or the first of September when I hit the mountains. I spent that winter and probably the next in the Sawtooth Ridge.

Avery, Idaho, the place where Moreland obtained his maps, is still much the same as it was in the early thirties. Milwaukee Road trains continue to collect at the extensive marshalling yards there, where they are remade into shorter units for the trip down through the rugged mountains to the east.

A simple track leads in and out of this mountain hideaway, providing a link with Spokane, Washington, and Missoula, Montana. That Moreland stopped there is not unusual, given his propensity to travel, but why he took maps of such god-awful country, much less kept them, is a question that will never be answered.

During the early fifties, Moreland on several occasions told Burt Curtis, a local logger, that he had come to Idaho from central Arizona. Whether he came via Mountain Home as per the court records, or from Arizona, is probably immaterial, because before long, Moreland found himself deep in the mountains of central Idaho, heading north.

Two times, when the weather got really bad and the snow piled up, Moreland decided to head for town. However, he apparently heard rifle fire and assumed that it was directed at him. His past encounters with the law plus the already great solitude clouded his mind. It was just elk season in Idaho, but Moreland thought that officers were trying to get him, and he reacted accordingly. When he came out in 1945, Moreland dated his departure by saying that he had left just before Roosevelt was elected the first time (in 1932). As the years went by, he kept semi-informed by reading old newspapers and magazines left in Forest Service lookouts and cabins.

Given the ruggedness and depth of the area, packers and guides who work the county have questioned not only if Moreland crossed it in two years of walking, but if any man could perform such a feat without ever coming out to civilization to resupply.

Later, when Moreland established himself on a semipermanent basis in the St. Joe and Clearwater national forests, he set up regular supply caches. All were well hidden far from regular trails. As far as is known, none were ever discovered until Moreland himself showed them to searchers. His caches included hollow logs, pits dug under large rocks, rock shelters, caves, and holes under windfalls. All were on the ground, accessible to animals. Although there is no record, Moreland must have suffered mightily from bears, pack rats, porcupines, and chipmunks. Principally the caches comprised items of clothing and footwear taken from cabins and lookouts, as well as stores of packaged food. Some of the food was stolen Forest Service rations, but much was grub that Moreland put up himself.

Moreland was acutely aware that the disappearance of anything gave away his position. Often he had to steal to stay alive, but always he took the worst, the dirtiest of anything, perhaps thinking that nobody would miss what he took. Bill's appearance on the Clearwater during the summer of 1934 can in retrospect be documented on the basis of the cabins he entered. However, at the time, the owners assumed that the pilferage was the work of many different people.

During the warmer months, Moreland used old telephone wire to snare deer and elk. He cut the meat into strips and dried it over a fire. Thus prepared, it lasted quite well, but as one old woodsman who knew him later said, "It was tough fare. I don't think anybody but Bill could have lived on it."

Another trick that Bill used often—after he had acquired a rifle—was to preserve wild huckle and thimble berries in old tin cans. He accomplished this seemingly impossible task by shooting a fat bear in the fall and rendering the animal's lard. The molten grease poured over the berries sealed and preserved them. But probably even Moreland had to be half-starved before eating such a mixture.

However, there can be no caches of food and clothing for one heading through the country on a line. As the crow flies, it is about 250 miles from Mountain Home to the Pierce/headquarters area where Moreland finally stopped. On the ground, the distance had to approximate 750 miles. Obviously, given the fact that he made it in two years and that extensive travel was impossible several months of the year, the man had to have pressed on with a great deal of determination.

Later in life, when Bill started talking to people again, he claimed that he settled where he did in the St. Joe and Clearwater because the game was abundant. This is probably true. Even today, elk and deer are scarce in the primitive areas where the forests have grown up and destroyed the natural browse.

So what kept him alive? During spring and fall, when few people were around, Moreland might have used some of the Forest Service rations stored in the various lookouts. After the disastrous fires of the 1900s, the United States embarked on an ambitious fire control plan that included an extensive system of fire watchtowers. Today, most of the fire surveillance chores are handled by airplane, but in the 1930s, even the remote areas had a lookout on every high peak.

Forest Service pack strings visited the stations once every two weeks during the fire season. Between times, the watchers kept in touch via a primitive network of field telephones. Grub for the stations was transported in advance in stout green Forest Service chop boxes. It wasn't fancy, but each box contained enough food to last one person ninety days. Traditionally, a full chop box was left at every lookout and cabin after the fire season, when the watchers departed.

Obviously, Moreland had few compunctions about helping himself, but more important, the Forest Service did not get all that excited about providing a handout back in the bush. Part of the agency's plan in leaving food in its cabins was to provide emergency rations for lost hunters and other persons in distress in that part of the world.

If the Forest Service had been more concerned about its chop boxes, it might have been possible to accurately document Moreland's progress through the primitive area. Thirteen years later, after a consistent pattern of disappearing food had developed, traceable to one culprit, the Forest Service still did not consider the petty thievery to be the principal problem. At the time that Moreland was absconding with whole chop boxes full of grits and caching them for winter use, there were more compelling reasons for solving the mystery of the lone intruder than the loss of a few dollars worth of beans.

But for Bill Moreland, as he pressed on north through the central Idaho mountains, the food in the lookouts might as well have, in many cases, been stored on the moon. Always the lookouts were on top of the highest mountains—places that had little natural game but lots of snow from October through June. During August and September, he had to contend with firewatchers, which left him precious little time in which to get a free handout. In all likelihood, Moreland traveled the low trails along the rivers and creeks. Later in the fall, when winter started to set in, he might have grabbed a full chop box. But even this was a dilemma. An early storm might dump two feet of snow on the ground that five days later would completely melt. Should he hole up with the food, or press on? Always there was a risk.

Although deer and elk were few, other small animals were available. He snared rabbits and giant four-pound blue grouse, ruffled grouse, and fools' hens. In the high country, these creatures are so unwary that it is often possible to kill them with a stick or stone. Another staple was porcupine. Bill roasted it in an open pan and often soaked up the grease with a puffball or cauliflower mushroom.

Years later, Moreland described Meadow Creek, Deep Creek, and Fish Lake in detail. Those who personally heard his tales were convinced that he had been there, but proof was still lacking that he had actually walked from the Idaho desert through all those rugged mountains.

"I arrived at Chamberlain Meadows in the spring and tried to steal an airplane," he said. "But I couldn't get it started. I found keys in one of the planes and tried everything, but it wouldn't start. I don't know anything about flying planes," he said.

Moreland never learned to ride a horse or drive a car, much less fly a plane. What makes this incident important is that years later a pilot out of Missoula, Montana, remembered it. Someone had indeed tried to start one of his planes on the remote Chamberlain strip, proving that Bill Moreland had been there, as he said he had.

When Moreland first came to the Clearwater/St. Joe country, he created something of a stir. After a few years, he learned to make keys for the Forest Service locks using a piece of tobacco can backed with a thin knife blade. Broken lock clasps or pried windows no longer gave away his presence — now it was the filth he created. Bill Moreland never washed a dish in his life. Instead of opening the stove damper, he always pulled down the pipe and let the smoke pour into the cabin. He threw coffee grounds on the floor, fish guts on the bunks, and relieved himself in the corner. His messy habits were one of the reasons why the Forest Service finally decided to find out who he was.

But of course, Moreland did not spend much time in cabins. One especially bad winter he did stay in a remote Forest Service cabin, but mostly he avoided them like a plague. Through the years, several of his "hole ups" have been discovered. One was nothing more than a five-foot hollow cedar log. Bill had a bunk rigged inside with a single piece of stovepipe cut in the ceiling. He built a fire on the floor and closed the entrance with pine boughs. Another shelter was merely a hollowed out area under an earthen bank, much like a woodchuck's den. Both the log and the den were high up on the headwaters of major creeks, away from the trails. The snow came early at those elevations, and on several occasions, Moreland found himself snowed in. Forced to spend two or three months holed up away from the game that had retreated to lower elevations, he lived on martens and piney squirrels.

It was a desperate existence. Often meals were as much as five days apart. Later, after the snow hardened, Moreland was able to move to the warmer valleys, where he could raid a cabin or catch a fish. Fishing in the many rivers and creeks was excellent. If the salmon and steelhead were not running, trout and whitefish were available. To a hungry man, even the abundant squawfish and suckers probably looked good. Bill got them on a hook and line that he had "borrowed" or in rock traps that he constructed in the creeks.

But always there were tremendous hardships. Some winters he had no rubber boots. When he could, Moreland solved this problem by making boots out of old inner tubes. Shoes and clothing were a problem. He stole what he could, improvising as necessary. Although he wore a size five shoe, he stuffed rags in a borrowed set of size elevens and wore those one winter. He made shirts from blankets, using nails to lace up the sides. Years later, Moreland said the dearest tool that he lacked in the woods was "something to sew with. Nobody ever leaves that material behind."

And Moreland was personally dirty. He never bathed. The layer after layer of long underwear that he wore simply rotted on his body, giving it a vile odor. His skin had an oily dark hue and shed water like a simonized car.

His eating habits were more like those of a wild animal than those of a human being. When food was plentiful, Moreland gorged himself, eating with both hands, tearing at the flesh. Once, while roasting a rabbit on a spit, he was jumped by a bobcat that made off with the last of Bill's food, causing no end of grief. Next summer, Moreland tried his best to snare or shoot every wildcat in the drainage, he was still so angry.

Through the years, Moreland learned. When he finally was able to steal a .22 rifle, he felt that his future was much brighter.

He made snowshoes out of vine maple and laced them with raw buckskin strips. But snowshoes did not always help. One time he tried to cross a frozen slope by cutting footholes in the ice with his ax. He carried one pack across and was returning for the second when he slipped and fell down the slope. Over and over he tumbled, until, bruised and battered, he lay at the bottom of the mountain. His ax and snowshoes were with his packs above on the mountain. The bedroll and tent sheet were there — both essential. Bill had to climb back up for the needed supplies. They were all that kept him alive. So he did. But it took him two full days. Can anyone truly imagine the suffering he must have endured the first night — cold and wet, with no protection or fire, he camped in five feet of snow!

Bill Moreland was a small man, standing 5'2", weighing about 130 pounds. Perhaps his small stature was an advantage in finding shelter and securing enough food. Later, when he came out of the woods, the Forest Service gave him a medical examination. They found him to be in reasonably good health. However, the feast-or-famine diet had taken its toll in at least one regard—Bill had lost most of his teeth. He had pulled them himself as they rotted and loosened in the gum by fastening a piece of wire to a bent-over sapling and jerking them out. Compared to the rest of his life, his dentistry was probably only a minor inconvenience.

Bill continually prowled around for food. At times, the fruits of his labors would have been humorous if the situation had not been so grim. He sat down and ate most of a case of canned peanut butter. Moreland could not look a peanut in the eye after that until he had not eaten anything for another week. Then he finished the stuff with relish. Another time he happened on a sack of frozen onions. The nine-tenths wasted man sat down and ate them like so many apples. Soda crackers were a particular favorite of Bill. He ate so many that later some people thought they were all he lived on.

Any man who voluntarily endures such grief and hardship has to be at least "half a bubble out of plumb." Normal people are not able to take that kind of punishment without developing a strong desire to escape their present circumstances.

By the winter of 1944, the Forest Service had begun a concerted, organized effort to find out who was living back in their Idaho snow country. Several factors had contributed to this decision. Probably foremost was the conclusion that the theft of food and the trashing of the cabins was not the random work of many different people.

Eight thousand miles away, a war raged. Women took the place of men in the fire towers, giving rise to other concerns and rumors regarding the mysterious creature living back in the mountains. Also, Bill's petty thievery from individuals, while not serious, was an aggravation, especially when he took boots from trail crews or wool shirts from packers. The loss of pants, socks, and .22 ammo greatly infuriated the owners. Rumors spread. The most credible was that the mysterious mountain man was actually a hardened criminal known as Baldy Webber. Webber had escaped from the Idaho pen a few years earlier, and it was reasonable to assume that he might be hiding out in the Clearwater or St. Joe national forests.

As a result of the increased search activity, Moreland became even more paranoid. He seldom visited the cabins or lookouts unless absolutely forced by hunger. During the summer months, he completely abandoned his home territory and went afield, visiting areas as much as 200 miles away. He never traveled the established trails, electing instead to walk parallel to and above them. When he had any doubt, he moved an hour after sunrise and an hour before sunset. By so doing, he could see and smell smoke from campers' fires and know from the condition of the deer and elk if anyone was near. A favorite was to strap his snowshoes on backwards and walk into creeks. He would wade up the creek to a rivulet, then climb up the little tributary to safety. Often, he left confusing sets of tracks. Forest rangers reported double prints and concluded that they were made by somebody else. However, it was Moreland—with a second set of shoes fastened to a couple of walking poles. Bill even used stilts shod with elk hoofs to throw off pursuers.

Moreland kept two rafts, one on each side of the river. When followed, he would dismantle one raft and hide in the bush on the riverbank. Invariably, the pursuers thought that he had crossed to the other side, because that was where the whole raft was.

The end of Wild Bill Moreland's grim saga came February 9, 1945. Two crack Forest Service woodsmen climaxed a dramatic six-day chase in twenty-below-zero weather and stormed his tiny camp high up on the mountain above Skull Creek cabin. They found a frightened, raggedy little man wearing an old pair of holey rubber boots, a pair of threadbare pants, and an old mackinaw. He had no long underwear at the time, a fact that amazed everyone who saw him during the next few days.

His tent was a small piece of canvas strung over a low line. It was open on both ends. A government-issue sleeping bag hung out, wet and pathetic, from both ends. Other possessions included a jackknife, fishing line, matches, some bottles of boric acid and oil of cloves, and a tiny sack of .22 cartridges. Another bottle containing the tin can key that he used to open the Forest Service locks hung around his neck. The last dab of Moreland's food supply lay sizzling in an open frying pan. A tiny cedar chip fire provided heat. Obviously, it would not have been long until hunger had pressed him again, something that probably had occurred many times in the last thirteen years.

It took the better part of two days to walk to the railhead, where the trio caught a handcar back to civilization. During that time, four of the finest Forest Service walkers made a concerted effort to wear down Moreland. They succeeded, but it took all four of them.

Moreland adjusted poorly to civilization. He had numerous brushes with the law and generally did not get along with people. Several times he reverted to his old haunts, only to be brought out again.

Early in the fall of 1963, Moreland escaped from a state mental institution in Orofino, Idaho. He was sixty-two at the time. Several people saw him on the road back to his old territory, but that was all. Bill Moreland was never found. Perhaps his bones lie on one of the lonely, snow-swept ridges back in the Clearwater, the cruel mountains finally having taken their toll.

Note: Today the country over which Bill Moreland traveled is made up almost entirely of three wilderness areas: the Sawtooth, the Selway, and the Idaho.

Ragnar Benson is an outdoor writer and businessman currently living off the land in the Rocky Mountains.

3

City Survival

Introduction

Our prophets have long been predicting that sudden disaster will strike the good old U.S.A. in one form or another; and because we have not ruled out the possibility that our Cassandras are right, several books containing just-in-case instructions have been included in this chapter. But why, one asks, do so many of the depression and emergency survival manuals seem strangely relevant to our present, precataclysmic way of life? It could be that our prosperity, and with it our national stability, is going not with a bang but a whimper. Or is that rather a groan one hears increasingly amplified throughout the land, as more and more citizens tighten their belts? Ouch. For many, everyday life in the city or suburb has become an exercise in survival.

The city dweller, several steps removed from the land, has traditionally been more dependent on other people for food, shelter, and clothing than has his country counterpart. He or she may also have to be prepared to fight off muggers in the streets. For those of us who find ourselves in this predicament, consumer-oriented publications, self-defense manuals, and how-to guides have been included. One does not, after all, have to live outside the city limits in order to be self-reliant.

Who would have guessed, ten short years ago, that food was to become a luxury to be unstintingly enjoyed only by the well-to-do? But of course, this is an exaggeration. Food is a necessity; we just pay for it as if it were a luxury. Due to this sorry state of affairs, the news media have been making much of so-called "shopping tips," aimed at the citizen who wants to feed the family and still have a little left over to put toward rent and utility bills. Many of these hints, unfortunately, turn out to be less helpful than the shopping tipsters would have us believe.

Generic brand products, despite all the hype, are generally inferior in quality to name brands, and the shopper has to be wise indeed to get a good buy. Paper products that do not absorb liquids properly will not save you money; you end up using twice as much as you would with a brand name product. Canned fruits and preserves tend to have more syrup than fruit, and dish-washing detergents usually are watered down. Manufacturers, it seems, are not prepared to give the consumer more for his money. Their packaging costs are minimal, but the temptation to take advantage of a money-making opportunity must be irresistible. People are, after all, buying the products. And if the goods are disappointing, to whom will consumers complain? Manufacturers of generic brands are going incognito and consequently feel little need to stand behind their wares. No one complains much anyway; the old adage, "you get what you pay for," has become a part of the national folklore. "So what do you expect for forty-nine cents?"

And what about coupons? Well, it's too bad, but an informal survey conducted by the editor reveals that they are frequently not worth the paper on which they are printed. Check and see whether the product advertised on your coupon is cheaper with the discount than another brand that you like just as well. Often, even with ten or fifteen cents off, you pay more than you would for an equivalent, couponless brand. Besides, coupons are seductive. Do you really need a large, economy-size bag of chocolate chips, or a can of gravy enhancer, or a box of artificially flavored and colored meat extender? It is disconcertingly easy to enter the supermarket full of good intentions and rich with clippings and money-saving offers addressed to Occupant and come away realizing that your grocery bill was higher than ever. Just who is this Occupant, anyway, and how did he get on all of these mailing lists?

Another suggestion that has been receiving considerable press these days may be helpful. Most staples—produce, dairy products, bread, and meat—are usually arranged around the perimeter of the store. If you travel along following the wall like a cockroach, making only a few grim forays into the heart of the market for items you truly need, like tomato paste, flour, or tuna, all the while resisting the attractively packaged grocery bag filler shelved at eye level, you may be able to get out with some of your savings intact. And trite but true: a well-thought-out list, religiously followed, and a full stomach are worth all the coupons that Occupant is likely to receive during the year. By the time this goes to press, however, the super-

market brains may well have become wise to the cockroach strategy and begun to rearrange the goods—so be prepared. Supermarket survival requires great shrewdness and steadfastness of purpose.

If you can find local manufacturers or wholesalers in your area and enough people willing to cooperate, you can save money by buying in large quantities. You may need to buy a wholesaler's or resaler's license for this; many wholesalers will not sell to you unless you can reel off a license number. Most big cities have farmers' markets, where an enterprising co-op can buy large amounts of inexpensive fresh fruits and vegetables, which can then be distributed among the members. It is always a good idea to have the money up front when purchasing anything in bulk this way, especially if you are the one doing the buying. Then, all you have to worry about is the gofor who gets carried away at the thought of a swell bargain and spends everyone's money on bushels of rutabagas that were dirt cheap but that no one else in the co-op happens to like.

Since utility bills are another big concern these days, both for renters and home owners, a section on energy conservation has been included here. If you have made, or are considering making, weatherization or other fuel conservation improvements on your home, check with your local IRS branch and find out about the National Energy Act. By installing approved, energy-saving equipment, you may be entitled to a lower tax bill.

Household repair, auto repair, and car buying have also been covered with a view to saving money. Maybe the reader will have something left over to enable him—or her—to take advantage of the financial section. And the books on self-defense might just save you some money, too.

Photo by Janet Snow Ritchie

Western Historical Collection, University of Colorado Libraries.

Access

General

Books

The Book of Survival
Anthony Greenbank.
Paper, $1.95.
Harper and Row, Publishers, Inc.
10 E. 53 St.
New York, NY 10022

Greenbank explains the proper procedures to follow when attacked by dogs, drunks, ghosts, and bullies or when confronted with a burning building or other crisis. Much practical and original advice, sometimes with a twist of gallows humor.

City Survival/City Resistance
William Hanson.
Paper, $4.00.
Loompanics
Box 264
Mason, MI 48854

Emergency tactics for urban folk. Such matters as water, food, first aid, and sanitation are discussed in the survival section; the resistance section details organization, intelligence, evasion, and escape tactics.

Praeger Publishers, Inc.
386 Madison Ave.
New York, NY 10017

How to Live on Nothing
Joan Shortney.
Paper, $1.50.
Laissez Faire Books
206 Mercer St.
New York, NY 10012

Learn to live without the help of doctors, plumbers, and other expensive professionals.

Skills for Survival
Esther Dickey. 1978.
$6.95.
Horizon Publishers and Distributors
P.O. Box 490
50 S. 500 W.
Bountiful, UT 84010

This book gives extensive guidance on home-produced products, health measures, emergency preparedness, home gardening, and preparing and preserving nutritious health foods. The book begins where others end—it provides plans for a fall-out shelter, tells how to raise food in a drought, describes how to keep cool without air-conditioning, etc. Practical, creative new ideas make this book unusual and important.

The Survivor: Vols. I-IV
Kurt Saxon.
Oversize paper, each vol., $10.00.
Paladin Enterprises
P.O. Box 1307
Boulder, CO 80306

Twelve consecutive issues of Saxon's *Survivor* newsletter make up each volume in this series. A wealth of how-to information is contained in every book. Examples: burglar-proof your home, make black powder, survival kits, arc and spot welders, furniture, a boomerang—you name it, the instructions are here. Much of the information was gleaned from old-time sources, maybe the same sources your grandparents used. As my grandmother might have put it, there's more information in each of these books than you can shake a stick at.

Pamphlets

Free consumer education pamphlets from:
Consumer Information Center
Pueblo, CO 81009
Consumer Handbook of Credit Protection Laws
How to use your credit to your best advantage.

Consumer Resource Handbook
Government agencies that handle consumer complaints and how to fight back if you get ripped off in the marketplace.

A Consumer's Shopping List of Inflation Fighting Ideas
Ways to save money on such essentials as food, housing, medical costs, and energy.

More Than You Ever Thought You Would Know about Food Additives
What additives are and what they are doing in the foods we eat.

National Consumer Buying Alert
Monthly listing of the best foods and housewares for your money, with updated information on housing, medical care, energy, and other subjects.

Shopping by Mail
Protect yourself from mail fraud.

Generic Drugs: How Good Are They?
Comparison of generic and brand name drugs.

Ya Gotta Eat, But Can You Afford It?

Books

Eating Better For Less: A Guide to Managing Your Personal Food Supply
Ray Wolf, ed.
Hardcover, $11.95; paper, $8.95.
Rodale Press
33 East Minor St.
Emmaus, PA 18049

"... how to incorporate homegrown products and outside purchases into a nutritious lifetime eating plan, starting at the supermarket or seed catalog and ending at the dining table."

How to Cut Your Food Bills by Half or More: City Survival During the Famine to Come
Kurt Saxon. 1972.
Atlan Formularies
Distributed by Paladin Press
P.O. Box 1307
Boulder, CO 80306

It is Saxon's contention that the United States is spreading itself thin by exporting grain and other foodstuffs so that extensive crop failures in the Grain Belt could cause a severe, but temporary, famine for Americans. With this in mind, he spells out food storage procedures designed to tide us over during emergencies. The book also contains information on eating well at low cost, making foods without using harmful additives, and kicking nicotine and booze habits without having to summon up a lot of willpower. And for those who desire to improve, rather than to eradicate, these habits, there are sections on home fermentation and distillation and an article on the advantages of snuff. Entertaining and enlightening. But remember that food prices quoted herein were collected in 1972, another economic age entirely from 1980.

The Supermarket Handbook: Access to Whole Foods
Nikki and David Goldbeck. 1976.
Paper, $2.25.
New American Library
1301 Avenue of the Americas
New York, NY 10019

The Goldbecks take you around the supermarket pointing out the best nutrition for the least money. Specific information is given for brand name products in different regions of the United States.

Social upheaval or a similar disaster could easily put an end to food processing and manufacturing. Customers will once again buy goods from the local miller, butcher, beekeeper, baker, etc. However, this does not mean that the problem of food adulteration will end. The following list shows how foodstuffs were commonly adulterated before reaching the nineteenth-century consumer. Should you be in a similar situation, this information could be most useful. (Reprinted from the *New Century Book of Facts*, King-Richardson Co., 1913.)

ADULTERATION OF FOOD.

Beer has been known to contain vitriol, potash, poppy heads, tartar, linseed, licorice, alum, wild cherries, henbane, chicory, pine sprouts, camomile, salicylic acid, picric acid, etc. Several deaths have resulted from adulteration with arsenic.

Bread is often improved in color by the use of alum and sulphate of copper.

Butter has been found to contain water, buttermilk, animal and vegetable fats, gypsum, chalk, flour, cheese, salicylic acid, boric acid, borax, glucose, alum, anilin yellow, and other dyes. More than 12 per cent. of water and 5 per cent. of salt is adulteration.

Oleomargarine or artificial butter or butterine is made from the fat of beef animals, and, while not a bad product, must not be sold as pure butter. It originated in France as a result of a prize offered at the suggestion of Napoleon III for the best substitute for butter. Hippolyte Mege was awarded this prize in 1869.

Cheese is often adulterated with foreign fats and potato flour.

Chocolate and Cocoa sometimes contain flour, potato meal, sawdust, mutton tallow, and oils.

Coffee, when ground, has been found to be adulterated with chicory, roasted beans or peas, tan bark, sawdust, iron rust, etc.

Confectionery is not adulterated to the extent to which it was formerly subjected. The harmful matter often lies in the coloring or as starch, sawdust, artificial extracts of fruits, benzaldehyde, and many other substances.

Drugs are often adulterated by mixing in substances which closely resemble the drug but which contain none of the medicinal properties.

Flour often contains cheaper grain products, gypsum, and mineral matters. These frauds are more practised in Europe than in the United States.

Honey often contains syrups, meal, cornstarch, cane sugar, and grape sugar.

Jams and **Jellies** sometimes contain gelatin, glue, coloring matter, artificial flavors, and zinc oxid.

Mustard is very frequently adulterated with flour, grain, or starch.

Pepper and **Spices** are commonly adulterated, and samples sold as pepper have contained no black pepper at all, but were mixtures of mustard-husks, red pepper, starch, gypsum, sand, etc.

Olive Oils often contain cottonseed oil, sesame oil, or ground-nut oil.

Pickles and **Canned Goods** frequently contain preservatives and mineral salts such as green copper salts in French peas and pickles to impart a brighter color. These are highly dangerous and harmful adulterations.

Spirituous Liquors are often wholly artificial products. Fusel oil and the use of methylated alcohol (wood alcohol) are extremely harmful ingredients.

Sugar is, on the whole, a pure article. Sometimes glucose, terra alba, and sand are found in white sugar, but adulteration of the brown sugar is more common.

Tea sometimes contains the leaves of linden, sage, strawberry, and similar plants. Iron salts are sometimes added to dried or used tea leaves to give the required strength.

Tobacco is artificially colored and flavored — the so-called artificial fruit flavors being much used.

Vinegar contains added water and sulphuric or hydrochloric acid.

The accumulation of vital statistics provides for the collection of information upon every detail of the work of the authorities in connection with the promotion of public health, and throughout the civilized world these departments are building up a vast amount of authoritative information upon an important subject.

Do-It-Yourself Foods—City Farming

Books

All About Vegetables
Walter L. Doty, ed. 1977.
Paper, $3.95.
Chevron Chemical Corp., Ortho Division—Garden and Home
200 Bush St.
San Francisco, CA 94104

Raising vegetables with or without a garden. Detailed information about soil, fertilizers, composting, seeds and transplants, and individual vegetables. Zone map, full color illustrations, line drawings, bibliography.

Success with Small Food Gardens Using Special Intensive Methods
Loise Riotte and Walter Hard. 1977.
Paper, $5.95.
Garden Way Publishing
Charlotte, VT 05445

How to grow food of high nutritional quality in a small garden plot. "Even the tiniest spaces can be made to attractively produce luscious, fresh vegetables, fruits and berries."

Tub Farming: Grow Vegetables Anywhere in Containers
Mary Johnson.
Paper, $5.95.
Garden Way Publishing
Charlotte, VT 05445

Indoor and outdoor vegetable, fruit, and herb gardening.

Colorado Libraries.

Do-It-Yourself Foods — City Kitchen

Books

These foods could be prepared anywhere. Why include them in the city section? Well, because they can be prepared anywhere. You do not need a farm or a lot of extra room for equipment. And the feeling of self-reliance that an urbanite or sub-urbanite experiences when he provides for himself is highly fulfilling. Even the city dweller does not have to depend on the market for everything!

Country Skills Library
Phyllis Hobson.
Paper, $2.95 each; seven volumes, boxed, $14.95.
Garden Way Publishing Co.
Charlotte, VT 05445

Making Homemade Cheeses and Butter
Making Breads with Homegrown Yeast and
  Homegrown Grains
Making Your Own Wine, Beer and Soft Drinks
Making Your Own Ice Cream, Ices and Sherbets
Home Drying Vegetables, Fruits and Herbs
Making Homemade Soaps and Candles
Making Homemade Apple Pies and Crusts

Catalogs

Continental
Box 68016
Indianapolis, IN 46268

"Yeast, books, concentrates, malts — everything necessary to make your own wine and beer."
Free catalog.

Duane Imports, Ltd.
508 Canal St.
New York, NY 10013

Equipment and supplies for brewing premium U.S. and European beers at home.
Free information.

International Yogurt Co.
628 N. Dohemy Dr.
Los Angeles, CA 90069

Yogurt and kefir cultures.
Free information.

Kraus
Box 7850
Independence, MO 64053

Yeasts, concentrates, malt, hops, barrels, etc. for beer and wine. Free catalog.

New England Cheesemaking Supply Co.
P.O. Box 85
Ashfield, MA 01330

Cheesemaking supplies and book.
Catalog, $1.00, refundable.

The Sausage Maker
1067 Grant St.
Buffalo, NY 14207

Equipment and supplies.
Free catalog.

A Man's (or Woman's) Home is His/Her Castle: Conserving Energy in the Home

Books

Complete Energy-Saving Home Improvement Guide
James W. Morrison. 1978.
Paper, $2.95.
Arco Publishing Co., Inc.
219 Park Ave., S
New York, NY 10003

Find out where your house is losing heat and learn how to correct it. Safety suggestions and emergency procedures.

Consumer Reports Buying Guide Issue, 1980
$3.50.
Consumers Union of United States, Inc.
256 Washington St.
Mt. Vernon, NY 10550

This is the December 1979 issue of *Consumer Reports* magazine. Pages 110–141 discuss home energy conservation: fuel-saving devices; energy-saving thermostats; flue heat recovery devices; foam caulks; weather stripping; window sun controls; "energy-saving" windows; insulation; insulation for air conditioning, high-efficiency room air conditioners and fans—attic, window, oscillator, and so on. General discussion and test results—advantages and disadvantages—of different manufacturers' products are given in detail for each category.

547 Easy Ways to Save Energy in Your Home
Roger Albright.
Paper, $4.95.
Garden Way Publishing
Charlotte, VT 05445

Simple home energy conservation. Original and not-so-original ideas.

The Fuel Savers: A Kit of Solar Ideas for Existing Homes
Dan Scully, Don Prowler, and Bruce Anderson. 1978.
Paper, $2.75; add $1.00 postage and handling.
Total Environmental Action, Inc.
Church Hill
Harrisville, NH 03450

This is a sixty-one-page booklet that may be one of the best buys around for anyone looking for ways to save energy at home. Among the ideas discussed are insulating curtains and shutters; additional glazing; stone walls transformed into solar collectors; greenhouses; and solar water heaters. Each topic is broken down into the following sections: variations; where this works; advantages, disadvantages, and economics. (With the economy the way it is, you will hardly need to be reminded that allowances must be made for the listed approximate cost of materials for each project.) *The Fuel Savers* is clearly written and illustrated and contains no extraneous filler.

Home Energy for the 80's: Plus Complete Catalog on Alternative Energy Systems
Ralph D. Wolfe and Peter Clegg. 1979.
Garden Way Publishing
Charlotte, VT 05445

Supercedes Clegg's *New Low-Cost Sources of Energy for the Home* but is comprised of new material—not a revision. Supplies information on devices such as thermostat timers, glazing, insulating window shades, and other devices.

SOLAR HOT WATER SYSTEMS:
Operational Description

The solar hot water system usually is designed to preheat water from the incoming water supply prior to passage through a conventional water heater. The domestic hot water preheat system can be combined with a solar heating system or designed as a separate system. Both situations are illustrated below.

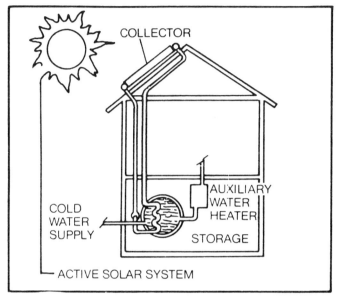

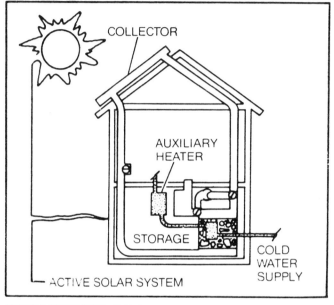

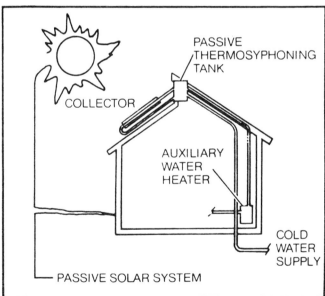

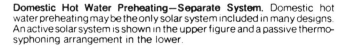

Domestic Hot Water Preheating—Separate System. Domestic hot water preheating may be the only solar system included in many designs. An active solar system is shown in the upper figure and a passive thermosyphoning arrangement in the lower.

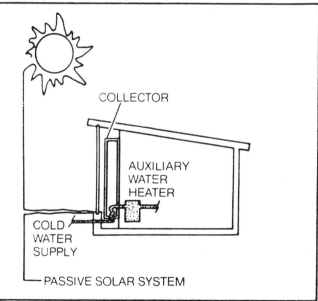

Domestic Hot Water Preheating—Combined System. Domestic hot water is preheated as it passes through heat storage enroute to the conventional water heater. An active solar system using air for heat transport is shown in the upper figure and a passive solar system in the lower

Earth Berming to Window Sill:
Standard Practice House
Energy Savings 6.6%

The Homeowner's Energy Guide: How To Beat the Heating Game
John A. Murphy. 1977.
Paper, $6.95.
T. Y. Crowell Co.
Distributed by Harper and Row, Publishers, Inc.
10 E. 53 St.
New York, NY 10022

Homeowners' Guide to Saving Energy
Billy L. Price and James T. Price.
Paper.
Tab Books
Blue Ridge Summit, PA 17214

Includes weatherizing techniques, appliance maintenance, and home lighting and wiring methods designed to save energy.

How to Cut Your Electric Bill and Install Your Own Emergency Power System
Edward A. Lacy. 1978.
Paper, $2.95.
Tab Books
Blue Ridge Summit, PA 17214

How to Cut Your Energy Bills
Ronald Derven and Carol Nichols. 1976.
Paper, $4.95.
Structures Publishing Co.
P.O. Box 423
Farmington, MI 48024

Insulation, appliances, ventilation, lighting, heating, cooking, etc.

How to Cut Your Energy Costs
G. Kimball Hart and the editors of U.S. News and World Report Books. 1977.
$7.95.
U.S. News and World Report Books
Distributed by Simon and Schuster
1230 Avenue of the Americas
New York, NY 10020

How to Improve the Efficiency of Your Oil-Fired Furnace
Free booklet.
Consumer Information Center
Pueblo, CO 81009

Insulate Your Water Heater and Save Fuel
Free pamphlet.
Consumer Information Center
Pueblo, CO 81009

In the Bank or Up the Chimney? A Dollar and Cents Guide to Energy-Saving Home Improvements.
GPO-023-00-00297-3
Abt Associates, Inc.
U.S. HUD. 1975.

Available from:
Superintendent of Documents
U.S. Government Printing Office
Washington, D.C. 20402
$1.70.

Chilton Book Company
Radnor, PA 19089
$1.95.

Abt Associates, Inc.
55 Wheeler St.
Cambridge, MA 02138
$1.25

The cost estimates in this booklet are now outdated, but much of the information is worthwhile. How to decide what your house needs in the way of energy-saving features; select tools and materials; install various energy-wise devices; and use energy safely.

Insulating the Old House: A Handbook for the Owner
Sally E. Nielsen, ed. 1977.
Paper, $1.90.
Greater·Portland Landmarks, Inc.
165 State St.
Portland, ME 04101

Insulation and Weatherstripping
Sunset editors. 1978.
Paper, $2.95.
Lane Publishing Co.
Menlo Park, CA 94025

The Integral Urban House: Self-Reliant Living in the City
Farallones Institute
$12.95.
Sierra Club Books
530 Bush St.
San Francisco, CA 94108

Learn from the Farallones Institute how to convert an existing city house to self-sufficiency. They have done it themselves and supply blueprints and working plans that they used in a prototype urban dwelling.

Keeping Warm for Half the Cost
Phil Townsend and John Colesby. 1975.
Conservation Tools and Technology
143 Maple Road, Surbiton
Surrey KT6 4BH
England

Hailed by the *Energy Primer* as one of the best guides for reducing energy use in the home, with one qualification: increase the recommended amount of insulation by at least 100 percent.

Save Energy, Save Money
OEO pamphlet 6143-5.
Free.
Eugene Eccli and Sandy Eccli.
Community Services Agency
Washington, D.C.

Penny-pinching heat conservation techniques employing such readily available materials as old blankets, newspaper, and leaves. Definitely low-tech.

Stopping Power Meters
John J. Williams, M.S.E.E.
Paper, $7.95.
Rebel Press
Distributed by Loompanics Unlimited
Box 264
Mason, MI 48854

Here is a real energy conservation alternative. This publication is just what the title claims—a treatise on stopping or slowing down power meters, resulting in a sharp decrease in utility bills. Several methods are illustrated with diagrams, none of which requires meter by-passing. Although the booklet costs roughly one dollar per page, consider the savings if you actually put it to use! The truly rebellious individual who is sick of OPEC, not to mention sanctimonious U.S. officials telling him to curtail his energy consumption, could have a heyday with this one. But of course, because it is illegal to tamper with a utility meter, this publication is sold for informational purposes only.

Thermal Shutters and Shades
1979.
$12.00, plus $1.00 shipping.
Brick House Publications
3 Main St.
Andover, MA 01810

Do-it-yourself projects and descriptions and evaluations of currently available commercial products. The overall emphasis is on saving money. Fully illustrated; includes a bibliography.

Weatherizing Your Home
George Drake.
$16.95.
Reston Publishing Co.
11480 Sunset Hills Rd.
Reston, VA 22090

Recommended by *Organic Gardening Magazine*.

Home Repair and Maintenance

Books

Fix-It-Yourself Manual
The Reader's Digest Association. 1977.
$12.99.
Pleasantville, NY 10570

Homeowner's Quick Repair and Emergency Guide
Max Alth. 1978.
Paper, $3.95.
Harper & Row, Publishers, Inc.
10 E. 53 St.
New York, NY 10022

Homeowner's Survival Kit: How to Beat the High Cost of Owning and Operating Your Home
A. M. Watkins. 1971.
Paper, $2.95.
Hawthorn Books, Inc.
260 Madison Ave.
New York, NY 10016

How Things Work in Your Home (And What to Do When They Don't)
$14.95.
Time-Life Books, Inc. 1975.
Alexandria, VA 22314

Hyde Surface Preparation How-To Book
Paper, $1.00.
Hyde Tools
Southbridge, MA 01550

Well, technically this is a Hyde Tools catalog, but instructions for surface preparation of inside and outside surfaces should prove useful to those contemplating home improvement projects.

Protecting Your Housing Investment
Free booklet.
Consumer Information Center
Pueblo, CO 81009

How to fix leaks, get rid of termites, maintain heating and plumbing systems, and other home maintenance advice.

Simple Home Repairs
Paper, $1.00.
Bulletin A-28
Garden Way Publishing
Charlotte, VT 05445

Self-Defense

Books

Below the Belt
Bradley Steiner.
Hardcover, $12.95.
Paladin Enterprises
P.O. Box 1307
Boulder, CO 80306

Self-protection guide designed to enable a woman to fend off even violent attack. Hundreds of illustrations.

Black Medicine I
N. Mashiro, Ph.D.
Paper, $8.00.
Paladin Enterprises
P.O. Box 1307
Boulder, CO 80306

". . . over 150 parts of the human body where a minimum amount of force will produce a maximum impact on a person's ability to fight."

Black Medicine II
N. Mashiro, Ph.D.
Paper, $8.00.
Paladin Enterprises
P.O. Box 1307
Boulder, CO 80306

An outgrowth of the first volume. Presents 112 parts of the body that are natural weapons and a section on hastily improvisable weapons, listed alphabetically. The basting syringe listing may give you an idea of Mashiro's rather macabre humor with which the heavy subject matter is leavened: "Basting syringe: Who says that the terrorists won't come after you on Thanksgiving? A squirt of searing grease. . . ."

Get Tough
Captain W. E. Fairbairn
Hardcover, $12.95
Paladin Enterprises
P.O. Box 1307
Boulder, CO 80306

Originally used to teach the famed British commandos how to defeat the enemy with bare hands, this long out of print book is both a collector's item and a fact-crammed manual that could save your life.

Ju-Jutsu And Judo
Percy Longhurst
Paper, $6.00
Paladin Enterprises
P.O. Box 1307
Boulder, CO 80306

A classic reprint — one of the first English language books about this famous martial art. A very practical introductory self-defense text.

Principles of Personal Defense
Jeff Cooper
Paper, $4.00.
Paladin Enterprises
P.O. Box 1307
Boulder, CO 80306

"How alertness, decisiveness, speed, aggressiveness, coolness, precision and surprise can save your life when you are faced with a violent confrontation."

Save-Your-Life Defense Handbook
Matthew Braun. 1977.
Paper, $5.95; hardcover, $10.00.
Devin-Adair Co., Inc.
143 Sound Beach Ave.
Old Greenwich, CT 06870

A comprehensive, illustrated, how-to-do-it instruction book explaining everything that the citizen-homeowner needs to know to protect his home and family from unwanted intruders.

Auto Maintenance

Books

Auto Body Repairs and Painting Made Easy
By the editors of *Consumers Guide*.
Spiralbound $3.98.

Auto Tune-ups Made Easy
By the editors of *Consumers Guide*.
Spiralbound, $3.98.

Both books available through:
Publishers' Central Bureau
One Champion Ave.
Avenel, NJ 07131
Add $1.95 shipping and handling.

Automotive Operation and Maintenance
VITA
3706 Rhode Island Ave.
Mt. Rainier, MD 20822

"Do-it-yourself guide to troubleshooting and dealing with problems, especially valuable when service facilities are not available."

At the time of this writing, Publisher's Bureau is offering *Chilton's Auto Repair Manual 1978* for $6.95, plus a shipping charge of $1.95. This edition covers service, troubleshooting, and overhaul for all U.S. mass-produced cars from 1971 to 1978.

Publishers Central Bureau
One Champion Ave.
Avenel, NJ 07131

Chilton Auto Repair
Chilton Book Co. 1979.
$15.95.
Chilton Way
Radnor, PA 19089

This is the preferred car repair text of many U.S. auto mechanics. An old standby (continually updated).

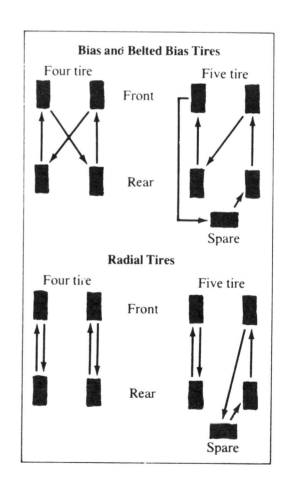

How to Keep Your Volkswagen Alive
John Muir. Rev. ed. 1979.
Paper, $9.00.
From the author.
P.O. Box 613
Santa Fe, NM 87501

Well-illustrated, complete with cartoons that may or may not lift your spirits when your VW is malfunctioning, the information in this book has put many a car back on the road. Clear enough for the beginner to follow, with step-by-step instructions.

Buying A New or Used Car

Books

Car and Driver Buyer's Guide 1980
Annual.
Paper, $2.95.
Ziff-Davis Publishing Co.
2002 Hogbank Rd.
Ann Arbor, MI 48105

"Prices, specifications, fuel economy for every car, light truck and van sold in America." Lots of photographs.

Cherries and Lemons: Or, How to Buy a Good Used Car for Under $1000
Joe Troise. 1977.
Paper, $2.75.
Barkfeather Publishing Co.
519 Concord St.
Boulder, CO 80302

This book offers plenty of useful tips. The only problem is this: just as for wines, automobiles have good years and bad years. Troise describes the vintage models, but they are difficult to find when you are in the market for a used car. Many have long since succumbed to rust and hard driving, or their owners are holding onto them. Still, it is good to know about them, just in case.

Consumer Guide Auto Test 1980
$2.95.
Consumers Union of United States, Inc.
256 Washington St.
Mt. Vernon, NY 10550

Detailed report of the results of CU testing of new models.

Consumer Reports 1978-79 Guide to Used Cars
By the editors of Consumer Reports Books. 1978.
Paper, $5.50; plus 50¢ handling.
Consumers Union of United States, Inc.
256 Washington St.
Mt. Vernon, NY 10050

"Consumer Reports summary judgments of 255 domestic and foreign cars plus detailed test reports on 131 cars for the 1974-77 model years; frequency-of-repair records for 626 makes and models from 1972 to 1977, 162 good bets in used cars and 125 used cars to avoid."

Gainful Self-Employment

Books

The Mother Earth News Handbook of Home Business Ideas and Plans
By the staff of Mother Earth News.
Paper, $2.25.
Bantam Books, Inc.
666 Fifth Ave.
New York, NY 10019

"This, as you'll soon discover, is not your usual 'home business' book. It does not vaguely promise overnight wealth in mail order. It contains no 'miracle' accounts of the manner in which 'a woman with an invalid husband devised a wonderful item she could manufacture at home and now enjoys a $50,000-a-year income.' It was written by no 'expert' with six degrees in business administration. It is not filled with dry discussions of proper markup ratios, tax reserves, and double entry bookkeeping systems." — Introduction. Well then, what is it? A conglomeration of first-person accounts by people who are now in business for themselves in all kinds of fields, ranging from baking to cartooning. Many ideas and plans can be adapted to other endeavors. Enjoyable reading.

Working for Yourself: How to Be Successfully Self-Employed
Geoff Hewitt.
Hardcover, $9.95; paper, $6.95.
Rodale Press
33 East Minor St.
Emmaus, PA 18049

"Selecting a business or trade; promoting, financing a new endeavor; getting professional help, from bankers, lawyers, etc. and actually getting started in business. The major part of the book contains stories and advice of almost 100 self-employed people."

Financial Opportunities

Books

Age of Inflation
Hans F. Sennholz. 1979.
$8.95.
Western Islands
395 Concord Ave.
Belmont, MA 02178

An enlightening and sobering analysis of the history and theory of inflation in the twentieth century. Written from the perspective of the subjective theory of value of the Austrian School, this book recounts the German experience with inflation and price controls from World War I to the end of World War II, deftly exposes the errors of the monetarists and their recommendations for living with inflation, examines the creation, policies, and consequences of the Federal Reserve System, and offers recommendations for restoring a sound monetary system.

This work will prove an invaluable aid to those interested in economics, for it includes not only an index and a bibliography, but also a glossary of economic terms and a list of persons influential in twentieth-century economics.

The New York Gold Room on "Black Friday," September 24, 1869.

Barter Way to Beat Inflation
George W. Burtt. 1980.
$10.95; paper, $6.95.
Everest House
1133 Avenue of the Americas
New York, NY 10036

An in-depth explanation of trade options open to any of us—skilled or unskilled—who choose not to deal exclusively in cash. You will be astonished at the ease and variety of barter techniques that are detailed in this informative new look at a classic tradition. Written in a clear style, this book explains barter from its simplest level—babysitting in exchange for firewood, for example—through the organization and operation of barter clubs, trading co-ops where services can be credited against future trades. Barter clubs provide for exchange of professional services as well, i.e., an accountant can do the taxes of a dentist and get root canal work done as payment. Protecting yourself against the too-shrewd trader and developing trading skills are also described.

Biggest Con: How the Government Is Fleecing You
Irwin A.   1977.
Paper, $5.95.
Freedom Books
P.O. Box 5303
Hamden, CT 06518

With irrefutable evidence and driving logic, the author accuses the federal government of converting the U.S. economy to national socialism and turning U.S. workers into federal peons. With facts and figures he shows how, when, and why the federal government: causes inflation; steals more from the public in a week than the Mafia does in a year; declared official bankruptcy three times since 1970; created the energy crisis; legislates unemployment, poverty, and crime; fraudulently conceals the nation's eight-trillion-dollar public debt; unconstitutionally enforces a fraudulently acquired power to tax income; why Social Security is a gigantic fraud that taxpayers can now legally "drop out"; why the federal government is nothing but a profit-making business monopoly (for those who run it); and why the author has paid no income taxes since 1973.

Black Market: A Study of White Collar Crime
Marshall B. Clinard. 1969.
$15.00; paper, $5.00.
Patterson Smith Publishing Corp.
23 Prospect Terrace
Montclair, NJ 07042

A study of the black market in meat, tires, sugar, and other rationed goods in the United States during World War II. Author Clinard was chief of the Analysis and Reports Branch of the Enforcement Department of the Office of Price Administration. Topics include: counterfeiting and theft of ration currency; comparison with ordinary crimes in wartime; voluntary methods of control; opposition to volunteer price panels; the problem of using volunteers in enforcement work; the meat black market; the gasoline black market; landlords as violators; enforceability of the regulations; investigative techniques; economic factors in the black market; suggestions for future controls.

Bleeding of America
Herman Dinsmore. 1977. (3rd ed.).
Paper, $3.00.
Western Islands
395 Concord Ave.
Belmont, MA 02178

The author analyzes the forces that are determined to transform the United States into a socialist state in order to merge with the Soviet Union. This book presents a concise overview of the policies that are now being executed for the purpose of furthering world socialism.

Building Your Fortune with Silver
Robert L. Preston. 1973.
Paper, $2.00.
Hawkes Publishing, Inc.
3775 S. 500 W.
P.O. Box 15711
Salt Lake City, UT 84115

The author reveals the dynamic profit potential of silver and explores the new uses to which silver is being applied. It explores the economic conditions of today and explains how to capitalize on the strength of silver in the future.

Business End of Government
Dan Smoot. 1973.
Paper, $1.00.
Western Islands
395 Concord Ave.
Belmont, MA 02178

An in-depth look at how federal regulations threaten to destroy the U.S. free enterprise system. The author, one of America's foremost conservative commentators, describes the dangers that all Americans face from OSHA, EPA, ICC, FDA, and a whole alphabet of agencies and

inspectors spawned by the federal government. The author proves that the "energy crisis" was deliberately created by the same bureaucrats who now propose more governmental controls to solve it.

Christians Will Go Through the Tribulation: And How to Prepare for It
Jim McKeever. 1978.
$10.95; paper, $5.95.
Alpha Omega Publishing Co.
P.O. Box 4130
Medford, OR 97501

Every believer should read this book that could affect every major decision he makes. Most Christians have only heard about a pre-Tribulation Rapture and probably believe in it because they have not heard a viable alternative presented intelligently. This book is solidly based on the Word of God and shows clearly why Christians will go through all, or at least part, of the Tribulation. The book discusses both physical and spiritual preparation for the Tribulation and gives practical "how to" suggestions.

The Coming Real Estate Crash
Gary Emerson Cardiff and John Wesley English.
1979.
$12.95.
Arlington House Publications
165 Huguenot St.
New Rochelle, NY 10801

The authors think that the real estate boom is about to burst. They look into the future crash to see what will happen to homeowners, real estate investors, and the institutions on which they rely. The authors review past real estate booms and crashes and reveal the forces behind today's booming real estate market to explain why the crash will come. More importantly, they explain exactly how to profit and protect yourself from any such crash.

Common Sense Economics: Your Money—What It Is and How to Keep It!
John A. Pugsley. 1976 (rev. ed.).
$12.50.
Common Sense Press
711 W. 17th St., G-6
Costa Mesa, CA 92627

Your key to a clear understanding of what is really happening in the economy. It is not the gospel according to the politicians and their hired economists, but the truth as it exists in the real world. The author defines and clarifies the concepts of money, inflation, and devaluation. He shows how the banks and politicians work together to siphon off the wealth of the individual producer, and in so doing, create inflation. They then mount programs to fight inflation, and these programs further destroy the productive ability of the country. If, as the author asserts, inflation will not be controlled, then you must make your financial plans based on the reality of the future, not on political promises and wishful thinking. The author discusses in detail each investment area including the stock market, bonds, gold, and art and shows what must happen to the values of these products in the future. In essence, the book is a survival manual that offers clear steps on how to protect your wealth.

Complete Guide to Financial Planning for Your Family
J. K. Lasser.
$8.95; paper, $2.95.
Simon and Schuster
1230 Avenue of the Americas
New York, NY 10020

Complete guide to personal finance. Whether a person is single or married, self-employed, working for a company, or on a fixed income, the need to plan for everyday living as well as the future is becoming more and more necessary, especially in these times of high inflation and increased service costs. All aspects of wise money management are discussed: how to apply for and protect your credit rating; the pros and cons of buying a house, co-op, or condominium; how to plan for retirement by careful investment; dozens of ways to save money everyday; how to plan a weekly budget or secure a loan.

Crash of Seventy-Nine
Paul E. Erdman. 1976.
$8.95; paper, $2.75.
Pocket Books
Simon and Schuster
1230 Avenue of the Americas
New York, NY 10020

A book so real that its plot reads like today's headlines: fifteen of the top U.S. banks are broke. The Dow-Jones is plummeting. The Arabs will bail out the banks, but only in exchange for arms. The Shah of Iran is scheming for control of the entire Middle East and the world's oil supply. His chief negotiating weapon—the bomb. And Bill Hitchcock, a financial wizard with a keen eye for big money and magnificent women, is manipulating billions for the super-rich from the power centers of the world, holding the answers that could save America from ruin—or plunge it into an economic abyss.

Creative Retirement: Planning the Best Years Yet
Murray Hoyt. 1974.
$5.95; paper, $3.95.
Garden Way Publishing Co.
Charlotte, VT 05445

Contents: retirement economics, various housing alternatives, part-time employment, when to retire, personal adjustments and goals.

Crisis Investing
Douglas R. Casey. 1979.
Hardcover, $14.95.
'76 Press
P.O. Box 2686
Seal Beach, CA 90740

If we are headed for another Great Depression—and Casey discusses his reasons for assuming that we are headed straight for the precipice—our present savings and investments are not going to protect us from economic hardship. This book offers advice on how to survive, even prosper, during the hard times ahead.

Cycles of War: The Next Six Years
R. E. McMaster. 1978.
$11.00.
Cycles of War Institute
P.O. Box 1673
Kalispell, MT 59901

The result of thirteen years of preparation, this is a stimulating, fast-moving work that cyclically builds the case for war, both international and civil, within the next six years. Beginning with the concept of international war as a social activity subject to the principles of mass psychology and the concept of civil war as a breakdown of society, the author, step by step, leads the reader through the following factors that predict the coming violence: a study of the nation's literature and how accurately it predicts war; primary causes of previous historic revolutions and how they apply to the United States today; the similarity between the "mass mind" of the international markets and the "mass mind" that goes to war; resource shortages and man's aggressive tendencies are explored; the work of cyclical historians is reviewed and shown to predict war; the long-term downturn of major economic and business cycles is presented, with the implications for those living in the cities explained in light of both international and civil war; the Russian economist, Kondratieff, and his economic and warfare cycle is examined; lack of military preparation is shown to be a prelude to war; prophecies of war by visionaries are brought to light.

Diamond Connection: A Manual for Investors
Anthony C. Sutton. 1979.
$19.95.
JD Press
P.O. Box 22674
San Diego, CA 92122

The author elaborates on the strengths and weaknesses of diamonds as investments: how to choose investment diamonds wisely and safely, even whether you should be a diamond investor at all. Topics covered include: the four "Cs" of diamond grading; how diamonds fare in recessions; how different sizes and shapes of diamonds perform in the market; where to sell diamonds; the dangers and pitfalls for the unwary; how to identify synthetic and simulated diamonds; will the Russians take over the diamond market?; the future of the De Beer's cartel; how diamonds are marketed and how much you should pay; where to buy diamonds.

Double Your Dollars: The Investment Opportunity for the 1980's
Ira U. Cobleigh. 1979.
$9.95.
Crown Publications, Inc.
1 Park Ave.
New York, NY 10016

Dow Jones-Irwin Guide to Commodities Trading
Bruce G. Gould. 1973.
$17.50.
Dow Jones–Irwin.
1818 Ridge Rd.
Homewood, IL 60430

This book will prepare you to trade successfully in commodities, and you will clearly understand every step of the process. It is divided into three parts, starting with a general overview of the market, why it exists, who uses it, how it is used, and the position of the trader in all of this. Part two is limited solely to commodity price factors that determine the cash price, which, in turn, determines the price of the futures contract held by the trader. Part three contains specific facts and trading systems. The author has also included a "Guesstimator" table to help you develop a successful trading strategy of your own.

Dow-Jones–Irwin Guide to Put and Call Options
Henry K. Clasing. 1978, (rev. ed.).
$14.95.
Dow Jones–Irwin.
1818 Ridge Rd.
Homewood, IL 60430

This revised edition has been almost completely rewritten, and much new material has been added. The author has developed new easier-to-use timing tools and has added new chapters on spreading, put premiums, and the interrelationship between puts and calls. He also covers different strategies to use with combinations of puts, calls, spreads, hedging, etc. As in the previous edition, the book coordinates the dynamics of the stock market, strategy, selection and human emotions, and places at the reader's fingertips all of the current tools used by professional option money managers. Without resorting to complicated mathematics, the book presents graphs for estimating option premiums and even includes a simple formula for premium estimating that requires nothing more than a hand calculator.

Dow Jones–Irwin Guide to Stock Market Cycles
Michael Hayes. 1977.
$19.95.
Dow Jones–Irwin.
1818 Ridge Rd.
Homewood, IL 60430

The most important decision you need to make for investment success is how much of your capital should be in the market at any time. This decision determines when you should buy or sell. The author discusses the risks and potential returns from stock market investment, develops a profile of a typical stock market cycle, provides rough guidelines for determining whether the market is too high or too low, covers analysis of individual indicators, price trends, and price movements in typical stocks. He also covers the influence of economic factors on the market and concludes with a test of the composite indicator against market data of past cycles to demonstrate its usefulness.

Economics in One Lesson
Henry Hazlitt. 1979.
$8.95.
Arlington House Publications, Inc.
165 Huguenot St.
New Rochelle, NY 10801

Extensive, revised, and completely updated edition of Henry Hazlitt's classic exposition of general economic principles in layman's terms. In this new edition, the author applies the basic truths of economics to the problems and opportunities of today and tomorrow.

Economics in Plain English: All You Ever Need to Know About Economics — in Language Anyone Can Understand.
Leonard Silk. 1978.
$7.95; paper, $3.95.
Simon and Schuster, Inc.
1230 Avenue of the Americas
New York, NY 10020

At a time when inflation seems to be uncontrollable and the daily news is an impenetrable mystery to the thousands of people who lack a sound understanding of economics, the author takes on the task of explaining what economics means to everyone. He lucidly demonstrates the workings of economic theory; dramatically illustrates the differences among the theories of such great economists as Adam Smith, Ricardo, Malthus, Marx, and Keynes. He explains not only how you can learn to understand economics, but how you can profit from it.

Eco-Spasm Report: Why Our Economy Is Running Out of Control
Alvin Toffler.
Paper, $1.75.
Bantam Books, Inc.
666 Fifth Ave.
New York, NY 10019

What we are seeing today is not simply an economic upheaval, but something far deeper, something that cannot be understood within the framework of conventional economics. This is why increasingly mystified economists complain that "the old rules don't work any longer." What we are seeing is the general crisis of industrialism — a crisis that transcends the differences between capitalism and Soviet-style communism, a crisis that is simultaneously tearing up our energy base, our value systems, our sense of space and time, our epistemology, as well as our economy. What is happening, no more, no less, is the breakdown of industrial civilization on the planet and the first fragmentary appearance of a wholly new and drastically different social order: a superindustrial civilization that will be technological but no longer industrial.

The End of Affluence: A Blueprint for Your Future
Paul R. Ehrlich and Anne H. Ehrlich. 1978.
Paper, $2.25.
Ballantine Books, Inc.
201 E. 50th St.
New York, NY 10022

America's economic joyride is coming to an end. Thus far, we have met each new piece of bad news with disbelief and sometimes outrage. There has been a lot of talk about "who is to blame," and some groups have taken the position that they have been singled out for unfair treatment . . . charges and countercharges fill the air, clog the media, and do nothing to hasten an adjustment to new ways of life.

Expatriate Investor
(Originally published as *The International Man*).
Douglas R. Casey. 1979.
Paper, $9.95.
Everest House Publications
1133 Avenue of the Americas
New York, NY 10036

The complete guidebook to the world's last
frontiers. Become an international person.
Explore the various possibilities in 200 or more
nations. You will find everything you need to
know about five "Last Frontier" nations—plus 45
more with enough advantages to make them
worth considering. Details on: business and work,
the economy, residency requirements and citizen-
ship, social and political conditions, the people,
passports and visas, land and housing, tax levels,
money and foreign exchange, future trends, etc.

*Financial & Physical Survival in Times of Inflation,
Depression, and Other Crises.*
Deane E. Kogelschatz. 1976.
$9.95.
Sycamore Island Books.
P.O. Box 1307
Boulder, CO 80306

Throughout mankind's history, what began as
purely economic crises have often culminated in
complete social chaos. Physical survival has then
become the individual's only day-to-day goal.
This book is an in-depth study of this historical
phenomenon and how it will directly affect us all
in the near future.

Food, Shelter and the American Dream
Stanley Aronowitz. 1974.
$7.95; paper, $3.95.
Seabury Press, Inc.
815 Second Ave.
New York, NY 10017

The author addresses the issues that increasingly
plague most Americans: are there real shortages
of food, oil, and other basic commodities? Or are
these manipulated shortages, generated to secure
higher profits for the new agribusiness and oil
companies? What consequences for U.S. foreign
policy may result from competition between
America's need for agricultural resources and
energy and the demands of other countries? Will
Americans accept deterioration of their living
standards? If a new "scarcity" economy is generated, what are its consequences for work disci-
pline? Will American prosperity have to be maintained by a constant high level of military spending in the wake of declining consumption of

durable goods? This book explores the reasons for
the reversal in the fortunes of the U.S. economy,
the consequences for politics and culture that
may arise from the new situation, and the possible solutions for our national dilemma.

Great American Bond Market
Sidney Homer. 1978.
$14.95.
Dow Jones–Irwin.
1818 Ridge Rd.
Homewood, IL 60430

This book consists principally of twenty-seven
speeches on the bond market and bond investment techniques. The book's main value to
money managers will be found in parts 4 and 5
dealing with bond investment strategy and the
stock market.

Great Inflation: Germany 1919–1923
William Guttmann & Patricia Meehan. 1975.
$13.95; paper, $4.95.
Saxon House.
Distributed by:
Atheneum Publications
122 E. 42nd St.
New York, NY 10017

Inflation run riot. What would happen if we lost
control and money went mad? Germany in the
1920s. Fortunes were made and life savings were
lost, overnight. Any alternative seemed better—
even Hitler.

Grow or Die; The Over-Population Myth
James A. Weber. 1977.
$11.95.
Arlington House Publications
165 Huguenot St.
New Rochelle, NY 10801

America is underpopulated. Our central cities
actually have shrinking populations. Once pros-
perous farm areas in New England and the South
are underutilized or have reverted to forest. Zero
Population Growth (ZPG) threatens the retirement
income of millions, the prosperity of those still
working, and the future of the young. The myth
of overpopulation has sinister roots, the author
shows. Advocates of abortion on demand, hedon-
istic sex protected by the pill, and selfish life-
styles are building the overpopulation myth to
justify their own conduct and to satisfy their lust
for power. The result of six years of research, this
hardhitting, documented answer to the doomsayers reopens the great debate on which our
future will turn.

Guide to Intelligent Investing
Jerome B. Cohen, Edward D. Zinbarg, and Arthur Zeikel. 1977.
$12.50.
Dow Jones–Irwin.
1818 Ridge Rd.
Homewood, IL 60430

This work is geared to the investor who wants to create and manage his or her own investment portfolio. The authors deal with the basics of sound investing and answer questions such as: Is this the time to buy common stock? What kind, in what industry, and in what company? What are your investment objectives? Are you aggressive, conservative, or a speculator? Should you choose blue chips or speculative options? Income stocks, growth stocks or performance stocks? In short, if you are looking for answers to investment questions, the chances are that you will find them in this book. The authors are all recognized authorities in the field of investment.

Hard Money Book: An Insider's Guide to Successful Investment in Currency, Gold, Silver & Precious Stones
Steven K. Beckner. 1979.
Paper, $19.00.
Capitalistic Reporter Press
1212 Avenue of the Americas
New York, NY 10036

Contents: the basics of currency analysis; how to make money through over-the-counter trans-actions in currencies, precious metals and stones, and gold and silver; currencies; precious stones; leverage; the futures market; commodities.

Harry Browne's Complete Guide to Swiss Banks
Harry Browne.
$12.95.
McGraw–Hill Book Company
1221 Avenue of the Americas
New York, NY 10020

Nonstop inflation, a recession that will not go away, "problem" banks, lack of privacy—these are just some of the reasons why thousands of investors have moved their money out of the United States and into Swiss banks. The author shows you how the right Swiss bank can be your avenue to financial safety, profits in currency that will hold its value, and the kind of privacy that exists nowhere in North America. This com-plete guidebook tells you which banks are safety-minded, what services are available, which invest-ments are the safest, what little known risks are

involved (and how to eliminate them), how to assure absolute privacy, and what to tell the tax collector.

How the Experts Buy and Sell Gold Bullion, Gold Stocks & Gold Coins
James E. Sinclair & Harry D. Schultz. 1975.
$8.95.
Arlington House Publications
165 Huguenot St.
New Rochelle, NY 10801

The authors talk candidly about: the crucial minute—how to time your purchases and sales; how to use Swiss and Canadian banks legally for gold trading; strong points and potential weak-nesses in South African gold shares; price projec-tions for the long haul, for the short term; U.S. gold mines; silver revisited—pluses and minuses in today's oddball economy; the jargon of gold trading.

How to Be Prepared for Any Crisis
Roland Page. 1974.
Paper, $2.95.
Hawkes Publications, Inc.
3775 S. 500 W.
P.O. Box 15711
Salt Lake City, UT 84115

A good, helpful book from the Mormons. Covers complete medical, food, clothing, and miscel-laneous inventories; specific storage know-how; how to drill your own well; how to get out of debt; how to prepare and use herbs; primitive sur-vival; the importance of gold and silver; how to make dried jerky; how to build a fish smoke-house; how to sprout a kitchen garden; edible wild plant life; how to distill water; etc. Nothing radical or profound—just good old common sense.

How to Beat the Money Grabbers: The Essentials of Estate Planning
Victor P. Whitney. 1979.
$14.95.
Arlington House Publications
165 Huguenot St.
New Rochelle, NY 10801

Introduces you to the important ideas and concepts of estate planning that can help you avoid the "Money Grabbers," such as the IRS agent who can confiscate up to 70 percent of your estate. What is estate planning? What taxes will your estate face? What are the tools of estate planning? These and other questions are answered in a straightforward style that will de-mystify one of the more complex tax angles. Case studies for estate planning are presented for the elderly retired, the professional person, the business owner, the corporate executive, the farmer, the single person, and the handicapped.

How to Invest in Bonds
Hugh C. Sherwood. 1974.
$7.95; paper, $2.95.
McGraw–Hill Book Company
1221 Avenue of the Americas
New York, NY 10020

How to Invest in Diamonds, Metals & Collectibles for Maximum Profits
Arthur C. Simon. 1980.
Paper, $9.95.
Future Shop
P.O. Box 111
Camarillo, CA 93010

How to Invest in Gems: Everyone's Guide to Buying Rubies, Sapphires, Emeralds, & Diamonds
Benjamin Zucker. 1976.
$12.95.
Times Books.
The New York Times Co.
3 Park Ave.
New York, NY 10016

How to Invest in Gold Coins
Donald J. Hoppe. 1975.
Paper, $2.95.
Arlington House Publications
165 Huguenot St.
New Rochelle, NY 10801

The author concentrates for investment purposes on the gold coins of the United States, but the investor interested in Mexican and other foreign coins is not ignored. Indeed, this comprehensive work surveys every modern nation that has minted gold coins. Extra features abound in these pages: forty tables, twenty charts, a helpful glossary, a bibliography, sixteen photographs, four appendices, and a comprehensive index.

How to Locate in the Country: Your Personal Guide
John Gourlie. 1973.
$3.95.
Garden Way Publishing Company
Charlotte, VT 05445

Evaluating different locales and geographic areas to suit you personally; cost of living; medical facilities; zoning; economic and educational opportunities; government; taxes; population trends; twenty-one-point checklist.

How to Prepare for the Coming Crash
Robert L. Preston. 1975.
Paper, $2.95.
Hawkes Publishing Inc.
3775 S. 500 W.
P.O. Box 15711
Salt Lake City, UT 84115

"We will soon witness the greatest crash and depression this nation has ever known!" The author's ten-step program prepares you to survive comfortably, shows you how to store foods wisely, and tells you what investments to make or avoid.

How To Prosper During the Coming Bad Years: A Crash Course in Personal and Financial Survival
Howard J. Ruff.
Hardcover, 1979, $8.95, Times Books.
Paper, 1980, $2.75.
Warner Books, Inc.
Independent News Company
75 Rockefeller Plaza
New York, NY 10019

This book tells you: why most "conservative" investment programs will wipe you out soon; why financial chaos is coming and how you can beat it; why and how inflation will win and how you can join it; the financial errors that can endanger your life and how to correct them with bad-news-is-good-news investments; how the sexual revolution is leading the assault on your pocketbook; why you will never collect social security.

Hungry Planet: The Modern World at the Edge of Famine
George Borgstrom. 1972.
Paper, $3.95.
(Collier) Macmillan Publishing Company, Inc.
866 Third Ave.
New York, NY 10022

In this updated second revised edition of his 1965 work, the author repeats and reemphasizes his warning that man is threatening to deprive himself of a future through his insane procreation and his waste of resources.

Inflation-Proofing Your Investments: A Permanent Program That Will Help You Protect Your Savings Against Inflation or Depression
Harry Browne and Terry Coxon. 1980.
$12.95.
William Morrow & Co., Inc.
105 Madison Ave.
New York, NY 10016

Introduction to Christian Economics
Gary North. 1979.
Paper, $6.50.
Presbyterian and Reformed Publishing Co.
P.O. Box 817
Phillipsburg, NJ 08865

This work is an attempt to set forth the biblical presuppositions in several areas of economics, but primarily in the field of monetary theory. Some of the implications are then explored, though hardly in an exhaustive fashion. The book is intended to supplement the more rigorous secular economic textbooks that, for all their rigor, are virtually worthless in the area of epistemology, and nearly so in the area of monetary theory.

Invisible Government
Dan Smoot. 1977 (3rd ed.).
Paper, $3.00.
Western Islands
395 Concord Ave.
Belmont, MA 02178

A classic analysis of the establishment that runs the executive branch of the federal government. This new, larger edition contains an updated membership list of the Council of Foreign Relations, a list of the members of the Trilateral Commission, an updated list of the leaders of the Atlantic Council, and a new introduction by the publisher. This work helps to explain why the United States is rapidly moving toward a socialist state.

Mark Skousen's Complete Guide to Financial Privacy
Mark Skousen. 1979.
$14.95.
Alexandria House Books.
901 N. Washington St.
No. 605
Alexandria, VA 22314

Today we live in a brash, uninhibited, bare-all society. Government corporations and the press intrude on every aspect of our lives. Your freedom is at stake. This book tells you how to: keep your bank account confidential; set up a secret foreign bank account; become a private investor; use a registered company name legally; purchase real estate, stocks, gold, and collectibles anonymously; avoid swindlers who prey on your desire for privacy; get your name off mailing lists; use an unlisted telephone number and post office box; find out if your telephone is bugged; travel incognito; borrow money confidentially—by mail—without revealing the purpose of the loan; build secret safes in your home; maximize privacy on your tax return and avoid an audit; write a private will; use cash, money orders, and cashier's checks to do business discreetly.

Money and Man: A Survey of Monetary Experience
Elgin Groseclose. 1977.
$13.95; paper, $5.95.
University of Oklahoma Press
1005 Asp Ave.
Norman, OK 73019

What is money today? "We see all about us," says the author, "the capitulation of the money managers to the cry noted by Adam Smith, that of more money, more purchasing power—a cry which they seek to satisfy by printing more paper, progressively destroying the integrity of money. This has gone on to such an extent that no one knows what money is. We need to return to a new valuation and appreciation of the importance of integrity, of character, in the management of money, as indeed, we need to relearn its importance in the entire economic realm of production and distribution."

Money Market: Myth, Reality, and Practice
Marcia Stigum. 1978.
$22.50.
Dow Jones–Irwin.
1818 Ridge Rd.
Homewood, IL 60430

A comprehensive guide to the U.S. money market. Since the money market will be relatively new to many readers, the book begins by providing all of the background necessary to read and understand it. Much of the material in this book is the result of primary research and has never appeared in print before. Key topics covered in depth are: how big banks operate in the money market; the operation of the Eurodollar market; the operation of money market dealers; treasury debt management policies, past and present; Federal Reserve open market operations; the characteristics of each money market instrument, including risk, liquidity, and return; how the market for each money market instrument is made by dealers, brokers, and investors; the T-Bill futures market—hedging, speculation, and arbitrage; the principles of managing a liquidity portfolio; yield calculations for the portfolio manager; glossary of money market and bond market terms.

New Money Dynamics
Venita Van Caspel. 1978.
$11.95.
Reston Publication Co., Inc.
11480 Sunset Hills Rd.
Reston, VA 22090

A personal guide to lifelong financial stability that will lead you ultimately to financial independence. The author maintains that you can plan to protect your assets based on monetary strategy, not luck. Presented in a clear, easy-to-follow style.

New Profits from the Monetary Crisis
Harry Browne. 1978.
$12.95.
William Morrow & Co., Inc.
105 Madison Ave.
New York, NY 10016
Orders: Wilmot Warehouse
6 Henderson Dr.
West Caldwell, NJ 07006

Whether you count your investment dollars in the hundreds or in the millions, this book will help you understand why the economic chaos of the 1970s will continue. It will help you find the way to financial survival; it offers you a variety of strategies and tools. You will find clear, complete explanations that allow you to create an investment program suited to your own needs, talents, and objectives. Among the many subjects covered are: why there are economic crises and why they will continue; why the U.S. economy is on the brink of a deflationary depression; why the real estate boom is nearing its end; why gold, silver, and currencies are no longer buy-and-hold investments but are still important; why stocks and bonds move in cycles, and how you can spot the beginning and end of an uptrend; how to know when a foreign currency is a bargain; which investment (not gold) is the only pure inflation hedge; why your bank is vulnerable and what you should do about it; how you can use low-risk warrants to profit from the stock market; why you should ignore the boom in rare objects, art, postage stamps, and other "collectibles."

Nineteen Seventy-Nine Insider's Banking & Credit Almanac
Mark Skousen. 1978.
$14.95.
Alexandria House Books
901 N. Washington St.
No. 605
Alexandria, VA 22314

Topics covered include: one credit union that pays 9 percent on unrestricted savings accounts; a checking account that lets you write checks in any currency you wish; a U.S. checking account backed by gold bullion; how to earn 12 percent on an 8 percent CD; how to get free life insurance; how to manage without a U.S. checking account (if you seek privacy from government snooping); how safe is your bank?; a credit union that pays 6 percent on its checking account; how anyone can use an out-of-state checking account locally; postpone bankruptcy forever; save $100 a year on checks.

None Dare Call It Conspiracy
Gary Allen and Larry Abraham. 1972.
$5.95; paper, $1.00.
Concord Press
P.O. Box 2686
Seal Beach, CA 90740

Fact upon fact is compiled to prove that conspiratorial forces behind the scenes control the U.S. government and dictate its policies.

Panics and Crashes . . . and How You Can Make Money Out of Them
Harry Schultz. 1975.
Paper, $1.50.
Pinnacle Books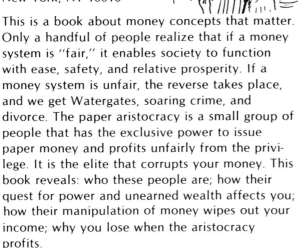
1 Century Plaza
2029 Century Park E
Los Angeles, CA 90067

What will happen to you, your family, your business, your dreams, when the next panic strikes? Are you protected? Are you taking the steps that could double, even triple, your money? In this bestselling handbook of financial protection, one of the most influential financial authorities in the world takes a hard look at how you can prepare for the worst.

Paper Aristocracy: The Elite that Controls America's Money System
Howard S. Katz. 1976.
$7.95; paper, $4.95.
Books in Focus, Inc.
160 E. 38th St.
Suite 31B
New York, NY 10016

This is a book about money concepts that matter. Only a handful of people realize that if a money system is "fair," it enables society to function with ease, safety, and relative prosperity. If a money system is unfair, the reverse takes place, and we get Watergates, soaring crime, and divorce. The paper aristocracy is a small group of people that has the exclusive power to issue paper money and profits unfairly from the privilege. It is the elite that corrupts your money. This book reveals: who these people are; how their quest for power and unearned wealth affects you; how their manipulation of money wipes out your income; why you lose when the aristocracy profits.

Playing the Price Controls Game: How Some People Will Profit from the Coming Controls
Mark Skousen. 1977.
$9.95.
Arlington House Publications
165 Huguenot St.
New Rochelle, NY 10801

This work grapples with the number one problem facing the U.S. economy in the late 1970s: government controls on wages, prices, rents, and profits. But this is not a doom-and-gloom book. The author does not leave the reader with a feeling of hopelessness. Rather, he provides numerous historical examples of how controls have been anticipated, survived, and eluded; how people in all walks of life can prepare for the coming controls and thus avoid their nastier consequences.

Profiting from Uncertainty
Patrick Wood. 1977.
The August Corporation
P.O. Box 582
Scottsdale, AZ 85251

Contents: politics; economics; social trends; investing for profits; investing for survival.

Robert Kinsman Guide to Tax Havens
Robert Kinsman. 1978.
$17.50.
Dow Jones–Irwin
1818 Ridge Rd.
Homewood, IL 60430

Contrary to popular belief, foreign tax havens still make sense for many people. This book will show you if they make sense for you. And if they do, it will tell you where to look, whom to contact, and how to use them legally. This book was designed for the layman as well as for the professional tax planner. In it you will find ratings of eight major tax havens; the new U.S. laws regarding foreign trust and companies; a seven-step action list explaining what you should do before using a haven; addresses and phone numbers of respected financial institutions in key havens; a real-world view of four havens through the eyes of three very different potential haven users; and a detailed discussion of the current financial scene in Switzerland.

Rules for Financial Survival 1979: The Questions and the Answers
Julian M. Snyder. 1979.
Paper, $15.00.
International Moneyline Press
25 Broad St.
New York, NY 10004

As the year 1978 moved toward its closing hours, and its curious place in world economic and political history, International Moneyline editor Julian Snyder engaged in an intensive series of private meetings and discussions designed to cast light on future events. Attending these sessions were economists, government leaders, scholars, bankers, financiers, journalists, money managers, political analysts, and investors. This book treats the most incisive questions asked at those sessions—and the answers presented by the author.

Stock Market Logic: A Sophisticated Approach to Profits on Wall Street
Norman G. Fosback. 1976.
$30.00; paper, $20.00.
Institute for Econometric Research
3471 N. Federal Hwy.
Suite 501
Fort Lauderdale, FL 33306

The author analyzes a multitude of technical and fundamental approaches to market timing and stock selection, combining the best into a practical, profit-oriented, investment program.

Tax Havens: What They Are and What They Can Do for the Shrewd Investor
Adam Starchild. 1979.
$12.95.
Arlington House Publications
165 Huguenot St.
New Rochelle, NY 10801

Tax havens: those odd little countries in the Caribbean, Europe, and out-of-the-way corners of the world with no or minimal taxes where U.S. investors can shield their profits from the clutches of the IRS. In this compact, informative book, the author reveals the secrets of tax haven investment.

Tax Target: Washington
Gary Allen. 1979.
$8.95; paper, $2.45.
Seventy-Six Press
P.O. Box 2686
Seal Beach, CA 90740

Since the passage of California's Jarvis-Gann Amendment, known as Proposition 13, beleaguered taxpayers across the nation have begun to realize that something can and should be done about the incredible burden that they have been forced to bear. The formerly "silent majority" is now beginning to swell the ranks of tax reform groups in every state, and this potential for political clout has big spenders everywhere running for cover. In this concise book you will begin to discover the extent of the abuse suffered by U.S. taxpayers, and you will learn that the problem is not completely revealed by your Form 1040.

Time for Truth
William Simon. 1979.
Paper, $2.50.
McGraw-Hill Book Company
1221 Avenue of the Americas
New York, NY 10020

The author presents both his personal philosophy

and an insider's revealing picture of the Nixon and Ford administrations. He substantiates his message with the wider perspective that he gained as Secretary of the Treasury from 1974 to 1977. His aim is to inspire all Americans to a critical awareness of the real and unbreakable connection between economic and political freedom. To lose one is to lose the other. And we are losing both, he warns, in the wake of the expanding state. He also offers a blueprint for a "counterintelligentsia" to preserve our freedom.

Trilaterals Over Washington
Antony C. Sutton and Patrick M. Wood. 1979.
Paper, $4.95.
The August Corporation
P.O. Box 582
Scottsdale, AZ 85251

Drawing from the voluminous writings of the Trilateral Commission, the authors document the unseen power structure in the United States. Also covers taxation, the energy crisis, the death of the dollar, gold, and the coming financial panic.

Troubled Times: A Survival Plan for the Future
Isao Horinouchi. 1978.
Paper, $4.95.
Hawkes Publications, Inc.
3775 S. 500 W.
P.O. Box 15711
Salt Lake City, UT 84115

A book to help those who are seeking useful advice for an uncertain economic future in the United States. Basic guidelines and principles. How to prepare physically, emotionally, psychologically. Shows the problems and consequences of a depression and how to prepare for and survive difficult times.

Understanding Runaway Inflation: An Investor's Guide to Inflation Hedges
Jerome F. Smith. 1979.
E R C Publishing Company
204-1760 Marine Drive
West Vancouver, British Columbia
Canada V7V 1J4

The simple act of destroying most of the value of the U.S. dollar (now about 20 percent of its 1940 value) has unleashed powerful and far-reaching forces of economic, political, and social destruction. These forces of chance will increasingly exert themselves in international markets and in the U.S. domestic markets, including the stock market. The present fundamentals of the world economy or the U.S. economy can in no way be compared to the post-World War II period when the dollar was redeemable and fixed exchange rates were honored. We are in a new period of disorder that calls for new criteria and new methods in investing.

Understanding the Dollar Crisis
Percy L. Greaves. 1973.
Paper, $4.95.
Western Islands
395 Concord Ave.
Belmont, MA 02178

Professor Greaves has, for many years, been in wide demand both in the United States and abroad as a lecturer on free market economic theory and the events that led to the 1929 Depression. It is from a series of such lectures that this book has been compiled. The questions and answers following each lecture have been included. They provide emphasis and clarification of the ideas expressed.

Unusual Investments That Could Make You Rich: Revised and Updated Edition of the Speculator's Handbook
David Smyth and Lawrance F. Stuntz. 1978.
Paper, $6.95.
Contemporary Books, Inc.
180 N. Michigan Ave.
Chicago, IL 60601

Contents: the international portfolio; options; overseas banking; gold—the ultimate security; silver—the hoarder's metal; copper—a political commodity; diamonds—a global monopoly; worldwide real estate; tax shelters; defaulted bonds and old shares; foreign currencies; how to speculate and win; some tropical bonanzas; some all-American products; some food staples; some dietary luxuries.

Using Warrants: Safe Investment Programs Using Stock Warrants and Dual-Purpose Funds
Terry Coxon. 1979.
Paper, $10.00.
Investors Perspectives Publishing.
P.O. Box 1187
Burlingame, CA 94010
Warrants are long-term options to purchase stocks. By themselves, warrants are risky and speculative; but properly matched to other assets, they can add to the safety of your investment program. This booklet tells you how to handle warrants.

War on Gold
Antony C. Sutton. 1977.
$9.95.
Seventy-Six Press
P.O. Box 2686
Seal Beach, CA 90740

Throughout history, a paper fiat currency, not backed by gold, has always spelled disaster. But today, the U.S. Treasury and the Federal Reserve System are waging a political and propaganda war against gold. The author warns that it is a war the United States is bound to lose. This work is the definitive study of the past, present, and future of the precious metal that Keynesian economists and political schemers have denounced as a "barbarous relic." The war in gold began several centuries ago, when politicians discovered that they could print limitless amounts of paper currency for a small fraction of the cost of using gold as money. This practice has accelerated in recent years as the United States acquired a paper debt of a trillion-plus dollars, massive federal deficits led to double-digit inflation, and internationalists plotted to create a New World Order.

Warmongers
Howard S. Katz. 1979.
Ed. by Stephen A. Zarlenga.
$11.95.
Books In Focus, Inc.
160 E. 38th St.
Suite 31B
New York, NY 10016

They started World War I. They engineered World War II. They are moving the world toward war now! Who are they? In this book you will discover the distressing link between the creation of paper money and major wars, present designs to lead the United States into major war, and why the author predicts that the United States and China will be fighting Russia and Japan in the near future.

What Has Government Done to Our Money?
Murray N. Rothbard. 1979.
Paper, $2.00.
Libertarian Publishers
1035 6th St., No. 4
Novato, CA 94025

Of all the economic problems, money is possibly the most tangled and perhaps is where we most need perspective. Money, moreover, is the eco-nomic area most encrusted and entangled with centuries of governmental meddling. Many people—many economists—devoted to the free market stop short at money. Money, they insist, is different—it must be supplied and regulated by government. They never think of state control of money as interference in the free market; a free market in money is to them unthinkable. Governments must mint coins, issue paper, define "legal tender," create central banks, pump money in and out, and "stabilize the price level."

What You Should Know About Individual Retirement Accounts
L. L. Unthank and Harry M. Behrendt. 1978.
$12.95.
Dow Jones–Irwin.
1818 Ridge Rd.
Homewood, IL 60430

More than a quarter-million persons have already established IRAs, and it is estimated that over 45 million additional people are eligible for such accounts. This book will aid you in determining if you are among those who are eligible, plus it will illustrate how to go about getting the new and very important tax benefits to which you may be legally entitled. The unique question-and-answer format of the book makes it ideal for reference and getting clear-cut answers to specific points.

When and How To Profit from Buying and Selling Gold
Lawrence R. Rosen. 1975.
$14.95.
Dow Jones–Irwin.
1818 Ridge Rd.
Homewood, IL 60430

Despite the verbal thrashings about of some doomsayers, gold still remains one of the best hedges against runaway inflation available to the average person. This book will tell you how much to pay for gold; it will tell you when the price is too high; and it will tell you, based on price and charges, which to buy—gold coins, gold bullion, gold futures contracts, or gold mining shares.

Winning with Money: A Guide for Your Future
Beryl W. Sprinkel and Robert J. Genetski. 1977.
$10.95.
Dow Jones–Irwin.
1818 Ridge Rd.
Homewood, IL 60430

The authors discuss the implications that various policies will have on your investments and analyze the performance of investments in different inflationary settings. Whether future governmental actions are responsible or irresponsible, the authors' prime objective is to provide you with winning strategies. This book will show you how to cope with future economic crises.

You Can Profit from a Monetary Crisis
Harry Browne. 1974.
$8.95.
Macmillan Publishing Co., Inc.
Orders to:
Riverside, NJ 08075

The biggest crises lie ahead, but so do the biggest opportunities. Important changes in the economy include the opportunity for profit. This book tells the investor what to look out for now that gold ownership is legal—and how to hedge against both runaway inflation and depression. Interesting suggestions that could be of value to every income earner.

Your New Swiss Bank Book
Robert Kinsman. 1979.
$14.95.
Dow Jones–Irwin.
1818 Ridge Rd.
Homewood, IL 60430

The author takes a new, 1979 look at Swiss banks and divulges many surprising and some not-so-surprising facts about the "Gnomes of Zurich" and other Swiss banking centers. He tells how you can use the services of a Swiss bank to your advantage and shows you how to do it. Among the topics covered are: how to select a Swiss bank; how Swiss banks help you to beat inflation and recession; the four important new limits to Swiss bank secrecy since 1975; what amount of capital gets you the most for your money at Swiss banks; the significance of the Iranian revolution on Swiss bank secrecy; whether Swiss annuities and insurance are better than Swiss banks; what to do

before U.S. foreign exchange controls are initiated; when to use Swiss banks to buy gold and silver; three U.S. political reasons for using Swiss banks. The book also contains a complete reference section on gold and on Swiss history.

Emergency Procedures

What to do in case of nuclear attack, flood, tornado, or other disasters? You might want to contact your local branch of the Defense Department's Office of Civil Defense to find out about warning systems and public shelters for your area. Look under "Federal Emergency Management Agency" or "Defense Civil Preparedness" in the U.S. Government section of the phone book.

Books

In Time of Emergency: A Citizen's Handbook on Nuclear Attack, Natural Disasters
1968. 0-297-579
Department of Defense, Office of Civil Defense
Available from the Superintendent of Documents
Washington, D.C. 20204
Free booklet.

Although first published in 1968, the information contained herein is still usable, and the booklet is still distributed by local Civil Defense Preparedness offices.

Survival Directory: A Guide to Personal Survival
Mutual Association for Security and Survival
P.O. Box 6
Lakehurst, NJ 08733

Packed with well-thought-out advice for surviving nuclear attack. City dwellers, for the most part, are advised to evacuate, and Saxon details the methods for doing so. High-risk cities are listed; also, low-risk campgrounds and other public lands where retreats may be established in a crisis.

The Ten Most Dangerous Areas of the United States in a Nuclear Attack

These ten areas will certainly be hit in the opening minutes of a nuclear attack on the United States.

1. The Washington, D.C. area. (Military command centers)
2. Most of north central Montana. (Minuteman missile silos)
3. Everything within seventy-five miles of Minot, North Dakota. (Minuteman missile silos)
4. Everything within eighty miles north, west or south of Grand Forks, North Carolina. (Minuteman missile silos)
5. The area lying within 100 miles north or east of Rapid City, South Dakota. (Minuteman missile silos)
6. Everything within 120 miles north or east of Cheyenne, Wyoming. (Minuteman missile silos)
7. The area within fifty miles of Tucson, Arizona. (Titan II missile silos)
8. The area within fifty miles of Wichita, Kansas. (Titan II missile silos)
9. The area within 125 miles east or south of Kansas City, Missouri. (Minuteman missile silos)
10. The area within fifty miles north of Little Rock, Arkansas. (Titan II missile silos)

Excerpted from *Life After Doomsday* by Bruce D. Clayton, Ph.D. All rights reserved by the Publisher: Paladin Press, Post Office Box 1307, Boulder, Colorado 80306.

Urban Survival

Ragnar Benson

On two different occasions in my life I have had to live in large cities. Both times I was so dirt poor it was awful. But both times we made it without government help. What government assistance I did get was of the negative kind. The authorities didn't approve of what I was doing and did everything in their power to stop me. Our family got the strong impression that anybody who thought they could be self-reliant was a bad actor to be dealt with severely. The word was dependence but we didn't want to be somebody else's ward, and we weren't.

I have a strong and lasting conviction that there is an incredible amount of wild products going to waste in the average city. The suburbs and the various city neighborhoods have a lot of grass, trees, parkways, hedges, parks, ponds and similar game habitat. The potential harvest from these can be quite impressive.

I have never lived right downtown in the inner city and doubt if it would be possible to exist by poaching in that type of environment. But cities are not all core area. Most people don't live on just pavement and brick. The following are some suggestions that worked for me. The wise and prudent person might keep them in mind.

Squirrels

By far and away the best source of good meat in the cities are tree squirrels. From east coast to west coast I have only been in a few cities that didn't have sizeable populations of these animals. As an added advantage, squirrels can often be lured to the poacher rather than the other way around.

City squirrels are probably best taken in a box trap. They are out of sight, out of mind and easy to handle in a box trap. No one suspects the little boxes sitting around one's yard in the bushes.

113

Under some circumstances, box traps can be set in parks.

If the yard is surrounded by brush or there is a window to shoot out of, try BB caps or other quiet rifles.

Steel traps will also work. They can be set up in a tree, along a roof line or other place that is out of sight.

Robins and Blackbirds

The British eat both, so some years ago we got a recipe for Robin Pie and tried it. Not bad, but not all that good either.

On the other hand there are a lot of these birds in many cities. They are easily taken with various methods so in an emergency situation it may be worth a try.

The best, in my estimation, is to use a bird snare. Bait with a few kernels of wheat, some flour or even cherry pits. Anything of that nature will work.

Another good method is to build a bird trap. These are handy in the wide range of situations, and it certainly won't hurt to have one sitting around taking a few birds now and then.

Shooting robins is too destructive and slow. Better to make up a batch of bird lime and get them that way.

Pheasants And Quail

The Chicago suburb we lived in had a fair population of pheasants and quail. Over the years these creatures had become incredibly elusive. I first realized they were around when I saw their tracks in the snow.

The best plan, if these game birds are around, is to use a game bird trap or some snares. The best trap is probably a net trap or closure trap. Steel traps tear them up too much. A standard bird snare also works very well.

During the winter it is often possible to shoot pheasants and quail from a window or porch as they scratch around for food. At that time it may also be profitable to bait them in for harvest.

Pigeons

Every city has a large number of pigeons. I have eaten hundreds of them and they all tasted fine. It's just the idea, I guess, because I won't eat any more unless things get pretty desperate.

Pigeons in cities are everywhere. For a time I disposed of pigeons for the police department in three medium sized cities. During that time I killed pigeons out of old barns, from the eaves of houses, under bridges, out of old cars, out of the attic of a school and a hundred other weird places.

Pigeons in a city are best taken in a bird trap. Bait with cracked corn and leave several in the trap at all times to call the others.

Bird snares also work well, but at three or four per trap per week the pigeons can usually breed faster than the poacher can catch them.

Bird lime works, as does shooting them.

A very good method is to blind pigeons on their roosts with a powerful flashlight. Then either shoot the critters or grab them live. Most people want to get rid of the damn things, so it generally isn't hard to find a place to shine and shoot them.

Muskrats

I am constantly amazed at the number of muskrats that live in the ponds and rivers that flow through our cities. Other than one killed by a cat or dog every now and then, I don't think they have any enemies. Don't forget muskrats are vegetarians, and are not related to rats. They are very good to eat.

Keep watch in the sheltered city parks and you will probably be as surprised as I was at their numbers.

Most rats in parks have bank dens. Use a box trap or two and work on through the area till the harvest is made. People who would recoil in horror over a steel trap never give the square boxes a second thought.

Bees

People in cities are continually having problems with bees. They take up residence in the walls of their houses, in old trees, in attics, and harass passers by.

If the swarm has been there for a while, I usually agree to take it out if they will let me neatly cut into the side of the building or do what ever to get the honey and the wax.

Most of the time in cities the colony can't be saved so I use a CO_2 fire extinguisher and freeze the bees. It is the safest, easiest, non-destructive method of dispatching bees that I know of.

Possums And Coons

These are some fur-bearers that are far more abundant in many cities than anybody except the police (who get nuisance calls about them) would ever believe. They are also hard to trap since they get plenty to eat and won't come to bait well. City coons and possums are used to living around people. Even dumb old possums wise up to a certain extent, making it difficult to collect them.

If there is both an old large stand of trees and some creeks near town I can guarantee that at least raccoons live nearby. With only one or the other there is still an excellent chance that coons will be there.

About the only set that works for coons and possums is a steel trap and bait. Place the trap so it is obscured and plan to leave it for long periods without getting anything. Best bait? Probably peanut butter.

Rabbits

I probably don't have to remind readers that there are a lot of wild rabbits in most towns and cities throughout the U.S. Conditions are generally fairly good for them. There is food and cover and, other than dogs and cats, few enemies.

Best methods for rabbits are either snares or box traps. One is about the same as the other so the decision then becomes one of expedience.

Some poachers learn to set snares and become very good with them. Others like box traps. At times it is better to set a box trap than a snare or vice versa, but usually good sets can be found for either.

Shooting rabbits with a quiet .22 works in town if there is enough cover.

Mushrooms

Since this is not a text on mushrooms, I won't labor the point. But good outdoorsmen know their mushrooms and take advantage of any opportunity to collect them.

Puffballs, cauliflower mushrooms and morels grow in cities. Keep a lookout for them.

4 Building and Alternative Energy

Introduction

This chapter begins with house building, covers building that incorporates the use of solar energy, then eases into wood heat, methanol, and finally to sources of general energy information. The unifying theme here is the self-reliant owner-builder, and most of the materials included are geared to people who would rather do it themselves.

A few words of solace on the subject of solar confusion. Solar energy—or at least the *idea* of solar energy—has become popular of late due to rapidly rising petroleum product prices. Because solar heating and cooling is a new field, however, few of us have a good grasp of its principles, let alone its economics. The subject can be intimidating.

In which climatic regions can solar energy be used effectively to heat a home? What are conversion tables, and how do they work? How long will an active solar hot water heating system take to pay itself off, considering the projected cost of public utility bills? These are just a few of the most commonly asked questions about solar energy. While the editor would like nothing better than to answer all of them, the scope of this book does not permit it. Besides, you will remember the answers better if you look them up yourself. The books, magazines, tapes, and other information sources listed in this chapter will help you. Whether you are an energy amateur wanting to start out small with maybe a solar cooker, or an architect with specific questions about solar design, you should find what you need in these pages. (If you are considering solar heating and/or cooling for your home, and you pay taxes, contact your local IRS office and ask for information on the National Energy Act. Going solar may entitle you to a reduction in your tax bill.)

For farm building, see also Chapter 1, *Homesteading*. The *Wilderness Survival* chapter includes books that have instructions for fashioning survival shelters. Home energy conservation is covered in the chapter on *City Survival*.

Access

Building

Books

Building Construction Illustrated
Francis D. Ching. 1975.
Paper, $10.95.
Van Nostrand Reinhold Co.
135 W. 50th
New York, NY 10020

Thorough information, detailed instructions.

Building Construction in Warm Climates (two vols.)
Richard L. Fullerton.
(*Oxford Tropical Handbook*) 1967-1968.
I: paper, $8.00.
II: paper, $8.50.
Oxford University Press, Inc.
200 Madison Ave.
New York, NY 10016

Building the House You Can Afford
Stu Campbell.
Paper, $9.95.
Garden Way Publishing
Charlotte, VT 05445

"The objective of this book is to help you save at least 20 percent on home building without sacrificing quality."

Building Your Own Stone House: Using the Easy Slipform Method
Karl and Sue Schwenke.
Paper, $5.95.
Garden Way Publishing
Charlotte, VT 05445

Materials, sites, excavation; making and using slipforms, footings, foundations, walls, roofs, fireplaces.

Build it Better Yourself
Editors of *Organic Gardening Magazine.* 1977.
Hardcover, $16.95.
Rodale Press
33 East Minor St.
Emmaus, PA 18049

The Complete Book of Masonry, Cement and Brickwork
(A Drake Home Craftsman's book) 1975.
Paper, $4.95.
Drake Publishers, Inc.
801 Second Ave.
New York, NY 10017

A basic, no-nonsense text with diagrams. Complete, and a good value.

Design and Construction Handbook for Energy-Saving Houses
Alex Wade. 1979.
Hardcover, $15.95.
Rodale Press
33 East Minor St.
Emmaus, PA 18049

Contains, along with other information, floor plans, elevations, and site plans; lists of recommended contractors, architects, and suppliers of materials; sophisticated wood-heating systems.

Design with Climate
Victor Olgay. 1963.
$30.00.
Princeton University Press
41 William St.
Princeton, NJ 08540

Architectural design to correspond with various climatic conditions.

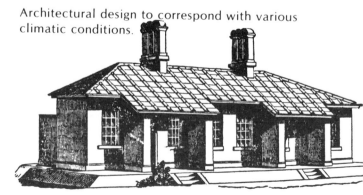

Energy, Environment and Building
(Urban and Architectural Studies: No. 3)
Phillip Steadman. 1975.
Paper, $7.95.
Cambridge University Press
510 North Ave.
New Rochelle, NY 10801

Compendium on solar energy, wind power, small-scale water power, with bibliographies and appendices. Listing of solar hardware manufacturers now outdated.

The Fifty Dollars and Up Underground House Book
Mike Oehler. 1978.
$6.00.
Mole Publishing Company
Rt. 1, Box 618
Bonners Ferry, ID 83805

How to build an innovative and cheap home using the post-shoring polyethylene method, which in most areas does not meet building code requirements, enabling the builder to go underground in two senses of the word.

From the Ground Up: The Shelter Institute Guide to Building Your Own House
John N. Cole and Charles Wing. 1976.
Paper, $7.95.
Atlantic Monthly Press
Little, Brown & Co.
200 West St.
Watham, MA 02154

The energy-efficient home, from site selection through construction.

How to Build a Low-Cost House of Stone
Lewis and Sharon Watson. 5th ed., 1978.
Paper, $7.95.
Stonehouse Publications
Sweet, ID 83670

How to Build a Wood-Frame House
L. O. Anderson. 1973.
Paper, $3.50.
Dover Publications, Inc.
180 Varick St.
New York, NY 10014

Wood-frame construction procedures, from beginning through completion.

Illustrated Housebuilding
Graham Blackburn. 1977.
$4.95.
Overlook Press
Woodstock, NY 12498

Well-illustrated, easy to follow.

Low-Cost, Energy-Efficient Shelter for the Owner and Builder
Eugene Eccli, ed. 1976.
Hardcover, $10.95; paper, $5.95.
Rodale Press
33 East Minor St.
Emmaus, PA 18049

Plans and specifications for fourteen low-cost, energy-efficient homes.

Making the Adobe Brick
Eugene H. Boudreau. 1972.
Paper, $3.50.
Bookworks
Distributed by:
Random House, Inc.
Box 10128
Palo Alto, CA 94303

How to design and build your own adobe house.

Other Homes and Garbage: Designs for Self-Sufficient Living
$9.95.
Sierra Club Books
530 Bush St.
San Francisco, CA 94108

Solar, wind, and water energy are combined with building design and suggestions for alternative water and waste systems. Other than discussion on sewage, there is no garbage in this book. Useful for both the beginner and the professional builder or architect.

The Owner-Builder and the Code: Politics of Building Your Home
Ken Kern et al. 1976.
Paper, $5.00.
Owner-Builder Publications
Box 550
Oakhurst, CA 93664

Kern details and gives examples of hassles and legal obstacles that commonly confront the individual trying to build his own home. The advice offered herein may save you from finding out the hard way what you are up against.

Planning and Building the Minimum Energy Dwelling
Burt et al. 1977.
Paper, $10.00.
Craftsman Book Co.
542 Stevens Ave.
Solana Beach, CA 92075

Small-Scale Manufacture of Burned Building Brick
Paper, $2.25 (add 15% surface mail, 40% air mail).
VITA
3706 Rhode Island Ave.
Mt. Rainier, MD 20822

How to make clay bricks for building a house or a kiln.

Survival Home Manual
Joel M. Skousen.
Survival Homes
903 State St.
Hood River, OR 97031

Architectural design, construction, and remodeling of self-sufficient residences and retreats.

The Timber Frame Raising
Stewart Elliott and James Brooks. 1979.
Paper, $9.95.
Dovetail Press
P.O. Box 1496
Boulder, CO 80306

An old-fashioned building technique adapted to suit modern needs. Through text, photographs, and illustrations, the authors give a clear explanation of foundation, joinery, timber organization, tools, labor, and solar design.

Village Technology Handbook
Paper, $8.95 (add 15% surface mail, 40% air mail).
VITA
3706 Rhode Island Ave.
Mt. Rainier, MD 20822

Instructions and plans for basic shelter, sanitary facilities, etc., using local materials and community labor. The word "basic" should be stressed for all VITA projects—look elsewhere for high-tech design. Drawings, diagrams.

120

Your Energy-Efficient House: Building and Remodeling Ideas
Anthony Adams. 1975.
Paper, $4.95.
Garden Way Publishing
Charlotte, VT 05445

Site planning, landscaping, insulation, and construction. "Drastically reduce your fuel bills by not wasting bought energy and using 'free' energy all around you."

Magazines, Newsletters, and Periodicals

Building Construction Cost Data
Means Co.
100 Construction Plaza
Duxbury, MA 02332

Covers most building materials and construction processes. Used for making cost calculations by architects, engineers, contractors, and do-it-yourselfers.
Annual, $19.50.

Housemiths Newsletter
Dovetail Press, Ltd.
P.O. Box 1496
Boulder, CO 80306

"The purpose of this . . . newsletter is to act as a central forum for people concerned with quality homes and lives. Based on the growing popularity of timberframe construction and owner-builder housing, the newsletter will answer questions, give encouragement and provide hard knowledge to its readers. Each issue contains a how-to section, a question-and-answer column, and a classified exchange of subscribers' products and services. Feature articles will address current problems and directions in home-energy and building strategies, and give working drawings for the implementation of these developments."
Quarterly, $6.00/year; single issue, $2.00.

Consultation

Dovetail Press, Ltd.
P.O. Box 1496
Boulder, CO 80306

For details on building consultation, write to Stewart Elliott, in care of Dovetail Press. Working blueprints for nine houses and three barns are available from Dovetail Press for $35.00, each set. Their staff is busy with another book on timberframe building and solar energy, due for release this year (1980). Write for further information on blueprints, plans, and books.

Ekose'a
According to Lee Porter Butler, architect and organizer of Ekose'a, the Ekose'a house:
- is designed to perform as a solar collector and storage system
- contains a buffer zone of solar-tempered air between the house and cold air outside
- does not require mechanical, electrical, or fossil fuel backup systems, no matter where it is built.

Ekose'a Homes: Preliminary Planning Package
Lee Porter Butler and staff.
$24.95.
Ekose'a
573 Mission St.
San Francisco, CA 94105

"The information in this package illustrates many of the critical design considerations, principles and concepts incorporated in the Ekose'a design." These standard designs may be evaluated and modified according to the needs of the owner-builder, who then sends his modifications to Ekose'a for advice and suggestions.

The How-To Handbook/Case Study
Tom Smith and Lee Porter Butler.
$18.95.

"Follows the development of the Smith residence near Tahoe City, Lake Tahoe, California, from the point of conception through its operation during the 1977-78 winter and spring and summer of 1978. Information is not only textual, but graphic and technical, thus answering hundreds of questions which have been asked by readers and prospective builders."

Survival Homes Design Division
514 State St.
Hood River, OR 97031
503-386-6553

Contact Joel Skousen, president and chief architect of Survival Homes, Inc. for consultation on energy-efficient, security-minded building. If a truly autonomous living center is what you have in mind, either private home or retreat, Joel Skousen may be just the advisor you need. Call or write for information.

121

The Solar Home

Books and Plans

At Home in the Sun: An Open-House Tour of Solar Homes in the U.S.
Norah Deakins Davis and Linda Lindsey. 1979.
Hardcover, $14.95; paper, $9.95.
Garden Way Publishing
Charlotte, VT 05445

Interviews with solar home owners; detailed descriptions of each house. Floor plans and many photographs.

Buck Vaile's Underground House Plans
Through Mother's Bookshelf
P.O. Box 70
Hendersonville, NC 28739

"...full working drawings of this maintenance-free, passively heated, light and airy, spacious 2,038-square-foot, sun-tempered underground house—all ready to show the VA, mortgage institutions, zoning boards, etc."

One set of plans (84007), $100.00.
One set of plans and materials list (84008), $110.00.

The Mother's Bookshelf catalog (address above) is a good source for books on diverse modes of self-sufficiency. It costs $1.00.

Designing and Building a Solar House: Your Place in the Sun
Donald Watson. 1977.
Paper, $8.95.
Garden Way Publishing
Charlotte, VT 05445

Recommended reading. The author, who has done it all himself, tells how active and passive solar systems work, how to make the necessary design calculations, what works best in different climates, and how to build in units. Provides a complete checklist of the equipment needed. The source lists of publications, products, and designers are sound, although the reader may want to update them.

Earth-Sheltered Housing Design: Guidelines, Examples and References
Prepared by the Underground Space Center, University of Minnesota.
$17.95.
Van Nostrand Reinhold Mail Order Service
7625 Empire Drive
Florence, KY 41042

Insulation with layers of soil, passive solar heating. Warm and cold climate designs from plans, site selection, water-proofing to zoning codes and other policy issues: financing, building codes, and other considerations.

Homegrown Sundwellings
Peter Van Dresser.
Paper, $5.95.
Lightning Tree
P.O. Box 1837
Santa Fe, NM 87501

Passive solar home design with inexpensive ways to handle common problems.

The Integral Urban House: Self-Reliant Living in the City
Paper, $12.95.
The Farallones Institute. 1979.
1516 5th St.
Berkeley, CA 94710

The Farallones Institute is a nonprofit organization founded by a group of architects, builders, designers, agriculturalists, and biologists to research ecologically sound and self-sufficient dwellings. The Farallones urban and rural centers demonstrate the principles of appropriate technology at work and serve as showplaces and educational centers for the public. This book gives the designs and methods that they used in renovating and equipping a city house; includes blueprints and working plans. Write to the Institute for a list of other publications.

Natural Solar Architecture: A Passive Approach
David Wright. 1978.
Paper, $7.95.
Van Nostrand Reinhold Co.
135 W. 50th
New York, NY 10020

Informative resource for solar passivists, with good index and bibliography.

Nicholson Solar Energy Catalogue and Building Manual
Nick Nicholson. 1977.
Paper, $9.50.
British Book Center
Fairview Park
Elmsford, NY 10523

Step-by-step building instructions. Nicholson catalogs concepts rather than materials. Illustrated text comes with a year's worth of updates, mailed as published.

Passive Solar Energy Book: A Complete Guide to Passive Solar Home Greenhouse and Building Design
Edward Mazria. 1979.
Hardcover, $12.95.
Rodale Press
33 E. Minor St.
Emmaus, PA 18049

Designed to make passive solar technology comprehensible to the reader who would like to put it to use. How passive systems work, how you can make them work for you. Clear, comprehensive text supplemented with charts, illustrations, photographs, glossary, and bibliograpy.

Practical Guide to Solar Homes
(Bantam-Hudson Idea Book) 1978.
Paper, $6.95.
Bantam Books, Inc.
666 Fifth Ave.
New York, NY 10019

Thirty new solar homes; plans and sketches.

Solar Dwelling Design Concepts
AIA Research Corp. 1976.
Stock No. 023-000-00334-1
$2.30.
Available from the Superintendent of Documents
U.S. Government Printing Office
Washington, D.C. 20402

Architectural analysis of solar house designs. Information on solar heating systems, climatic factors, site planning.

Solar Heated Buildings of North America: 120 Outstanding Examples
William A. Shurcliff.
$9.80.
Solar Energy Digest
P.O. Box 17776
San Diego, CA 92117

Photographs, drawings, descriptions of working solar buildings.

The Solar Home Book
Bruce Anderson and Michael Riordan. 1976.
$8.50.
Cheshire Books
Church Hill
Harrisville, NH 03450

Using and conserving energy. Easy to understand, well-illustrated.

Solar Homes and Sun Heating
George Daniels. 1976.
$8.95.
Harper & Row Publishers, Inc.
10 E. 53 St.
New York, NY 10022

Construction and installation techniques with nontechnical explanation of solar principles.

Thirty Energy-Efficient Houses You Can Build
Alex Wade and Neal Ewenstein. 1977.
Paper, $8.95.
Rodale Press
33 East Minor St.
Emmaus, PA 18049

Beautiful, original, energy-efficient and inexpensive houses. Tells how to design efficiently without wasting space, attach a solar greenhouse, avoid hassles with banks and building code officials, use recycled materials. Photographs, floor plans, drawings, and specifications for each house.

The Solar Greenhouse

Books and Plans

Building and Using a Solar-Heated Geodesic Greenhouse
John Fontanetta and Al Heller.
Paper, $8.95.
Garden Way Publishing
Charlotte, VT 05445

Simple, step-by-step construction techniques. How to use a dome to raise vegetables, fish; preheat water; reduce hot water bills; and as an auxiliary source of home heat.

Building and Using our Sun-Heated Greenhouse: Grow Vegetables All Year-Round
Helen and Scott Nearing. 1977.
Paper, $6.95.
Garden Way Publishing
Charlotte, VT 05445

Complete Greenhouse Book: Building and Using Greenhouses From Cold Frames to Solar Structures
Peter Clegg and Derry Watkins. 1978.
Paper, $9.95.
Garden Way Publishing
Charlotte, VT 05445

The design, construction, and use of greenhouses. Foundations, floors, structure, framing, and mate-

rials. Recommended by *Publishers' Weekly* and *Library Journal.*

Provider Greenhouse
Helion, Inc.
Box 445
Brownsville, CA 95919

Plans for detached greenhouse, usable all year. $10.00.

Solar Greenhome
Helion, Inc.
Box 445
Brownsville, CA 95919

Helarium-heated house. Study drawing, photographs.
$6.00.

Solar Greenhouse Book
James McCullagh, ed. 1978.
Paper, $8.95.
Rodale Press
33 East Minor St.
Emmaus, PA 18049

Design features, including the collector, glazing, and storage. Emphasis on low-cost structures. Attached greenhouse may be home's primary heat source. Comprehensive, useful for all areas of the United States.

Solar Greenhouse Guide for the Pacific Northwest
$5.00.
The Ecotype Group
2332 E. Madison
Seattle, WA 98112

Recommended by *Organic Gardening Magazine.* Most of the information can be applied to all of the United States.

Solar Greenhouses: Food and Heat Producing, Design, Construction, Operation
Rick Fisher and Bill Yanda. 1976.
$6.00.
John Muir Publications
P.O. Box 613
Santa Fe, NM 87501

A worldwide overview. Nontechnical.

Solar Survival Frame Plans
$6.00.
Solar Survival
Box 119
Harrisville, NH 03450

Plans for a forty-square-foot growing frame. Insulated with styrofoam beads to retain solar heat during long, cold nights. Send for Solar Survival catalog.

Survival Greenhouse: An Eco-System Approach to Home Food Production
James De Korne. 1978.
$7.95.
Peace Press
3828 Willat Ave.
Culver City, CA 90230

How to build and operate.

Sundry

Books

Applied Solar Energy: A Guide to the Design, Installation, and Maintenance of Heating and Hot Water Services
David Kut and Gerald Hare. 1979.
Hardcover, $19.95.
John Wiley & Sons, Inc.
1 Wiley Dr.
Somerset, NJ 08873

Clearly written; reliable advice and instructions.

Build Your Own Solar Water Heater
Stu Campbell and Doug Taff. 1978.
Paper, $7.95.
Garden Way Publications
Charlotte, VT 05445

"All systems described can be built with off-the-shelf, readily available plumbing components."

Homeowner's Guide to Solar Heating and Cooling
Wm. M. Foster. 1976.
Hardcover, $8.95; paper, $4.95.
Tab Books
Blue Ridge Summit, PA 17214

How to Build a Solar Heater
Ted Lucas. 1978.
Paper, $2.25.
New American Library
1301 Avenue of the Americas
New York, NY 10019

Guide to building and buying solar collectors, heaters, and pool heaters. List of manufacturers, bibliography, and glossary.

How to Build a Solar Water Heater
D. A. Sinson and T. Hoad.
Pamphlet, $1.25.
Brace Research Institute
McGill University
Ste. Anne De Bellevue
Quebec, Canada H0A 1C0

How to Buy Solar Heating without Getting Burnt!
Malcom Wells and Irvin Spetgang. 1978.
Paper, $6.95.
Rodale Books
33 East Minor St.
Emmaus, PA 18049

How to decide whether you should use solar heating; choosing and financing a system; installation; finding a contractor.

How to Make a Solar Still
Pamphlet, $1.25.
Brace Research Institute
A. Whittier and G. T. Ward.
McGill University
Ste. Anne De Bellevue
Quebec, Canada H0A 1C0

How to Use Solar Energy in Your Home, in Your Business, In Your Car
Ted Lucas. 1977.
Paper, $7.95.
Ward Ritchie Press
474 S. Arroyo Parkway
Pasadena, CA 91105

The Solar Decision Book
Richard H. Montgomery. 1978.
$10.00.
Dow Corning Corp.
Midland, MI 48640

Flat-plate technology guide. Helpful in making design decisions and rough estimates.

Solar Energy and Your Home
Solar Hot Water and Your Home
Both publications free.
The National Heating and Cooling Information Center
Box 1607
Rockville, MD 20850

Solar Energy Thermal Processes
John A. Duffie and William Beckman. 1974.
$18.00.
John Wiley & Sons
605 Third Ave.
New York, NY 10016

Solar Heating and Cooling: Engineering, Practical Design and Economics
J. F. Kreider and F. Kreith. 1975.
$22.50.
McGraw-Hill, Inc.
1221 Avenue of the Americas
New York, NY 10020

Technical handbook emphasizing economic feasibility of heating and cooling systems. Extensive tables of reference data.

Solar Water Heater Plans
$5.00.
Zomeworks Corp.
P.O. Box 712
Albuquerque, NM 87103

Includes shower regenerator.

Manual on Solar Distillation of Saline Water
S. G. Talbert et al. 1970.
$2.00.
Available from the Superintendent of Documents
U.S. Government Printing Office
Washington, D.C. 20204

All about solar stills.

Practical Sun Power
William H. Rankins, III. 1974.
Paper, $4.00.
Lorien House
P.O. Box 1112
Black Mountain, NC 28711

How to make various solar projects, including parabolic reflectors and an oven and still.

Solar Access Law: Protecting Access to Sunlight for Solar Energy Systems
Gail Boyer Hayes, Environmental Law Institute. 1979.
$18.50.
Ballinger Publishing Co.
17 Dunster St.
Harvard Square
Cambridge, MA 02138

Solar Cooker Construction Manual
Paper, $2.25 (add 15% for surface mail, 40% airmail).
VITA
3706 Rhode Island Ave.
Mt. Rainier, MD 20822

The Status of Solar Refrigeration and Air Conditioning
R. K. Swartman.
Pamphlet, $2.00.
Brace Research Institute
McGill University
Ste. Anne De Bellevue
Quebec, Canada H0A 1C0

Sunspots, Collected Facts and Solar Fiction
Steve Baer. 1975.
$4.00.
Zomeworks Corp.
Box 712
Albuquerque, NM 87103

An interesting conglomeration of facts, helpful hints, and opinions.

Sun Up to Sun Down
Shawn Buckley. 1979.
McGraw-Hill Paperbacks
1221 Avenue of the Americas
New York, NY 10020

Solar Energy. We hear about it everyday, it
seems, now that fossil fuels have entered the
luxury category, but how many of us really understand it? Dr. Buckley explains solar principles for
those who would like to understand but who tend
to feel queasy when confronted with a lot of
graphs and higher math.

Wind Power

Books

Electric Power from the Wind
Henry Clews. 1973.
$2.00.
Solar Wind Co.
P.O. Box 7
East Holden, MA 04429

Good introduction to wind energy.

Harnessing the Wind for Home Energy
Dermot McGuigan. 1978.
Paper, $4.95.
Garden Way Publications
Charlotte, VT 05445

How to measure the wind power potential for
your site; which wind generators are best for
home installations; how to heat water inexpensively; figuring costs, payback on investment.
An especially helpful tool for the country homesteader, and one of the few available books with
a listing of commercial hardware.

Helical Sail Windmill
Paper, $3.95 (add 15% for surface mail, 40%
airmail).
VITA. 1979.
3706 Rhode Island Ave.
Mt. Rainier, MD 20822

Easy-to-build windmill for use where wind blows
regularly from one or two directions. Can be used
for water lifting, pumping, irrigation, and operation of processing machinery; full construction
details.

127

The Homebuilt, Wind Generated Electricity Handbook
Michael Hackleman. 1975.
Paper, $7.95.
Peace Press, Inc.
3828 Willat Ave.
Culver City, CA 90230

Low Cost Windmill for Developing Nations
Paper, $2.95 (add 15% for surface mail, 40% airmail).
VITA
3706 Rhode Island Ave.
Mt. Rainier, MD 20822

How to build a low-cost windmill with support tower using readily available materials.

Wind and Windspinners: A Nuts and Bolts Approach to Wind-Electric Systems
Michael A. Hackleman. 1975.
Paper, $7.95.
Peace Press, Inc.
3828 Willat Ave.
Culver City, CA 90230

A good introduction; clearly written.

Wind Machines
Frank R. Eldridge. 1979. (2nd ed.).
Van Nostrand Reinhold
135 W. 50th St.
New York, NY 10020

According to Eldridge, wind energy can be used for home heating, electricity generation, pumping water, and just about everything else short of fueling an automobile. Theory, discussion, and applications.

Wood Heat

Books

Be Your Own Chimney Sweep
Chris Curtis and Don Post. 1979.
Paper, $4.95.
Garden Way Publishing
Charlotte, VT 05445

How to clean your stove, chimney, or fireplace, by professional chimney sweeps.

The Chimney Book
$1.00.
Garden Way Publishing Co.
Charlotte, VT 05445

Complete Book of Heating with Wood
Larry Gay. 1974.
Paper, $4.95.
Garden Way Publishing
Charlotte, VT 05445

All about burning wood, from woodlot improvement to instructions for using your stove.

Fireplaces
Sunset Editors. 1973. (3rd ed.).
(Original title: *How to Plan and Build Fireplaces*)
Paper, $2.95.
Lane Publishing Co.
Willow and Middleford Rds.
Menlo Park, CA 94025

Fireplaces and Wood Stoves
M. E. Daniels. 1978.
Paper, $6.95.
Bobbs-Merrill Co., Inc.
4300 W. 62nd St.
Indianapolis, IN 46206

Fireplaces: The Owner-Builder's Guide
Ken Kern and Steve Magers. 1978.
Paper, $6.00.
Charles Scribner's Sons
Shipping and Service Center
Vreeland Ave.
Totowa, NJ 07512

The Forgotten Art of Building a Good Fireplace
Orton.
Paper, $2.50.
Yankee Books
Dublin, NH 03444

Heating with Wood
Neil Soderstrom. 1978.
Paper, $3.95.
Harper and Row Publishers, Inc.
Scranton, PA 18512

How to choose, cut, season, and burn woods.

Modern and Classic Woodburning Stoves and the Grass Roots Energy Revival
Bob and Carol Ross.
Overlook Press
Lewis Hollow Road
Woodstock, NY 12498

The authors, who prefer to discuss "going forward to wood" rather than "going back to wood," present solutions to woodburning questions, expound on all types of stoves, and end up with a list of eighty-eight stove manufacturers and importers, with addresses. Illustrated and nicely written:

"Felling trees is not something one should learn from a book. Learn from someone who has been at it a long time and still has all his good looks and extremities."

More Heat from Your Fireplace
Pamphlet, $1.00 (add 15% for surface mail, 40% airmail).
VITA
3706 Rhode Island Ave.
Mt. Rainier, MD 20822

Easy-to-build grate to increase the heat from your fireplace into the room. "Amazing results."

The New, Improved Wood Heat
John Vivian. 1978.
Paper, $7.95.
Rodale Press
33 East Minor St.
Emmaus, PA 18049

All about wood, stoves, fireplaces, furnaces, and ranges. Resource list.

The Woodburner's Encyclopedia
Jay W. Shelton and Andrew B. Shapiro.
$6.95.
Vermont Crossroads Press, Inc.
Waitsfield, VT 05673

Comprehensive guide to efficient woodfuel use; lists currently available ranges, stoves, furnaces, and accessories.

Wood Conserving Stoves: Two Stove Designs and Construction Techniques
Paper, $3.25 (add 15% for surface mail, 40% airmail).
VITA. 1979.
3706 Rhode Island Ave.
Mt. Rainier, MD 20822

One is a mud cookstove from Guatemala, the other a double-drum, sawdust-fueled heating stove. Fully illustrated, step-by-step instructions.

Wood Energy—A Practical Guide to Heating with Wood
Mary Twitchell.
Paper, $7.95.
Garden Way Publishing
Charlotte, VT 05445

Learn about woodburning furnaces and boilers; chimney and stove cleaning; installation of stoves; woodlot management; and best use of existing fireplaces. Book includes complete overview of available wood stoves and extensive catalog sections.

Wood Heat Safety
Jay W. Shelton. 1979.
Paper, $8.95.
Garden Way Publishing
Charlotte, VT 05445

How to evaluate the safety of your stove's installation and correct dangers; all about flues; installation as it relates to insurance coverage; how to use wood and other fuels; and safe operation and maintenance of your heating system.

Woodheating Handbook
Charles R. Self. 1977.
Hardcover, $8.95; paper, $5.95.
Tab Books
Blue Ridge Summit, PA 17214

Everything you need to know about wood, from finding it in the first place to burning it; selection, installation; use of wood-burning systems.

Wood Stoves: How to Make and Use Them
Ole Wik. 1977.
Paper, $5.95.
Alaska Northwest Publishing Co.
130 2nd Ave., S.
Edmonds, WA 98020

A comprehensive guide with a self-explanatory title.

Methane Fuel

Books

Here are three very different books explaining the hows and whys of home methane use and manufacture.

Brown's Alcohol Motor Fuel Cookbook
Michael H. Brown. 1979.
Desert Publications
Distributed by Paladin Enterprises
P.O. Box 1307
Boulder, CO 80306

Brown starts off describing the engine and explaining how to modify it for the most efficient use of alcohol fuel; then he launches into detailed instructions for making the home brew. Simple, straightforward text, supplemented along the way with cautions (to save the do-it-yourselfer from blowing up himself and his engine), make this a handy, basic manual. How much fuel will you actually have to produce to run your car? This is something the reader will have to find out on his own.

The Compleat Biogas Handbook
D. House. 1978.
Paper, $8.00.
At Home Everywhere, c/o Vahid
Rt. 2, Box 259
Aurora, CO 97002

House is coauthor of the highly regarded *Wind and Windspinners*. This book may not win any popularity awards in the methane how-to field. For one thing, it begins disclaiming any promise

of free and endless energy. "If you actually apply this information (and a great many will not)," states the author, "it is highly unlikely that your application will take place without a lot of hard work on your part." Furthermore, the text reads much like a school book, with mathematical formulae and technical terms bandied about freely. House even goes so far as to discredit some of the more enthusiastic claims for homemade alcohol fuel for use in automobiles. But for those who want to read an exhaustive exploration of biogas production and use, this should be a fine buy.

Methanol and Other Ways Around the Gas Pump
Joe Lincoln. 1972.
Paper, $5.95.
Garden Way Publishing
Charlotte, VT 05445

Tells how every driver can make minor auto adjustments and begin using methanol—or use a tested meth/gas combination without making any adjustments.

Mother's Methane Package
$13.00.
Mother's Bookshelf
P.O. Box 70
Hendersonville, NC 28739

Package includes *Bio-Gas Plant* by Bux Singh, famous Indian methanol expert; *Methanol Digesters*; newsletter no.3 of the New Alchemy Institute; text by *Mother Earth News*; plans for building a fifty-five-gallon drum methanol generator; *and* an alternative energy poster.

General Energy

Books

Alternate Sources of Energy: A Bibliography of Solar, Geothermal, Wind and Tidal Energy and Environmental Architecture
Barbara K. Harrah and David F. Harrah. 1975.
$8.00.
Scarecrow Press, Inc.
52 Liberty St.
Box 656
Metuchen, NJ 08840

The Book of the New Alchemists
$6.95.
New Alchemy Institute
Box 432
Woods Hole, MA 02543

Now you, too, can build the outlandish, ecologically appropriate, energy-efficient systems
devised, tested, and used by the New Alchemists.
This book tells how to build a home that incorporates a solar collector, greenhouse, fish tank,
and garden, and how to make water-pumping
windmills and solar heating systems.

Design Manual for Water Wheels
Paper, $4.50 (add 15% surface mail, 40% airmail).
VITA
3706 Rhode Island Ave.
Mt. Rainier, MD 20822

Instructions for building a water wheel with
overshot wheel design and pump attachment. Can
be used for pumping water, hulling rice, and
other homey tasks.

*Earth, Wind, Sun and Water: Our Energy
Alternatives*
D. S. Halacy. 1977.
$8.95.
Harper and Row Publishers, Inc.
Scranton, PA 18512

Overview of world use of geothermal water, tidal,
and sea thermal energy, wind, biofuels, and solar
energy.

Energy Dictionary
V. Daniel Hunt, ed. 1979.
Hardcover, $22.50.
Van Nostrand Reinhold
135 W. 50th St.
New York, NY 10020

Energy for Survival: The Alternatives to Extinction
Wilson Clark. 1975.
Paper, $4.95.
Anchor Press/Doubleday
501 Franklin Ave.
Garden City, NY 11530

Emphasis on solar energy. History of energy
sources, present use, and forecast. Roughly 1,000
sources supplied, some now outdated. The *Energy
Primer* dubs this book "one of the most important
energy books of the early 1970s."

Energy Primer. Solar, Water, Wind and Biofuels
Edited by Richard Merrill et al. 1978. (rev. ed.).
Paper, $7.95.
Portola Institute
540 Santa Cruz Ave.
Menlo Park, CA 94025

The Portola Institute brought you the *Whole
Earth Catalog*. Articles, hardware sources, and
book reviews on energy conservation and solar,
water, wind, biofuel, and integrated systems.

Energy: The Next Twenty Years
A Report of the Study Group, sponsored by the
Ford Foundation and administered by Resources
for the Future.
Hans D. Landsberg, Chairman. 1979.
$9.95.
Ballinger Publishing Co.
17 Dunster St.
Harvard Square
Cambridge, MA 02138

*Energy We Can Live With: Approaches to Energy
that Are Easy on the Earth and Its People*
Daniel Wallace, ed. 1976.
Paper, $3.95.
Rodale Press
33 East Minor St.
Emmaus, PA 18049

Harnessing Water Power for Home Energy
Dermot McGuigan. 1978.
Paper, $4.95.
Garden Way Publishing
Charlotte, VT 05445

An especially useful guide for the country homesteader. Includes information on available
hardware.

*How to Use Solar, Wind or Water Energy in Your
Home*
(Popular Science Books)
A. J. Hand. 1977.
Harper and Row Publishers, Inc.
Scranton, PA 18512

*Mother Earth News Handbook of Homemade
Power*
Mother's Bookshelf. 1976.
P.O. Box 70
Hendersonville, NC 28739

"Alternative energy sources you can use now . . .
how-to instructions."

Producing Your Own Power: How to Make Nature's Energy Sources Work for You
Edited by Carol H. Stoner.
Hardcover, $8.95.
Rodale Press
33 East Minor St.
Emmaus, PA 18049

Material by Henry Clews, Ken Kern, Eugene and Sandy Eccli, the New Alchemists, and others. How to get energy from the sun, wind, water, wood, and organic wastes. Includes source list of equipment and supplies, charts, tables, graphs, building plans, detailed instructions, conversion tables, bibliography, and glossary.

Survival 2001: Scenario from the Future
H. E. Voegli and J. J. Tarrant. 1975.
$5.95.
Van Nostrand Reinhold Co.
135 W. 50th
New York, NY 10020

Schemes for solving many environmental problems. Detailed engineering drawings.

Magazines, Newsletters, and Periodicals

Canadian Renewable Energy News
P.O. Box 4869, Station E
Ottawa, Ontario
Canada K155 B4
Monthly, $7.00/year.

Alternative Sources of Energy Magazine
Milaca, MN 56353

Solar, wind, water, and methane power developments. "Features, plans and projects for your home and future . . . unique reader information exchange."
Bimonthly, $12.00/year.

Coevolution Quarterly
(Published by the founder and editor of the *Whole Earth Catalog*)
POINT
Box 428
Sausalito, CA 94965

Not just about energy and building, but covers almost everything. Obviously written and compiled with an inspired zeal emanating from some mysterious energy source all its own. You never know what to expect from issue to issue or page to page, but frequently there are references to interesting but little-known books and new books and products in the alternative energy

field, and sometimes other survival-related information. Well-written and original.
Quarterly, $12.00/year.

The Energy Daily
National Press Bldg.
Washington, D.C. 20045

The exclusive Washington, D.C. scoop on federal government and the solar industry.
Monday through Friday, $500/year.

Home Energy Digest/Wood Burning Quarterly
8009 34th Ave. South
Minneapolis, MN 55420

Emphasis on woodburning, but also includes features on solar and other alternative energy and survival subjects. Includes book reviews, "Housing Project," and "New Products" departments.
Quarterly, $7.95/year.

New Alchemy Institute: Journal and Newsletter
Box 432
Woods Hole, MA 02543

Research, planning, design, and news from some of the most innovative and industrious people in the alternative energy field. Interrelated, harmonious systems are their specialty.
Membership, $10.00/year.
Includes subscription to publications.

Solar Age Magazine
SolarVision, Inc.
Church Hill
Harrisville, NH 03450

The leading U.S. solar magazine. Excellent articles keep the reader up to date on the state of the art—which is saying something, considering how fast the solar energy picture changes. Back issues are $2.50 each, or $2.00 each if you buy more than twelve. SolarVision will send a list of back issues with subject matter upon request.
Monthly, $20.00/year.

Solar Energy Digest
P.O. Box 17776
San Diego, CA 92117

Sample issue costs $1.00. Newsletter update on books, products, and developments in solar field. Concise news articles, editorial comments. Published by William B. Edmondson.
Monthly, $35.00/year.

Solar Engineering
Solar Engineering Publications, Inc.
8435 N. Stemmons Freeway
Suite 880
Dallas, TX 75247

The official publication of the Solar Energy Industries Association. Information on new products.
Monthly.

Solar Heating and Cooling
Gordon Publications
P.O. Box 2126
Morristown, NJ 07960

Aimed at the commercial reader. New product information.
Bimonthly.

Solar Energy Intelligence Report
Business Publishers, Inc.
P.O. Box 1067
Silver Springs, MD 20910

The solar industry and the feds; latest developments.
Weekly; 6 months, $50.00.

Sunworld
International Solar Energy Society
320 Vassar
Berkeley, CA 94708

Solar articles from all over the world.
Quarterly.

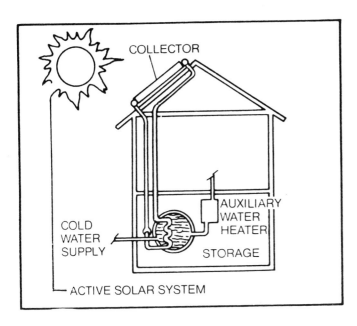

Sources of Energy Publications and Products

AIA Research Corporation Publications Dept.
1735 New York Ave., NW
Washington, DC 20006

Write for publications list. AIA Research publishes many fine reports, books, and videotapes on building design as it relates to solar energy, climate, and seismic factors.

The American Wind Energy Association
New Boston, NH 03070

Information on equipment manufacturers, etc.

Ann Arbor Science Publishers, Inc.
P.O. Box 1425
Ann Arbor, MI 48106

Send for free catalog. Ann Arbor Science publishes books on solar and other alternative energies.

Crowther–Solar Group Architects
310 Steele St.
Denver, CO 80206

Energy-Information Directory
Jill Ammon-Wexler. 1978.
Paper, $14.95.
Mercury Co., Inc.
730 Mission St.
Santa Cruz, CA 95060

Franklin Institute Press
P.O. Box 2266
Philadelphia, PA 19103

Books on solar energy, wind energy, bio-conversion. Write for list of publications.

Mother's Bookshelf
P.O. Box 70
Hendersonville, NC 28739

Lots of books and plans from many publishers on building, energy, do-it-yourself projects, and just about everything else you can think of.
Catalog, $1.00.

National Solar Heating and Cooling Information Center
Toll-free telephone, 800-523-2929 (PA 800-462-4983)
Box 1607
Rockville, MD 20850

Write or call with your questions. Services include: bibliographic search; performance, price, design, manufacturer, and legislative data; marketing and sales information; referrals; reading list for solar energy for heating and cooling. Designed to serve professionals (architects and engineers), the center was established by HUD in cooperation with the Energy Research and Development Administration. They will send you a listing of solar manufacturers in your state—or any state, for that matter—upon request.

Solar Age Resource Book: Complete Guidebook to the Dramatic Power of Solar Energy
SolarVision. 1979.
Paper, $9.95.
Church Hill
Harrisville, NH 03450

By the publishers of *Solar Age Magazine*. Articles, detailed listing of solar systems and equipment available now; geographical directory of architectural and design services and buyer's guides for wind products, wood products, and all types of solar products.

Solar Energy Information Locator
Solar Energy Research Institute (SERI)
Golden, CO 80401
303-234-7171

SERI is developing a computerized solar information retrieval service. Send for free booklet on solar organizations and publications and the "Solar Information Data Bank."

Solar Products Specifications Guide
SolarVision
Church Hill
Harrisville, NH 03450

Organization similar to that of the *Uniform Construction Index* published by the Construction Specifications Institute. Details on the latest hardware developments in the solar field. "Practical working tool for those who evaluate, select and specify solar equipment for all

building applications . . . no-nonsense technical data."
Six bimonthly updates over a 1-year subscription period: $120.00.

SolarVision, Inc.
Church Hill
Harrisville, NH 03450

SolarVision puts out many solar publications, including *Solar Age Magazine,* as well as a series of video tapes on solar energy.

SUN
P.O. Box 306
Bascom, OH 44809

"The only solar parts catalog for do-it-yourselfers . . . Collectors, absorbers, controls, glazing, tanks, energy-savers, books, etc."
Catalog, $5.00.

University of Cambridge,
Department of Architecture
Technical Research Division
1 Scroope Terrace
Cambridge CB2 1PX England

Cambridge publishes booklets about energy-autonomous houses. Useful, but some apply only to British climate.

Zomeworks
P.O. Box 712
Albuquerque, NM 87103

Innovative solar products and books.

Holding Tools on Stepladder

The problem of keeping a number of small tools at hand when working on a stepladder, is solved by inserting them into holes drilled through the top step of the ladder,

Preparing the Survival Home
How To Remodel A Home For Self-sufficiency

Joel Skousen

The choice to remain in your existing residence may well be your best financial alternative—*if* your location lends itself to long term social and economic stability. If not, you may still decide to remodel simply because you cannot leave your present location due to job or other ties. And even if you plan on relocating to a safer area eventually, it may be wise to take present funds and invest them in some self-sufficiency remodeling of your current residence rather than putting them all in the bank, Not only will they appreciate faster, but if your plans to relocate are set back or halted by

economic circumstances, you'll at least have a self-sufficient residence to help you through the rough times ahead. There are some real economic advantages for remodeling, too: unless you live in a deteriorated neighborhood, the resale value of a survivalized residence averages 10-20% above its non-prepared counterpart—even in peaceful times. And its value in a crisis will undoubtedly be significantly higher yet.

There are several major weaknesses and numerous minor ones which make the typical city or suburban home vulnerable in an economic, social or energy crisis. Eight primary failings are:

1. POOR INSULATION in ceilings, walls, floors, and windows.
2. EXCESSIVE AIR INFILTRATION.
3. SINGLE ENERGY SOURCE for heating and cooking.
4. LACK OF ADEQUATE STORAGE FACILITIES for food, dry goods, and fuel.
5. LACK OF SHOP AND REPAIR FACILITIES, and related equipment.
6. SINGLE SOURCE OF ELECTRICAL POWER.
7. LACK OF INDEPENDENT FOOD AND WATER SOURCE.
8. LACK OF SECURITY in windows, doors, walls. No intrusion monitoring or response equipment.

Insulation

Since warm air rises, most homeowners concentrate only on an insulated ceiling. But it is wise to remember that heat is exchanged to any surface in proportion to the temperature differential *inside* and *outside* the structure. For example: the air at the top of a room is usually only 5% warmer than the air at the floor level. Thus a ceiling is only capable of losing 5% more heat to the outdoors than the walls and floor, assuming it is of similar construction. Fortunately, it is not, having no windows or doors which are the primary sources of heat loss. So if you have to make a choice between adding more ceiling insulation or insulating windows and walls, choose the latter.

Windows deserve special treatment as they lose *twelve* times more heat than walls. Even though double glazing may reduce heat loss by half, it is still unacceptable in a real energy crunch. Without exception, and especially in cold climates, all windows should have temporary storm windows or plastic sheeting installed, even if you have double glazed windows. And don't worry too much about the highly publicized heat loss difference between metal and wood frames—in actual tests it is not significant. Sliding glass doors should be' closed permanently for the winter with plastic sheeting attached outside. They are notorious for creating a steady flood of convected cold air across the floor. Additionally, all windows and sliding doors should have drapes installed with enclosures on both the bottom and the top to prevent air drafts behind the fabric. Floor length drapes should be boxed in tight at the top and touch the carpet at the bottom. The sides should contact the walls.

There are some do-it-yourself options available, too. A more costly—but far more efficient window treatment—recently came on the market (see the January 1979 issue of POPULAR SCIENCE). This pull-down, aluminized mylar shade expands into an R-10 to 17 window covering as it unrolls. It does need a fairly tight framework surrounding it to be effective, however. Projected costs for the shade are realistically $4 per square foot, and are adaptable to sliding glass doors as well. They have the advantage of rolling up and out of sight, unlike the interior styrofoam-wood shutters which fold or accordion to one side or the other. But in the final analysis, we prefer you to take your $4-per-square-foot and add it to insulated EXTERIOR SECURITY SHUTTERS which will give you both insulation and impact resistance as well. If glass ever becomes a scarce commodity through shortage or mass violence, exterior insulated shutters will be far more useful than any amount of interior treatment minus the window pane. More on this in the security section.

Existing walls are fairly difficult to insulate because of the finished treatment on both sides. Consequently, you have two choices: you can bore 2-3 inch holes (inside or out) and blow in loose insulation. Or you can reface walls (inside or out) with an inch of rigid foam insulation. The latter is especially appropriate if you had planned to remodel the finished surfaces anyway. But if you are considering injecting liquid foam, hire a reputable installer who can give you local references to check out. Keep in mind, too, that many people have experienced problems with uneven insulation density and an after-odor of formaldehyde.

Ceilings usually have a minimal amount of insulation. This should be increased to at least the depth of the ceiling joists. Anything over 10 inches is "overkill"—unless you improve the walls and window insulation. Some attic treatment may be necessary to cut heat gain during the summer, as well as heat loss in the winter. Unfortunately, attic ventilation standards are woefully inadequate for summer cooling problems. The minimum "5 square feet vent area" should be increased to 25 square feet on both sides of the attic area. This is best accomplished by openable doors with screened entrances; these doors can be closed in the winter to capture attic heat. And additional insulation on the attic rafters will help guard against summer heat gain as well as winter heat loss. Closing off attic vents in the winter is a tricky subject. We recommend it *only* if you have an effective moisture barrier between your ceiling and attic. One sure way to tell is to tape plastic over attic vents and see if condensation occurs on the inside surface. If so, remove the plastic or dry rot will eventually set in. But if you have good interior moisture barriers and still have attic moisture, check to see that bathroom fan ducts are not pumping moisture into the attic. Even one untaped joint in the metal pipe leading to the outside can do significant harm.

Air Infiltration

The heating industry generally recommends that the air in a house be replaced or "exchanged" with fresh air once every hour. This standard may be acceptable in terms of room freshness, but is totally *unacceptable* in terms of heat loss. In fact, this exchange represents about 25 to 75 percent of total heat loss in a house, depending on the insulation. Weather stripping, if properly installed, helps. But nothing compares to caulked storm windows and air lock entries. At a minimum, the most used entrance to the home ought to have a double door air lock. Such a two-door entry way prohibits undue loss of heat since one door is closed while the other is being opened.

In general, if you shoot for one or two air exchanges per day, you should avoid most air stagnation problems and cut your heat loss to 1/24th the average. However, homes where smokers reside or which have a high concentration of people will need more air-per-hour to avoid odors. But forget about trying to calculate how many air exchanges you have per hour. Just seal the house up *tight* and see if you get any odor (the first sign of air stagnation). If you do, unseal one or two windows until you cease to notice any odors (or at least until they cease to be bothersome).

Alternate Heating Sources

Whatever heating system you now have, don't replace it—just add a different type to it. Most forced-air furnaces can be connected to a wood furnace utilizing the existing blower. Some new controls will be necessary if you want the existing oil or gas furnace to come on automatically when the wood unit ceases to provide sufficient heat. These dual stage thermostats and furnace controls are off-the-shelf equipment familiar to all manufacturers of multi-fuel furnaces (but may be totally unfamiliar to the conventional furnace dealer). Woodstoves can also be hooked up to your existing forced air systems if you are willing to have some custom sheet metal work done to enclose your unit for forced-air ducting.

An alternative to the cost of new furnace controls is a simple, manual-controlled reostat placed in the furnace blower circuit. This allows the owner to vary the blower motor speed to match the heat output of the wood burning unit, which varies from one hour to the next. Most blowers can be downgraded by a reostat to about ½ their normal CFM

capacity without overheating the motor. But check with an electric motor supply shop first (they'll usually know more than the furnace man who rarely ever does any modification of motors).

Certain areas in the country still have cheap electric power—especially those which have electric cooperatives. If you are living in such an area, you may well consider the installation of a heat pump. They are expensive initially, but will save on electricity in the long run. New and recent improvements are fast eliminating many of the previous maintenance problems. However, you should be aware of the basic heat pump liability which still remains: at very low temperatures, when the heat is really needed, their performance deteriorates to the point where built-in electric resistance heating coils (very expensive) come on to supplement with more heat. There are a couple of excellent ways to overcome this drawback, mostly through the use of a solar assist or latent heat from the earth or a nearby water source. But the key here is to keep the outdoor heat exchanger unit's temperature above 30 degrees where its efficiency is better. (See September 1978 issue of POPULAR SCIENCE).

137

Resistance electric heaters should be present in every home as a final backup in case all else fails. Although we may have severe blackouts in the future, people's vast dependence upon electricity will force the government into rapid action to keep electric power restored. But don't expect any such guarantees on keeping the cost low. Since electric resistance heat is generally the most expensive type, use it only as a back up.

Don't depend on your woodstove to cook on. Yes, it can be done, but not without driving you out of the house—especially in the summer time. The problem here is too much heating surface. Stoves designed for *cooking* only heat a small portion of the top surface hot enough to cook efficiently. Try that with your backyard-welded special and it will do some fancy warping. *Monarch* ranges (Malleable Iron and Range Co., Beaver Dam, Wisconsin) markets a full line of top quality wood and multi-fuel ranges. (Ask your grandmother for a recommendation—they have been a quality company in business for many years.) The *Monarchs* also have one of the finest water heating jackets available, which will provide all the hot water you'll need while the stove is going.

Almost without exception, I recommend solar hot water heating for residences. While solar space heating is still too costly (with lengthy pay-back periods), solar water heating is cost efficient almost immediately. Most systems can be purchased without installation (that is where some of the rip-offs occur) and piped into your existing hot water heating system. In cold climates, we have found that a water heating jacket in the wood furnace or Monarch range provides all necessary hot water during the winter. And just as these appliances begin to shut down, sufficient solar energy becomes available to take over your summer water heating needs.

Solar Space Heating

My primary objection to solar space heating in the survival or self-sufficiency context is not the cost *per se,* but rather its *percentage* of cost allocated to survival remodeling which prohibits the purchase of other, more valuable items. Heat is only *one* of the essential aspects of self-sufficiency. If you invest $10,000 or $20,000 in heat production to the exclusion of all the other aspects we are discussing, you may still have severe problems. There is a lot of talk about tax advantages and pay-off periods which are beginning to make solar look more tempting. But if all these advantages still keep you from purchasing the most important items first (food, dry goods, parts, equipment, etc),

then you've still been bilked into buying a $20,000 heating system for a cracker box. And on the social side of the issue, consider the vulnerability to vandalism and violence all that collector surface involves. Why would anyone want to do that? Consider the envy when you *have* heat and they *don't.* Now that isn't reason enough to stop living or making useful purchases, but it is certainly a security consideration. Architects who do a lot of glass design have nightmares about it, so beware of social unrest.

Storage Facilities

Remodeling to include storage facilities will represent a high percentage of new floor space. Because people have become so accustomed to miniscule storage space, typical of the American tract home, they have lost any concept of what amount it actually takes to store a year's supply of food stuffs, dry goods, and mechanical parts. Food storage alone will take a 10' to 10' room and the other items, nearly twice that much if you anticipate a storage system that allows fairly easy access to find what you want. But that doesn't include the need for some secret storage, which I'll leave to your imagination at the present.

Don't start thinking about all that wasted attic space; you can store dry goods up there, but not foods—they need cool, stable temperatures below 60 degrees for long shelf life. Fresh foods will require cellar space below ground level. Fuel storage tanks should also be buried below ground level with obscured vent stacks and filler caps some distance away to discourage discovery.

The secret to successful storage is "discretion." The family that brags about what they have will face a lot of pressure when they need their storage most. We do encourage sharing with those that are deserving, but it's nice to have that *choice* without the pressure of force.

It is far easier to design basement storage facilities into a new home than in single level remodeling. Sometimes excavation under a portion of the existing house is possible. But the better way is to design a small extension to the home, under which you can build a basement, since the new portion must have a foundation anyway.

Preparation, Shop and Repair Facilities

These facilities are the working spaces of the home. They are not found in most modern designs because of our specialized society, wherein everything is hired out to other specialists. But in future difficulties, we may well find ourselves faced with the necessity of producing many of our own goods and services. This means tools and equipment—all of which require separate space, ideally to seal-off the noise and dust production from the living areas of the home. The areas of primary concern should be a food preparation area (wheat grinding, food drying, canning, meat butchering, etc.), wood/metal shop area (full range of woodworking and basic metal working tools), auto repair, and electronic repair. Another option is an area to mix chemicals.

Independent Electrical Power

Almost every appliance in your home can be substituted for in some way, or at least be accomplished by manual effort. But the loss of electricity is hard to live without and hard to substitute. The primary functions of electricity such as light and heat for space, cooking or water heating can be replaced by other sources, though usually at a loss in convenience. But the secondary uses such as in automatic controls, fans, blowers for furnaces, security systems, or telephone and radio communication simply have few, if any substitutes. Refrigeration is the only appliance that presents a true hardship and possible health hazard, especially since people have generally forgotten how to cope without it. I have no doubts they would soon learn, but not without the loss of tons of valuable fresh food stuffs nationwide. Present ice making facilities hardly serve the drinking crowd, let alone everyone's refrigerator. And the greatest home labor-saving device (the washing machine) also has no other fuel substitute and would cause a great hardship to many mothers.

Without a doubt, every person reading this article will someday be faced with the need for independent electrical power. When clients come to our firm for consultation on land purchases for self-sufficiency, we send them looking for land with water power on it. When you have water of a sufficient quantity to produce power, it is usually very consistent and provides enough life-giving liquid for drinking and crop irrigation as well. Wind power is appropriate for certain sections of the country, but requires a good deal of technical know-how.

In the remodeling context, most homeowners are faced with engine-powered generators as their only alternative. Their cost is low, compared to water and wind power, but the fuel consumption is high and so is maintenance. As temporary back-up, the economics are digestable. But in a long term crunch, you become as concerned about fuel cost and availability as you do convenience.

Back-up power generators are marketed to match available fuel sources. You have your choice of engines, powered by diesel oil, gasoline, and natural gas—or special units which will burn two or more fuels. And combination carburetors are available which can use gasoline, natural gas or propane. But if your furnace burns oil, we suggest you go with a diesel generator, and have your tank filled with low sulfur fuel oil so it can be used for both furnace and generator. If your regular furnace burns gas, buy a combination carburetor model and install a propane tank and gasoline storage tank as well. If you purchase a set of propane jets for your furnace, both your generator and furnace can be switched to propane if natural gas is cut off. If you have a choice of oil or natural gas, we recommend going with natural gas. It is less subject to international politics, and thus a better long-term fuel. I also believe it will always be the cheapest fossil fuel. Not so with propane, however. Although a superlative storage fuel, it is expensive and will always be so due to its highly processed nature. Gasoline and diesel storage both must have special additives if you plan to keep them over a year and are available through fuel dealers.

A set of household storage batteries, though costly, are also an excellent addition to your emergency power system. In times of low power usage, and fuel shortage, you may not want to run your generator just to keep a fridge going periodically or a few lights. A battery system with an electronic inverter can be extremely useful during long-term electrical outages.

Independent Food and Water

Besides a family garden plot (which we highly encourage), self-sufficiency requires the addition of a solar greenhouse and a source of potable water other than public supply. Your food storage supplies will not adequately provide fresh foods and fresh water—two solid requirements for long-term health in a crisis. A south-facing solar greenhouse addition doesn't have to be excessively large or expensive, either. The most successful ones are those which are buried in earth at least four feet sharing some heat with your house, rather than have expensive heat storage mechanisms. Glazing should primarily be concentrated only on the south frontage with minimum glass on the sides. Some provision for interior heat blankets to cover the glass at night is helpful, too. But don't worry so much about letting the greenhouse save on your space heating bill. The fresh food it produces will be a much better payback at today's food prices.

Drilling a deep well to survive droughts is both expensive and illegal in many nonrural areas. Both of these drawbacks can be averted, however, by an owner-drilled well or by in-line water storage tanks in a reinforced attic. The small, owner-operated engine driven drill rigs can sink wells to fifty feet.

And they are small enough in diameter to not require well permits. Any well, except self-flowing "artesian wells," will require electricity to pump. So unless you also purchase a wind-operated pump or an electric generator, you will need some storage tanks with a well also. In-line pressure storage tanks will keep water fresh since water in the house flows through the tank first. And internal pressure bladders will continue to provide pressure if the water source is cut off. Tanks without such bladders (cheaper) must be placed above the highest plumbing fixture, equipped with a vent in order to gravity feed into the house.

Lack Of Security

In discussing security, most homeowners usually envision sophisticated electronic devices. While we do encourage their use, we recognize that all the intrusion warning devices in the world won't do any good if the intruder(s) has the power and desire to disregard the warning and you, the owner. Survival remodeling, therefore, involves some structural security features, making your home relatively destruction resistant, except to military hardware. (We don't recommend you defend your home as a fortress or bunker anyway.)

It is interesting to note that rarely will you ever find a home in Europe or South America constructed without roll-down metal security shutters. Only America seems to have avoided social unrest so long that no one prepares for possible street violence. Having lived in several foreign countries which dabbled in economic nonsense similar to our present domestic policy, I can testify that social unrest, like the New York City black-out lootings, will someday become more common. Our present wood structures will withstand many hand thrown projectiles. But no portion of your wood walls (not even the studs) will stop bullets. (Americans learned how walls are bullet proof from watching movies. Don't try to use walls for cover in real life. They simply don't work.) Brick homes are preferable in this regard, and provide a no-maintenance exterior as well. If your home needs a new exterior, we heartily recommend using brick veneer. The extra cost is worth it.

Windows can be protected by add-on, PVC plastic roll down shutters. These come with options for steel inserts for strength and foam insulation for energy conservation. But the big advantage of these commercial types over regular outdoor shutters is that they are operated from inside the house. This is important when danger is present. The only way to provide your home with bullet-proof window shutters is through custom-built sliding steel plates, which will be discussed in our next article. But do-it-yourselfers can actually beat the price of the commercial roll-down variety, and get better insulation too, by adding an inch or two of rigid foam to these sliding plate units.

Doors should have metal jamb guards installed to keep intruders from spreading the jamb with crowbars. And larger metal strike plates are also necessary to resist kicking doors in. Deadbolts should be on all outside doors, including the door between the garage and home since garage doors themselves are very vulnerable to forced entrance. The master bedroom door should always have a lock on it. This gives you time to telephone or react to intrusion before being presented with an ultimatum, or offensive situation.

During remodeling, all windows and doors should have seismic (detects vibration or breakage) detectors installed. Pressure sensitive pads can be installed under carpeting or mats in the path of outside doors and in major traffic areas of the home to indicate intruder position as well. And finally, area alarms (microwave or ultrasonic) can be installed to cover most other contingencies. The big drawback of the intrusion system is not the detectors, but the alarm indicators (sirens, bells, etc.). All they do essentially is scare the occupant. We prefer a more flexible home-built unit which has a floor plan of the home illuminated at night. The individual alarm detectors cause a small wake up tone to sound, and light up on the panel where the intrusion is occurring. This allows the owner to make a meaningful decision: a switch can turn on audible alarms either automatically or manually. Each child's room should be equipped with a panic button near the bedside so he or she can sound an alarm without noise.

Living Facilities

During remodeling, don't neglect a hard look at the efficiency (or lack of efficiency) of your present floor plan. Remember that in a crisis, your needs for in-house recreation and emergency accommodations for "guests" or relatives may require extra space. And if you are in nuclear fallout zones (check Civil Defense Preparedness Agency maps) you will want to design emergency living facilities, however limited, underground or in the basement. This is also true for people in tornado and hurricane areas. Each of these areas need specific attention, according to your individual assessment of where the greatest need exists. Avoid putting all your eggs into one basket. Try to budget your storage items and space first, and then work towards your other preparedness items, allocating some funds in each area.

Prior to implementing any of the foregoing remedies, it is essential to have a master plan which will link all of these areas into one unit. For example: many wiring and plumbing changes need to be done before walls are refinished to avoid future expense.

The scope of this article allows us to discuss only one sample home remodeling. Consequently, I have tried to pick a common type of home which may serve to illustrate general methods and remodeling procedures. Despite its small size, this typical tract home (see illustration) lends itself well to remodeling. Its backyard is oriented to the south, providing good solar requisites for a garden and future greenhouse. The kitchen/nook area is ample, although the refrigerator is somewhat bulky. And like most small, single-level American homes, storage space is almost nonexistent. You will usually find the $8,000 automobile sitting out in the rain while the garage is overflowing with miscellaneous storage tools and toys. The 20'x20' garage is definitely too small, having to share its minimal space with both furnace and laundry facilities.

Recommended Remodeling

First, the garage was brought forward 12 feet to the front "set back" limits. This allowed room for a laundry/mud room entry and a shop or storeroom. Additional space in the wall adjoining the kitchen provided a desk/phone area, a recessed refrigerator and a pantry. The traffic way between living and family room was altered to allow for a corner fireplace in the living room and a *Monarch* wood range/heater for the family room—both utilizing the same chimney system.

Since the home did not require new exterior siding, a brick wall was built across the front in line with the new garage to provide a security wall, as well as a visual shield for the air-lock entry and the new rain water collection reservoir. The reservoir concept is an excellent way to collect the watershed from the roof via gutters and gravel/sand/charcoal filters. And the reservoir blends nicely into front courtyard landscaping as a reflective pool.

Part of the master bedroom closet was taken for a shower stall so that the existing half bath becomes fully usable for the children. Useless corner space near the door of the master bedroom was taken for an additional closet to compensate for the lost closet space.

Another bedroom was added as an extension and a new, larger closet plus built-in desks provided more livability. The old bedroom closet now becomes a linen closet and utility storage in the hall. A solar greenhouse and a covered porch were added to the rear also. The greenhouse beds are designed in stairstep fashion to avoid shading each other. And the slope of the glass follows the same pitch of the existing roof. The outdoor deck/porch area can either have a trellis type covering or a full, waterproof roof (flat) as desired. The bedroom was then covered with a conventional gable extension as is the garage in front.

The rear extension has a full basement under it for use as cellar storage, food storage, emergency living quarters and some secret storage as desired. Generators can also go into the basement for sound insulation. Access is through a steep stairway in a simulated closet off the new bedroom.

Usable living space almost doubled as we expanded the habitable square footage from 1,250 to 2,250, including the basement. The cost of our sample remodeling, including equipment and facilities mentioned earlier, totaled approximately $35,000. That is expensive, though well spent in terms of actual dollar value. Much can be saved, depending on your do-it-yourself expertise: there is a lot that can be done on a modest budget if you sit down as a family and take a good hard look at where you presently spend your money. Many of those "nice to have" or "have to have" convenience appliances or recreation purchases might be re-routed elsewhere, if viewed in a survival or preparedness perspective. I fully realize that austerity cutbacks are never popular during relative peace and plenty—especially with kids. But never forget: he who waits until the daily newspaper announces a crisis before he acts has waited too long. In other words, WHEN THE TIME FOR ACTION ARRIVES, THE TIME FOR PREPARATION HAS JUST ENDED.

Joel M. Skousen is the president and head architect of the Survival Homes Corporation, 4270 Westcliff Drive, Hood River, Oregon 97031. He is the author of the 500-page Survival Home Manual, which may be ordered for $26.00 from the address above.

Photo by Janet Snow Ritchie

Survival Vehicles

Introduction

Here it is, the shortest chapter in the book; and this introduction will be correspondingly brief. The truth is, survival driving is a largely unresearched and uncatered-to field. You will not find much on the subject in car, or even four-wheel drive magazines, and if you ask your local dealer about survival models, he probably will not know what you are talking about. Automobile manufacturers generally do not pay much attention to survival design considerations.

Yes, this is definitely a do-it-yourself challenge, and the vehicle you end up with will be the result of your personal taste, knowledge of the terrain that you plan to cover, mechanical skills, and common sense. And fortunately, we have the experience and know-how of Rick Fines to guide us through this largely uncharted terrain.

Access

Sources of Information

Arrow Tanks, Inc.
1310 E. Katella Ave.
Anaheim, CA 92805

"Auxiliary and/or replacement gas tanks on your Jeep, 4X4, van, pickup, suburban or import truck . . . Rugged steel, arc-weld construction with inside baffles, pressure tested and guaranteed for two years . . . Double and triple your range."

Berens Associates, Inc.
5885 Hollis St.
Emeryville, CA 94608

Very complete for off-road equipment and accessories for four-wheel drive vehicles and pick-ups. Free catalog.

143

Car and Driver Enthusiasts' Information Center
Car and Driver magazine reprints
P.O. Box 278
Pratt Station
Brooklyn, NY 11205

Write for list of reprints of C/D road tests and articles.

Carbooks, Inc.
181 Glen Ave. D 94
Sea Cliff, NY 11579

Total service manuals and general interest books. Write for list.

Dick Cepek, Inc.
9201 California Ave.
South Gate, CA 90280

Four-wheel drive accessories, off-road tires, camping gear, etc. Excellent prices on wheels and tires. Cepek handles some survival items, such as water purification tablets, "Vietnam boots," police flashlights, first aid, survival and snakebite kits, and emergency signals. They offer a limited warranty on merchandise at customer's request. Catalog, 50¢.

Edgewood National, Inc.
6603 N. Meridian
Puyallup, WA 98371

Specializes in off-road parts. If it's not in Edgewood or in Berens, you probably don't need it. Free catalog.

Four Wheel Parts Wholesalers
1900 W. 135th St.
Gardena, CA 90249

Complete four-wheel parts wholesaler's catalog. Catalog, $2.00.

Hickey Enterprises, Inc.
1645 Callens Rd.
Ventura, CA 93003

Off-road. Best for winches and heavy-duty suspension kits.

Jack Furrier's Western Tire Centers
3645 S. Palo Verde Blvd.
Tucson, AZ 85713

Catalog title: "Off Road Tires and Accessories, Arizona Desert Rat."
Free catalog.

Western Historical Collection, University of Colorado Libraries.

Western Historical Collection, University of Colorado Libraries.

Warn Industries
9050 Empire Way South
Seattle, WA 98118

Tools. Old, dependable company with excellent
winches.
Free catalog.

Western Tire Centers
3645 S. Palo Verde Blvd.
Tucson, AZ 85713
Free catalog.

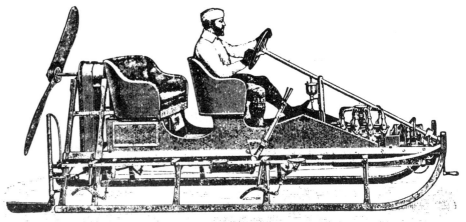

Photo by Janet Snow Ritchie

Survival Vehicles
Rick L. Fines

"Survival vehicle" is a term to which you have not likely been exposed, and for good reason. Four generations of very creative people have devoted their careers to designing advertising copy that makes certain you know what "economy cars," "luxury cars," and "recreational vehicles" are, but references to "survival vehicles" make less than sparkling ad copy.

Another good reason why you have heard little about survival vehicles concerns a peculiar, abstract trait in the American character. We seem to be a reasonably objective people except in the face of a few select topics. To the old cliche list of conversation topics guaranteed to start a fight, automobiles should be added right behind religion and politics. Most American males are willing to seek professional advice on other important topics

but have the curious idea that they were born with a degree in automotive engineering. The fact that the imaginary degrees are at best honorary is made painfully apparent when these same men walk into automobile showrooms brimming over with knowledge and conviction, then leave with what the white-shoed floor salesman wanted them to buy.

Admittedly, in most activities in which we use vehicles, the specifics are not all that important. It makes little difference whether we go to work in red cars or blue cars, or whether they have bucket seats or milk stools. The big, shiny, gadget-laden four-wheeler that your neighbor uses for arduous treks to the supermarket or the bowling lanes may be equipped with nearly any combination of engines, tires, or gear boxes, and the parking lot attendant will not really care one way or the other.

146

Survival is quite another case. The care and preparation used in selecting and equipping a survival machine can make the difference between survival—and the less than acceptable alternative. To consider the question in proper perspective, we must first define what we mean by the term, "survival vehicle." The consideration may be broken down into three basic categories:

(1) The vehicle in question is to be used to evacuate an urban area in the event of widespread civil disorder or natural disaster. Civil disorder would seem to be a simple concept, but it can take many forms. The folk in New York City who lived through the riots caused by an event as mundane as a power outage could certainly tell you so. Most normal services, including fuel, parts, and traffic control, will be disrupted or out. Looters likely will be roaming with little threat from civil authorities. The vehicle, after escaping the urban core, will transport its owner to an established retreat site a reasonable distance from disorder, i.e., 500 miles. The machine will be of use at the retreat site as a utility vehicle. The owner will plan to carry a basic, short-term supply of fuel, food, and clothing to supplement the support equipment already in place at the retreat site.

(2) This variation may best be described as the "land mobile" concept of survival. The vehicle becomes both the means of escape from the urban area as well as the retreat. The theory is that mobility is the most important consideration of survival. The vehicle must be large enough in which to live and must accommodate a vast assortment of supplies and impedimentia. At the risk of sounding less than objective, I will say at the outset that this theory is a lousy one with little chance of success. I will explain why in detail later.

(3) This situation presupposes a retreat site that is totally inaccessible by ordinary equipment, i.e., all-wheel drive capability is required. It should be noted that most four-wheel drive equipment is designed to take us places that we have no particular need to reach; we simply want to go there because it pleases us. Equipment designed to transport over rough terrain in time of need is a bit different than the Cowboy Cadillac–Blazer school of thought. Reliability and practical use are far more important than suburban showmanship.

One of the first advertising concepts that we must dispel to understand what constitutes an ideal survival machine is the idea that "new means best." The same ad copywriters who have tried to convince us what we need these many years have also devoted much ink to persuading us that any vehicle is just not worth owning after it is five years old. To bring at least some objectivity to the situation, consider the following:

(1) Even the wasteful U.S. military establishment commonly retains tactical vehicles for ten or more years.

(2) Other military organizations, i.e., the Israeli and Soviet armies, retain vehicles for as long as they have a tactical application. There are many machines in the thirty-plus age bracket in first-line service in Israel today simply because they do specific jobs better than any other equipment.

(3) Fire engines usually stay on the job for at least twenty years, often past thirty as reserve equipment.

(4) Commercial jet aircraft are depreciated against a schedule of from twelve to as many as eighteen years. At that age, they seldom go to the scrap heap but continue as freight haulers. About one thousand Douglas DC-3 transport aircraft are in service around the world, hauling everything from scheduled passengers to contraband dope. The last DC-3 was built in 1946.

So much for "new is necessary."

Recent trends in automotive engineering also make older equipment more attractive. Up until perhaps a decade ago, the direction of automotive engineering was to produce vehicles that went faster, carried more, and lasted longer. The only influences on the direction of engineering effort were those of a competitive marketplace. The construction of the Interstate highway system in the 1950s required vast changes in the design and perfection of far more durable engines than had been required before.

Starting about ten years ago, Ralph Nader's claimed consumer advocacy, combined with the bureaucrats' realization that empires could be carved from smog, changed the direction of engineering from what consumers wanted to buy to what government thought best for us to own. The result: technology is no longer concerned with making better cars, but rather with meeting a myriad of federal standards and deadlines. If the cars we have today happen to be as good as those we had fifteen years ago, the event is purely coincidental.

The specific effect that all of this political wheel spinning has on the concept of survival vehicle planning is more negative with each model year. As each new line becomes increasingly more "tamperproof," and controlled by still more black-box electronic components, it becomes less repairable by any source other than a dealer's shop loaded with complex diagnostic equipment. Since any repairs in a survival context must be performed by *you*, with no help from anyone, the effect is obvious.

If you believe that the admitted reliability inherent in 100 percent new components more than makes up for the complexity of late-model equipment, stop to think about the last time you delivered a new car to a dealer's shop for a routine warranty repair. Chances are, the dealer stalled you on the appointment. After you got to his shop, you consumed cup after cup of acidic coffee while several of his sharpest people disemboweled your shiny new toy. They surrounded themselves with all manner of diagnostic paraphernalia, all the shop manuals in print, and several thousand square feet of stored parts. After announcing that their expert tinkering and guessing had solved your problems, you drove home and discovered that your car ran worse than before.

Now, pretend that instead of minor irritation over the incompetency of Mr. Goodwrench, your very life depended on whether or not your vehicle operated as intended. Think how different things might be if no Star Wars electronic consoles, no herd of mechanics, and no half-acre of parts were available. Under the best of conditions, auto repairs are such a hit-and-miss proposition that complaints with garages take up more of the time of consumer protection types than any other single activity. Under the worst of conditions, you will have only yourself to keep the show on the road— any needed parts or tools must come from your own supplies and any expertise from your own experience.

Since few real advances have been made in the last decade in light truck and passenger car design, most of the benefits that you derive from going with an older vehicle come as a result of items with which you are not required to contend. Items like elaborate fuel evaporative control systems, smog pumps, nonadjustable carburetors, electronic ignition systems, sealed steering column ignition switches, etc., etc. are all potential maintenance hazards simply because they are there. Even if you luck out and they do not malfunction on their own, they get in the way of components that do require frequent servicing.

Someone always asks if it would be possible to buy a new vehicle and change all of the offending components back to older, simpler ones and to junk most of the smog gear. The answer is a qualified yes. The cost to do so naturally varies greatly with what type of machine is involved and what size engine is installed, but a figure of about $600 may be used with some accuracy to cover the dollar end of the question. The real problem rears

its head if a cop or other bureaucrat happens to poke his head under your hood. In some states, where inspections are mandated on a spot basis, you could find yourself charged with a crime against the people by tampering with the smog plumbing. Besides a fine, you would also face the expense of restoring every nut, bolt, and clamp to state standards. With an older machine offering the same utility, the legally required hardware standards are usually far less burdensome.

One disappointing aspect of the old versus new question relates to cost. By the time an existing machine is "zero times" to survival vehicle standards, the dollars invested will not be a lot lower than the tab for a new machine. Naturally, there are variables involved, and if you do a great deal of the work yourself, the tariff will be much lower. Licensing costs in many states will also be lower, as will the sales tax that you will avoid by staying away from the new machine.

To sum up the situation in which any category of survival machine must operate, we must presuppose the following circumstances:

(1) No repair sources or commercial parts sources are available.
(2) Parts are available only from your own supplies or from wrecked or abandoned vehicles.
(3) Roads are in poor condition and will get worse. Some roads may be blocked by bureaucrats who believe that they know better than you where you wish to go. Others will be blocked by looters. In the event of obstacles or washouts, no repair crews will be available for some time.

Besides the mandates of nonfunctional hardware, a number of very popular accessories should be avoided at all costs on any survival machine. Automatic transmissions are fine if they please you for supermarket transportation, but they have no place in survival planning. A manual transmission may be repaired or a clutch replaced by any reasonably competent individual with a moderate amount of tools. Automatics require very complex equipment for any sort of service. Under severe operating conditions, i.e., prolonged periods of low-speed operation over difficult terrain, automatics heat up and become far less reliable than manual transmissions. Power steering should be avoided. If the hydraulic pump should leak or a hose should fail, steering would become difficult if not impossible. Air conditioning in particular should not be considered. Air conditioner compressor belts are generally slaved in tandem with fan, water pump, and/or alternator belts. A seized compressor means that your engine stops and so do you. A shorted compressor clutch, which is often difficult to diagnose, can hazard your entire electrical system. If cool is all that is important to you, carry a flask of gin and tonic—but forget the air conditioner.

As you recall, we discussed the three basic categories of survival in which different types of rolling stock might figure.

Situation "1" presumes several conditions relating to your circumstances:

You are a city-dweller with a previously established retreat site, including permanent shelter. You have already moved your long-term food, fuel, and support equipment to safe storage at your retreat site, or nearby. Only you, your family, and short-term supplies need to be carried in your vehicle. If we deal in a context of reality, you will very likely need to use secondary roads or improved trails to get out of the city in the chaos certain to accompany any sort of sudden movement out of the urban core.

Perhaps the best way to begin any discussion of the most appropriate specific vehicles to consider is to review some very bad choices. For example, a Corvette would get you out of the city in a hurry. The Chevy engine and drive train are as reliable as any around, and parts may be had from the first abandoned station wagon by the side of the road. Good choice? Hardly. The last possible thing you would want is a machine as conspicuous as a Corvette. While you should be prepared to encounter looters and kill them if necessary, it is foolish to bait them with an attraction as flashy as a sports car. The utility of any sort of go-fast machine at a retreat site is someplace close to zero. Lack of ground clearance, no hauling capacity, and appetite for lots of clean, high-octane fuel rule out the use of just about any sporty cars for survival use.

Another pair of bad choices that have attracted much press coverage are the Subaru BRAT (also station wagon) 4X4 and the 4X4 AMC Eagle. A small, economical 4X4 with good gas mileage might seem to be a good program until you dilute the hype with some facts. In the case of Subaru, parts for the 4X4 may be had only from Subaru dealers. Your chance of salvaging parts from abandoned vehicles is about nil. Tying yourself to an obscure manufacturer and an odd model makes no great amount of sense, even if the Subaru were a good machine—which it is not. In the case of the Subaru and the Eagle, all body and interior hardware was designed for street use, with none of the peculiar torquing, banging, and slamming imposed by vigorous off-road operations. Try running the Eagle like a CJ7 and you will find all its feathers on the floor in short order.

The Subaru happens to have an engine best characterized as gutless, combined with no low-range transfer case capability. The lowest hanging parts are the exhaust pipes, which dangle below the axles. The Subaru might be fine for fetching up the mail at the end of a snowy driveway, but that's about it.

The Eagle is not at all bad in comparison to the Subaru. The only problem is that the Jeep Division of American Motors markets all manner of vastly superior equipment for about the same price. Why bother?

There are several types of vehicles we can strongly suggest, both old and new. You will note that most of our choices are not at the top of the EPA gas mileage charts, but for good reason: gas mileage in a survival context is not terribly important. If your retreat site is farther than the distance that a full tank of fuel and a reasonable on-board reserve will carry you, your strategic planning is faulty. If you plan on obtaining fuel from any source along the way, your tactics are muddled. After you reach your retreat site, driving will be drastically curtailed. You will have no office commute, no school and no supermarket runs. Mileage will become something you put on your machine to keep it running properly, even if you have nowhere to go.

Factors far more important than socially acceptable gas mileage must figure in your selection. For example, have you ever tried to drive through a locked, chain-link gate in a dune buggy? Don't try it. If you try the same act in a ¾-ton pickup or a Jeep, you will likely have no problems at all. How about moving an elderly derelict Cadillac out of the way with a Subaru? Same answer. We are not advocating that you amuse yourself by acts of property damage or destruction derby, but those very acts could spell the difference between getting out of a city and being buried in one. If your equipment is not up to the task, you will be walking with thousands of other unprepared folk.

The first practical category of survival machine that you should investigate is the full-size, ¾-ton pickup or van. Whether your choice of pickup is Ford or Chevy is of little practical importance, because parts are as available for one as for the other. Performance differences and design advantages of one over the other cancel themselves out equally. Since there is still some question about the continued presence of Chrysler in the marketplace, and certainly serious questions about its future in the truck business, I suggest that you give its products little attention. International has made some fine trucks and engines, but parts are something of a joke in the real world. Avoid I-H products for survival applications.

If you buy a new or old pickup, stay with the ¾-ton models. Many people who should know better make statements to the effect that bolting heavier springs to a ½-ton machine will somehow make it equivalent to a ¾-ton truck. The fact is that ¾-ton machines are built with heavier frames, axles, wheels, steering, and suspension. The heavier machines are much more likely to stay together under rough conditions than the ½-tonners. The light trucks are little more than passenger cars with cargo boxes and hold up no better.

If you have a choice about an engine-transmission combination, stay with six cylinders and a truck 4-speed transmission (not an automotive 4-speed, close-ratio street rod box). The truck 4-speed is equipped with a compound low gear that can be nearly as useful as four-wheel drive in tight spots.

Do not fall for all the printed trash about the virtues of headers, high-rise manifolds, multiple carburetors, ad nauseum. More than one self-anointed expert has proclaimed all the marvelous things to be accomplished by a set of headers bolted to a tired old clunk with bad rings, loose rods, and burned valves. The point to be made, beyond the unsuitability of many "performance" accessories to survival machines, is the fact that screwing one part onto any given engine is usually a waste of time and money. Headers, for example, installed in conjunction with engineered manifolding, proper carburetion, selected pistons, and a camshaft of carefully considered profile can yield tremendous changes over stock designs. It is possible to gain much more power, better torque range, and about the same fuel economy. However, the bottom line in survival applications is reliability and parts interchange with wrecks and abandoned equipment.

It would be stretching a point past credibility to suggest that any engine built is any more reliable than a mid-1960s factory product, and it is absurd to discuss parts interchange on a one-off custom engine. Since miserly fuel economy and flashing power are not part of the survival vehicle equation, they are best filed and forgotten.

Besides the advantages of less smog hardware, a few other points are to be made for the older, i.e., 1955–1967, trucks. While the carrying capacity on most of them was the same as for more modern equipment, most of the older machines were equipped with simple beam front axles. The later models, with their automotive-type independent front suspensions ride a bit better but are also far less durable and more difficult to maintain. Another advantage of old equipment is less apparent. If you are operating an old machine in excellent shape, you will find it possible to buy trucks of the same make and year, in less than excellent condition, for very low prices. The second truck may be treated as a complete parts stock of usable components. Such duplication is too expensive to consider if new equipment is in use.

Buying a new van is a simple proposition. Ford is the only make worthy of consideration for survival use. I have no irrational attachment to Ford products, but Ford happens to offer the only vans that feature frames as part of their construction. Chevrolet uses unit construction, which is perfectly acceptable for most uses but does not offer the strength inherent in the separate body-frame construction offered by Ford. Ford's front suspension is the twin I-beam type used on its pickup trucks. While not as rugged as the old single-beam designs, it is certainly a better bet than the GM automotive types.

A few features should be avoided on a van, no matter what the make. The first to be rejected is the sliding side door. The slider makes a great deal of sense in many commercial applications, but it has a habit of falling off into the dirt if subjected to hard use. The swing-out side windows, with their induction-welded hinges, have a similar propensity. Stay with the old-style doors and fixed side windows. Do not specify blind sides, as visibility is an obvious advantage in any survival situation.

While we should not have to tell you so, stay away from any of the "appearance" packages or trim groups on any new machine. Like military trucks, survival vehicles should be inconspicuous. While it is not likely that you will camouflage your machine, you should exercise common sense in selecting colors. The best commercial tones are nonmetallic medium greens and desert tans. Specify painted bumpers and as little chrome as possible. Since not being seen can avoid all sorts of needless confrontations, you should prepare to avoid detection while parked in remote areas. Keep a light coat of engine oil on the bright, plated surfaces of your machine. The road dust that adheres to the oil will kill any reflection. Cover the glass areas at night—and when parked during the day—with newspaper or grocery sacks held in place with masking tape. In open country, from a mile or so away, the outline of a vehicle seldom gives away its position as readily as the glint of the sun against glass. Without the glass to reflect glare, most vehicles appear as nothing more interesting than a clump of brush.

A term mentioned some time back bears clarification. "Zero time" in relation to a survival vehicle means that all moving parts are removed and inspected, or replaced with new components. The work involved is considerable. The axles must come out, the engine must be pulled along with the transmission, and the radiator and springs must be removed from the frame. It is amazing how many people can read such a summary, nod sagely, and lie through their teeth to themselves about how they could certainly complete such a major project in a reasonable period of time. Generally, those same folk have difficulty finding enough time for oil changes and lawn mowing under normal circumstances. Remember that no one is served by a hulk dragged home, disemboweled into a thousand greasy pieces, then never put back on the road. If you have the time, the knowledge, and the space to do a zero-time rebuild project, you will have a better survival machine, equipped closer to ideal, than if you bought new. If you take on the project without the equipment or determination to finish the job, you will only wind up with about twenty dollars worth of dirty scrap metal and a garage full of junk.

The next topic of consideration is the so-called "land mobile" survival concept. This philosophy, like some equally flawed and outmoded naval doctrine, emphasizes that speed and mobility are everything. Most people who subscribe to the land mobile thinking believe that some sort of motor home or trailer/truck combination are the ideal ways to equip. Their logic is that one may live out of the motor home and carry all necessary equipment aboard. Since, as we have already discussed, primary roads are not likely to be all that useful, it is reasonable to presume that the motor home will have to traverse some rough terrain while bearing its burden. A trip to a motor home factory will quickly show you that it is a bad idea to count on a motor home under any circumstances, let alone bad ones. Most motor homes are based on a truck chassis and are then covered with a box of composite construction. The composite often consists of many small wooden framing members fastened to each other by air-driven staples. Siding of one sort or another then sheaths the exterior, and the seams are concealed by molding screwed—or tacked—into place. The result of a few hours of off-road operation is often a stew cabinetry and interior fittings and gear on the floor, not to mention the toilet plumbing that was torn off by the first rock over which the machine passed. Motor homes are simply too complex and too flimsy to be considered for survival use.

If you insist that a motor home of some sort is an indispensable part of your planning, the closest thing to reliability that you might consider is a school bus conversion. While the dowdy old school hack offers little status, it does offer a substantial steel body shell, service access to the engine, and

nearly as much room as a conventional motor home. The retired Greyhound interstate behemoths require too much maintenance and too little rough country capability to warrant consideration.

The questionable tactical considerations of the land mobile survival concept are properly beyond the scope of this chapter, so they will not be addressed in depth. However, it should be pointed out that no matter how well planned a land mobile concept might be, the vehicle will run out of fuel, food, and places to go in a short time. As soon as the fuel runs out, the land mobile survivalist will be dealing with a fixed retreat site. The obvious disadvantage is that he will have no real advance idea where it will be.

The last, and certainly the most interesting, broad category of survival vehicle is the one on which the ad people have given us an almost useful body of information—the all-wheel drive, off-road machine.

Many people wonder why we do not suggest that all survival machines be all-wheel drive. The reason is that most drivers do not have the skill to use a driven front axle. The result is a very false sense of confidence ("I bet that there thing'll go anyplace!"), which can lead to disaster. The fact of the matter is that the great bulk of survival driving will be done on improved roads, improved roads in poor repair, or at least blazed trails. Perhaps the Baja road race hype has something to do with the conception that we all need a fire-breathing monster and a Nomex leisure suit to make us masters of off-road driving. The purveyors of that brand of B.S. forget that the residents of the Baja (they are called Mexicans) get around just fine in old Chevys, new Ramblers, or whatever strikes their fancy.

Another analogy to illustrate the futility of buying more machine than you can handle may be drawn from the habits of many who discover the craft of pistol shooting. They quickly learn that, as beginners, they can hit few of the objects at which they shoot. Rather than buy lots of ammunition and set aside time to practice, they try to see how much money they can fritter away on custom "accuracy" work on their handgun. Just as reading all the collected works of Mel Tappan and Jeff Cooper, then dropping a fortune into gunsmithing will not make an expert pistol shot, neither will buying a gadget-laden 4X4 guarantee that you can get where you most need to go in times of trouble.

If you are certain that you will take the time to learn your machine's 4X4 capabilities, by all means have at it. If you are going to kid yourself, you and your family may very well wind up on your heads in an overturned vehicle.

Again, the best way to talk about 4X4s on the market is to identify some of the popular equipment that you should avoid.

The first offender is the Toyota Land Cruiser. From the mid-1960s to about 1974, they sold well and were a good buy. I bought a new one in 1973 for the sticker price of $3,395, plus tax. The Toyota was at least $1,000 cheaper than a comparable Jeep CJ5, but there the similarity ended. The Toyota six-cylinder engine is close to a dead copy of the circa-1955 Chevrolet truck engine, which should be no surprise considering that Toyota was licensed to build Chevrolet trucks for many years. Unfortunately, the Toyota engine has always been plagued by a number of mechanical problems. My particular truck went through two engines before the 5,000-mile warranty was up. Then and now, parts for the Land Cruiser are a problem at the dealer level. Since the Land Cruiser is now priced closer to $9,000 than $3,400, sales are way down. It is a good bet that the Land Cruiser will be dropped from the U.S. market within the next year or so.

I have already discussed the Subaru and the AMC Eagle. Short of jacking up their radiator caps and rolling new machines under them, no amount of rationalization will make them good choices.

The British Landrovers are fine and very interesting machines. They are also about as gutless as a pet rock. They have not been sold in this country for some years, and parts availability reflects that fact. Some years ago, I owned one of the last 109 Series Landrovers imported to the United States and concluded that in some countries it might be a good bet. Sad to say, I was unable to think of a country on which I would wish a Landrover.

The International Scout had its beginnings back in the early 1960s. The first Scouts were helpless abortions and are best forgotten. The current product apes the Blazer Cowboy-Cadillac school of design, except it is as devoid of style as a pair of Russian underwear. As a more practical consideration, parts for the International 4X4 are as unavailable as for the rest of the I-H line. The parts problem has changed a little of late, because several of I-H's smaller engines were unable to meet federal 1980 smog regulations. As a result, some Scout engines now come from American Motors. Some improvement.

As in the ¾-ton standard pickup class, there is little need to be concerned over differences between Ford and Chevrolet. If you plan to buy a full-size truck, the ¾-ton offerings of 4X4s by either manufacturer will suit your needs. However, if you plan on buying a Blazer, scratch your head and think again. The current Ford Bronco requires the same sort of rethink, because it is as close to a mechanical clone as anything can be. The Bronco-Jimmy-Blazer have lousy visibility over the hood and out the side. They are as bulky and nearly as heavy as a full-size truck but offer the utility of a Jeep.

There is nothing the Cowboy Cadillacs can do that a Jeep Cherokee, Wagoneer, or CJ-series machine cannot do better. It was a shame that Ford just dropped one of the most modern and practical designs in recent memory—the "old" Bronco—to go to the corpulent GM clone.

The new Jeep CJ7 is probably the most practical of all the light 4X4 machines for survival use. The new four-cylinder engine is a vended product of the Pontiac Division of GM and is the powerplant of choice in the CJ5 or the CJ7. The Cherokee is the way to go if you require a vehicle large enough to sleep two. The similar Wagoneer should be specified if you have need for four doors.

As with every category—and more importantly with 4X4s—keep it simple. If the damn thing breaks down in the middle of the night, when rain is pouring down your neck, the wind is blowing, gasoline is running down your arm, and you have no light, YOU have to fix it all by your lonesome.

One add-on item that conjures up more myths than any other is the winch. Just as the term "I bet that thing'll go anyplace" is as asinine as a tow bill, most current winches are not all that much better. No matter what armchair adventurer tells you otherwise from the vantage point of a pair of white shoes, the winch of preference is the PTO unit; that is, a winch driven from an auxiliary gear case mounted on the transmission or transfer case. The bad advice has it that if you drive into water as deep as your nose and the engine stops, an electric winch will still run. Common sense says that if you drive into water of uncertain depth, you are stupid beyond all help. Electric winches are operated by automotive starter motors that are unsuited to extended operation. If you want a winch as a hood ornament, get whatever feels good. If you want to buy a winch and use it, try to get a power take-off type.

Like 4X4 capability itself, do not count on a winch as a cure-all. In more years of off-road operations than I now care to admit, I have done a great deal of digging and jacking to get unstuck but have seldom used a winch. Nature often conspires against you—when you find yourself in terrain likely to suck your truck down to its axles, you will also find that there is little to winch to.

At this point, my greatest awareness is the number of topics that cannot be covered in a single chapter. Hopefully, you now realize that the scam baloney you have read in the general interest automotive rags and the ads full of Beautiful People have little to do with survival. Probably the closest thing to a true survival machine that you are likely to see is a military tactical vehicle. Take some time and visit your local National Guard unit and look at their equipment. It would be time well spent.

The last thing to remember is that when you have assessed your needs and made a decision to buy, do not be swayed by endless compromise and empty advice. Do not walk into a dealership ready to buy a truck and drive out in a Pinto because some double-knit expert convinced you that his line was worth more than all your planning. It can be said with some accuracy that even a '52 Henry J beats no vehicle at all in a survival situation, but the results of thoughtful planning are certainly more likely to lead to success than are guesses. Always bear in mind what failure to survive amounts to.

Rick Fines is the senior product engineer for the Automotive Division of Exide Corporation. In addition, he is (and has been since its inception) an associate editor of Mel Tappan's Personal Survival Letter, *and is a former editor of the* Guns & Ammo Annual.

Photo by Janet Snow Ritchie

Photo by Janet Snow Ritchie

6

The Retreat

Introduction

In the 1950s, during the Cold War, a lot of Americans were running scared. Those were McCarthy days, home bomb shelter days, study science, and when the alarm sounded crawl under your school desk days.

The sixties brought us increased prosperity and the war in Vietnam. The United States seemed unbeatable then, the so-called military-industrial complex indestructible. It was hard to imagine one's own dreaming suburb disrupted by foreign attack or armed insurrection; that kind of thing happened in rice paddies and cities with unpronounceable and unmemorable names. Local disasters such as floods, tornadoes, and riots did occur, but they seemed to be isolated events. They did not affect the general public, who glimpsed the calamities on the evening news and then forgot. But the nation was in conflict with itself as citizens thought and argued about the United States' role and responsibilities as the greatest power in the world.

Then the seventies—a sobering decade, what with inflation, recession, losing our first war—a war that nobody was pleased with, from start to finish. The veterans came home and were hardly noticed, the first unsung U.S. war heroes. The country seemed embarrassed to recognize them. Was petroleum really running out, or was the gas shortage just an oil company rip-off? Either way, Americans began to envision an end to a way of life that

had heretofore been taken for granted. Eternal progress no longer seemed inevitable, or even likely. People began buying small cars and catching buses, turning down thermostats, and eating beans with brown rice. Cadillacs and steak began to reek of decadence to many. And besides, working for them was like running on a treadmill. What was happening to the American dream?

And, of course, there was the Watergate scandal, a severe blow to the self-esteem of the United States and to U.S. prestige abroad. The campuses quieted down as students became more interested in their books than in politics or psychedelic experience. Drugs and causes were considered alright in their places, but one did have to go out and scare up a job after college. The postwar baby boom had grown up and glutted the job market during the late sixties. At the time, unemployment had seemed a temporary problem; after years of prosperity, economic stagnation had been hard to accept.

TO THE WORLD'S END

155

Recession, inflation, loss of prestige, a huge national surplus of university graduates and skilled laborers, chemical pollution, radioactive waste—what else could go wrong? The peace/love movement had become the "me first" decade. And then we slipped into the 1980s.

At the time of this writing, the New Year's greetings are still ringing in our ears, and already Americans have new cause for alarm. Inflation, as the newscasters keep telling us, is skyrocketing—not that we need anyone to point this out. The only people making a profit these days, it seems, are oil company stockholders. Iran has taken over its U.S. embassy and is blackmailing the United States with U.S. hostages. How dare they, we ask. Americans are unaccustomed to such disrespect; yet many have the sinking feeling that we will have to get used to it.

Then the USSR invades Afghanistan, quite possibly with an aim toward Persian Gulf oil. There is talk in Washington about reinstating the draft and rumors of a Third World War that we are presently unequipped to win.

Meanwhile, this is an election year, and so we watch the candidates parade and preach on our television screens. We watch, we listen, we read what they have to say. But much has changed since Ike was president, and who believes politicians anymore? Once again, many Americans are afraid.

All along there have been people who considered it worth their while to plan and prepare for possible future emergency. Today the number is growing. The retreat provides both spiritual relief from the outside world and a means of surviving nuclear holocaust or other catastrophe. The retreatist is like Aesop's hardworking ant who turns away the frivolous grasshopper. This ant has stocked his larder and fortified his home against the hard winter that he has been expecting all through the summer and harvest time. First frost brings a shivering grasshopper to his door, begging food and shelter.

"What were you doing during the warm weather?" asks the ant.

"I was fiddling," replies the locust.

"Well then, go fiddle now," says the ant, and closes the door.

If and when national disaster strikes, retreatists will retire to their fortified hideaways and go about the business of surviving. Those who have made no provisions may not be welcomed. Would-be gate-crashers and raiders will probably meet armed resistance.

The retreat may be anything from a self-sufficient homestead to a wilderness camp, or even a small, tightly knit town. Other sections of this book provide sources of information and equipment useful to many possible aspects of retreating. This chapter deals more specifically with the retreat itself: how to plan, start, stock, get to, and live in it.

Just how and where to retreat is a decidedly personal choice. The books and newsletters in this chapter reflect the very personal and divergent opinions of their writers. For this reason, we suggest that the reader considering subscribing to a newsletter write to individual publishers for informative literature or for sample copies (sample copies often are sold for a small sum). In this way he can assure himself of receiving a publication that coincides with his own tastes and viewpoint.

Western Historical Collection, University of Colorado Libraries.

Access

General Information

Books and Tapes

Appropriate Technology Sourcebook
Ken Darrow and Rick Pam. 1977.
Paper, $4.00 (add 15% surface mail, 40% airmail).
VITA
3706 Rhode Island Ave.
Mt. Rainier, MD 20822

"Guide to practical plans and books for village and small community technology. Reviews of 375 selected U.S. and international publications on alternative sources of energy, shop tools, agriculture, low-cost housing, water supply, and so on."

Civil Defense Underground Construction Reprint
Paper, $5.00.
Stephens Press
P.O. Drawer 1441
Spokane, WA 99210

Twenty clipbound pages. "Information and drawings from the '60's on 'bomb shelters' no longer available from the government. Provides useful information for those interested in various underground construction techniques."

Complete Chicken Little Survival Catalog
From David G. Lee, author.
$5.95.
9108 Mt. Shasta, S.
Indianapolis, IN 46234

Prices and publishing information on over 1,200
survival-oriented books, 800 how-to articles, and
266 sources of this information and other publications and catalogs. Prices should be checked
before you send money, because some have gone
up since Lee did his exhaustive research. The
appearance of the book is somewhat unpre-
possessing due to dense print, but from acorns to
Yurt shelters, it's all here. An excellent reference
tool.

Design Guide for Light Aircraft Airport
VITA
3706 Rhode Island Ave.
Mt. Rainier, MD 20822

Complete instructions on building an airstrip in
remote areas. This may sound farfetched for
retreat purposes, but the airways will be less con-
gested than the highways in time of mass relo-
cation. Now all you have to worry about is
getting to your hangar.

Famine and Survival in America
Howard Ruff.
$5.00.
Laissez Faire Books
206 Mercer St.
New York, NY 10012

Contains Ruff's thoughtful alternative to the one-
year food storage program, and other ideas.

Also available from: Loompanics Unltd.
Box 264
Mason, MI 48854
$5.00.

Green Papers
Don Stephens.
Ringbound, $28.00.
Stephens Press
P.O. Drawer 1441
Spokane, WA 99210

Sixteen sets of reprints of personal survival
articles covering retreating, mobile retreating,
mental preparation for survival, retreat location,
and site selection, food, water, guns, storage,
nuclear safety.

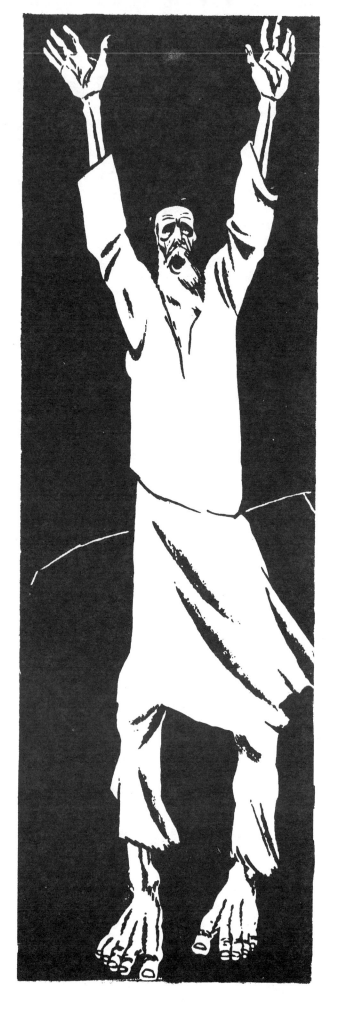

How to Plan and Develop a Survival Retreat
Sidney Ragsdale.
$10.00.
Loompanics Unltd.
Box 264
Mason, MI 48854

Location, roads, sanitation, water, building, and energy retreat considerations. Illustrated.

Also available from:
Rainier Books
P.O. Box 30753, Dept. B9
Seattle, WA 98103
$10.00.

How to Survive the Coming Depression
Paper, $5.00.
Alson Fry.
879 Park
Perris, CA 92320

"What may happen; how to get the necessities; how to protect yourself and your health; how to stay solvent and act in time." Many ideas and practical information are contained in this beautifully illustrated book. The copy that I have is hard to read, however, due to an unfortunate printing job. Let's hope that this has been corrected in later printing, as the sections on energy, survival foods, self-protection, and so on are very helpful.

In Time of Emergency: A Citizen's Handbook on Nuclear Attack, Natural Disasters
1968-0-297-579.
Department of Defense, Office of Civil Defense
Available from:
Superintendent of Documents
Washington, DC 20402
or
Your local Civil Defense Office

In simple terms, explains the hazards of nuclear attack—and the good news that it does not mean total decimation of the population. Covers fallout shelters, protection, supplies, water, food, sanitation, care of the sick and injured. Also discusses major natural disasters.

Life After Doomsday
Bruce D. Clayton, Ph.D.
Paladin Enterprises
P.O. Box 1307
Boulder, CO 80306

The most complete, detailed, and scholarly manual available on the effects of radiation, what areas will be affected most, survival shelters, physical and psychological first aid, and many other survival subjects. **$19.95**

The National Outdoor Living Directory
$3.00.
Live Free, Inc.
P.O. Box 743
Harvey, IL 60426

Lists more than 1,000 outdoor, survival, conservation, and homesteading organizations.

The Original Retreater's Bibliography
Don and Barbie Stephens. 1967/70.
$6.00.
Stephens Press
P.O. Drawer 1441
Spokane, WA 99210

Over 300 out-of-print listings and checklist. "May be largely of historical interest."

Personal and Family Survival
SM 3-11.
$5.00.
Loompanics Unltd.
Box 264
Mason, MI 48854

Civil defense manual on survival with two supplements by Hillcrest Publications.

Plan and Survive
Kurt Saxon.
Paper, $1.00.
Loompanics Unltd.
Box 264
Mason, MI 48854

Practical booklet on survival, whether the disaster is economic or atomic.

Plan to Survive: Programs for Individual and Group Survival
James C. Jones
Paper, $4.00.
Live Free, Inc.
Harvey, IL 60426

Retreaters' Maps
Don Stephens. 1977.
Seven maps, $3.50.
Stephens Press
P.O. Drawer 1441
Spokane, WA 99210

"Natural, political and demographic hazards in retreat site selection. Covers all fifty states."

Retreating on a Shoestring
Don Stephens. 1975.
Paper, $1.50.
Stephens Press
P.O. Drawer 1441
Spokane, WA 99210

Low-cost preparations and list of items for a basic survival locker to fit into a car trunk; designed for those with limited funds for retreating.

Survival Directory: A Guide to Personal Survival
T. A. De Mattis. 1976.
$5.00.
Mutual Association for Security and Survival (MASS). 1976.
P.O. Box 6
Lakehurst, NJ 08733

This booklet deals mainly with retreating from endangered urban areas. Much information on campgrounds that may be used as retreats.

Survival Guns
Mel Tappan
Paladin Enterprises
P.O. Box 1307
Boulder, CO 80306

The definitive work on the subject of armed personal, home, and retreat protection.

Survival Publications Directory
Survival/Security Associates
P.O. Box 30753
Seattle, WA 98103

Unbound listing of books, catalogs, magazines, manuals, newspapers, and survival equipment suppliers dealing with security and survival. Write for current price.

Survival Tape #1: An In-Depth Interview with Don Stephens
1977.
$40.00.
Stephens Press
P.O. Drawer 1441
Spokane, WA 99210

Three and one-half hours on three cassettes; question and answer format.

The Survivor's Primer and Updated Retreater's Bibliography
Don and Barbie Stephens. 1976.
Paper, $12.00.
Stephens Press
P.O. Drawer 1441
Spokane, WA 99210

Discusses hazards and possible reasons for concern, choices, advance preparation, and checklist of supplies, equipment, and trading goods. (Both the above offered as a package for $48.00, at a savings of $4.00.)

Village Technology Handbook
Paper, $8.95 (add 15% surface mail, 40% airmail).
VITA. 1970.
3706 Rhode Island Ave.
Mt. Rainier, MD 20822

Easy-to-read and use construction plans. Covers well digging, pumps, tools for agriculture, sanitation, food storage, and more, using readily available materials. Clear, basic instructions with many drawings and diagrams.

Where There is No Doctor
David Werner. 1977.
Paper, $4.50 (add 15% surface mail, 40% airmail).
VITA
3706 Rhode Island Ave.
Mt. Rainier, MD 20822

"Covers everything from diarrhea to tuberculosis, home remedies to modern medicines, family planning to childbirth."

Nobody Makes Housecalls Anymore

From *Life After Doomsday* by Bruce Clayton, Ph.D. (Paladin Press, Post Office Box 1307, Boulder, Colorado 80306).

In the space of the last three months, I have been brought into contact with physicians and hospitals altogether too frequently. In that period of time, an elderly relative became involved in a serious auto-mobile accident and subsequently suffered a stroke. A young woman who is a close friend of the family developed a brain aneurysm and had to have very dangerous surgery to correct it. Another close friend developed a 104-degree fever that ran on for days and turned into meningitis. He was in the hospital under codeine sedation for a week before he began to improve. My family and I participated in a holiday get-together after which everybody but me got sick (I don't like potato salad). Another friend developed a cyst in his head the size of an egg and had to have it treated. Yet another friend had a miscarriage. Last but not least, I spent five days taking care of a fourteen-month-old infant while his parents were out of town. He had the flu the whole time.

What would we do if we needed professional medical help and couldn't get it? The retreaters I have met regard that possibility as the single most difficult problem they face. After all, growing crops is not all that complicated. Pulling a trigger to bring in meat or defend your life is pretty simple, too. But if someone gets a small cut, and it becomes infected, and ominous red streaks start to spread—what do you do? If one of your sentries accidentally shoots himself in the foot—what do you do? If several members of your group arrive at the retreat suffering from flashburns or blast injuries—what do you do? Without a team of physicians, a fully stocked pharmacy, and a well-equipped hospital, these questions and others like them present life threatening dilemmas.

Obviously, the best answer to medical problems would be to have a physician join your group. This might not be as difficult as it sounds. A surprisingly large number of retreat groups are composed partially or wholly of physicians (particularly the commercial "rent-a-shelter" groups in California). I suspect that this is due to the fact that doctors are at home with emergency situations, death, and, particularly, preventive attitudes. Their profession makes them tend to think like retreaters; it is only a small step to full-scale emergency preparedness.

If you can't interest a physician in your group, there are several other medical professionals who could be of assistance. The Office of Civil Defense suggests the following "doctor substitutes," in order of priority: dentists, veterinarians, registered nurses, pharmacists, licensed practical nurses, trained medical corpsmen, podiatrists, and students of these disciplines.

And if your circle of friends does not include any veterinarians, podiatrists, or medical corpsmen? Don't despair. If you have to supply your own medical aid there is still quite a lot that you can do for yourself, even in severe emergencies.

There are two points to bring up here. Don't be complacent just because your brother-in-law the pediatrician has joined your retreat group. You will need to prepare for do-it-yourself medicine anyway. What will you do if he doesn't make it to the retreat site? What if he arrives but is so badly injured that *he* needs a doctor? Be prepared. And secondly, be aware that modern physicians are relatively inexperienced in medical techniques which lie outside of their fields of specialization, and may never have studied therapies which are more appropriate to a retreat than a hospital. They know the best way to treat a particular problem using the most modern hospital equipment and supplies, but the second-best way (using two spoons and a can opener) is something that they have never tried, seen, heard of, or thought about. You will have to provide the books, supplies, and equipment to assist your doctor in the difficult transition from modern medicine to retreat medicine. *Otherwise, the doctor may be unable to help you.*

Basic Medical Self-help

Public health authorities have begun to implement self-help training courses for the general public which go far beyond the traditional Red Cross "first aid" curriculum. These classes are intended to help a layman make the right decision about whether or not a particular medical problem requires the attention of a doctor. From 30 to 70 percent of the cases a family doctor sees each day are people who don't really need help. Most patients have discomforts that they can treat themselves or which are self-limiting. Medical self-help courses are designed to teach the layman how to tell the difference between these conditions and the more serious ones which do require professional treatment.

The basis of these programs is a course originated by Dr. Keith Sehnert, author of the best-selling book *How to Be Your Own Doctor (Sometimes)*. I highly recommend this book to all people who are concerned about their health, and to retreaters in particular. The book contains clearly written advice on teaching yourself how to monitor your family's health using simple medical instruments such as the stethoscope, thermometer, sphygmomanometer, otoscope, and penlight.

How to Be Your Own Doctor (Sometimes) includes chapters on general preventive medicine (living like you like to live), as well as extensive sections on understanding your doctor's medical jargon, putting together a "black bag" of your own, assembling a selection of emergency drugs and medical supplies, and evaluating your doctor. Sehnert also includes a really helpful section on how to interrogate your doctor to really find out what is wrong with you. It's the perfect preparation for the patient whose doctor says, "Take two of these pills and call me in the morning."

Within the main body of Sehnert's book is a second book, *The Self-help Medical Guide*. This manual is the heart of the matter for retreaters, because it guides one by a series of questions to a determination of what is wrong and to a decision about whether or not to see a doctor. If professional help is not called for, the guide includes complete instructions on treating the problem at home. I have used this guide with my family and I have found it to be comprehensive and easy to follow.

There is one book which you might consider buying as a supplement (or a poor substitute) for Sehnert's manual. This is *The Well Body Book* by Mike Samuels, M.D. and Hal Bennett. This book has an excellent section on self-examination but is heavily laced with Eastern mysticism and I cannot whole-heartedly recommend it.

A "Family Black Bag Home Health Kit" containing all the equipment necessary to complement Sehnert's book is commercially available from the Clayton Division of Marshall Electronics. The kit contains a special cut-down version of the book, but I suggest you visit a bookstore and get the complete text, too.

First Aid for Retreaters

For the emergency situations which retreaters may have to face someday, standard first aid

training will be hopelessly inadequate. You may be called on to administer first aid to persons, possibly loved ones, who have suffered severe injuries caused by blast, flash burns, flame burns, chemicals, or possibly even small arms. For these reasons a retreater needs a somewhat unusual manual on first aid technique and lifesaving.

The best manual I have seen along this line is the United States Army Field Manual 21-11, *First Aid for Soldiers*, available commercially from Normount Technical Publications under the title *First Aid for Soldiers and Sportsmen*. This is the manual to consult first in an emergency because it tells you what to do to keep the victim alive long enough either to get him to a doctor or to figure out how to treat the injuries yourself. This book contains all the standard information on bleeding, artificial respiration, closed-chest heart massage, bandaging, and treating shock. It also includes an unusual degree of information on first aid for victims of massive wounds, severe burns, bullet wounds, and poison gas. Have you ever stopped to consider how you would give artificial respiration to a person wearing a gas mask? This manual describes two procedures.

The chapter on psychological first aid is also unusual. Psychological injuries don't show like wounds of the flesh, but they can be just as incapacitating, and special skills are needed to deal with them. The manual discusses how to recognize a psychological casualty, how to give first aid, and how to control your own attitude toward a person who is helpless but apparently uninjured. (Saying "Snap out of it!" usually makes things worse.) If you contemplate being prepared for disaster, you will certainly need to give some thought to the psychological health of your group of survivors.

In one other aspect *First Aid for Soldiers* is unique. Most first aid manuals tell you never to move a wounded person for fear of aggravating injuries. This manual, designed for use on the battlefield, assumes that there will be times when the only thing you can do is to pick up and carry the casualty. The details of immobilizing the injury and protecting the patient under these circumstances are described at length. As a retreater, you may someday be forced to transport a member of your group under just such primitive conditions. If that happens, you will need this manual.

WARNING!

Self-medication under circumstances where a physician's care is available is not only illegal, it is *extremely dangerous*. The author and the publishers of this book do not recommend or endorse self-medication or the practice of medicine without a license in any way, shape, or form. The responsibility for any such activity is borne entirely by the reader. *Seek professional medical help if there is any possible way to obtain it.*

Keith Sehnert, *How to Be Your Own Doctor (Sometimes)* (New York: Grosset & Dunlap, Inc., 1975).

Mike Samuels and Hal Bennett, *The Well Body Book* (New York: Random House, Inc., 1973).

First Aid for Soldiers, U.S. Army Field Manual 21-11—D101.20:21-11/4.

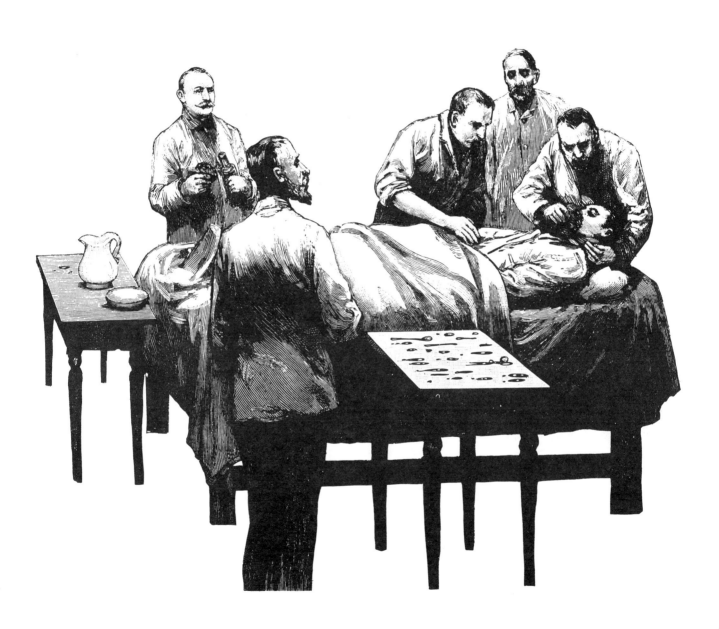

Plagues and Pestilences

Our present miracle age of medicine makes it easy to forget that plagues once took more human lives by far than did warfare. This listing of great plagues and pestilences of the past helps put this sobering possibility into perspective. Perhaps a super-virus will evolve that even modern medicine cannot contain. More probably, a nuclear war could devastate mankind's medical capabilities. Formerly innocuous illnesses could become plagues, because The War would have destroyed our great hospitals, research facilities, medical supplies—and the doctors themselves. (Reprinted from the *New Century Book of Facts*, King-Richardson Co., 1913.)

Date.	Locality.	Remarks.
767	Throughout the world	Plague; mentioned by Petavius.
534	Carthage	Infectious distemper; children offered in sacrifice as an atonement.
461	Rome	Plague; 100,000 persons died.
430	Greece, Egypt, Ethiopia	Plague; described by Thucydides.
188 A.D.	Egypt, Syria, Grecian colonies	Plague; according to Pliny, 2,000 persons perished daily.
80	Rome	Infectious disease; 10,000 persons died daily.
167 169 189	Roman Empire	Fatal contagious sickness.
250 to 265	Roman Empire	Plague (smallpox or bubo plague?); many provincial towns depopulated; in Rome itself, for some time, 5,000 persons died daily.
430	Britain	Plague; not enough survivors to bury the dead.
558 and after	Europe, Asia, Africa	Plague.
746 to 749	Constantinople, Sicily, Greece, Calabria	Contagious disease; 200,000 Constantinopolitans died.
772	Chichester (England)	Epidemic disease; 34,000 persons died.
954	Scotland	40,000 persons perished.
1094	London	Epidemic.
1095	Ireland	Epidemic.
1111	London	Distemper; great mortality among both human beings and domestic animals.
1172	Ireland	English invaders driven back by the plague.
1204	Ireland	Plague.
1267	England	Great mortality from plague.

Date	Locality	Remarks
1340	Italy, Germany	First appearance of "Black Death" in Italy; thousands perished in Germany.
1348	London	"Black Death"; 200 persons buried daily in the Charterhouse yard.
1362	England	57,376 persons died.
1362		
1367		
1370	Western Europe	Great mortality, especially near Paris and London, and in parts of Ireland.
1379		
1383	Ireland	"Fourth pestilence."
1407	London	Plague; 30,000 persons died.
1466	Ireland	Famine and pestilence; hundreds died.
1470	Dublin	Mortality very great.
1471	England	Plague; death of more people than in the constant wars of the fifteen years previous.
1478		
1485	London	"Sudor Angelicus" (sweating sickness).
1499		
1500	London	Plague; royal court removed to Calais.
1506		
1517	England	Sweating sickness; frightful mortality.
1522	Limerick	Plague; thousands died.
1528	England	Sweating sickness.
1529	North Germany	Sweating sickness.
1548		
1551	England	Sweating sickness.
1603		
1604	England, Ireland	Plague; 30,578 persons perished in London alone.
1611	Constantinople	Pestilence; 200,000 persons died.
1625	London	Plague; 35,417 persons died.
1630	Italy	Plague: 247,000 persons died.
1632	France	60,000 persons died at Lyons.
1656	Naples	Plague; in six months 400,000 persons perished.
1664		Great plague; 68,596 persons said to have died; fires kept burning to destroy the contagion; city not free from infection until the great fire (1666).
1665	London	
1720	Marseilles and vicinity	Plague; 60,000 persons died.
1741		
1742	New York City	Yellow fever.
1743	Messina	Plague.
1760	Syria	Plague.
1773	Persia	Infectious distemper; 80,000 persons died in Bassora.
1773	Saulica (France)	Out of 180 persons present at the opening of a grave, 174 were attacked by a putrid fever.
1784	Smyrna, Tunis	Plague; 20,000 persons perished in Smyrna.
1791	Atlantic coast of	
1795	North America	Yellow fever.
1792	Egypt	Plague; about 800,000 persons died.

Date.	Locality	Remarks.
1798	Baltimore, Philadelphia, New York	Yellow fever; one out of every twenty-seven died in New York, several thousand in and about Philadelphia, from the latter city 50,000 of its 70,000 inhabitants fled.
1799	Coast of Africa, particularly in Barbary	Plague; 3,000 persons died daily; at Fez, 247,600 perished.
1800	Morocco	Plague; 1,800 died in one day.
1804		
1805	Spain, Gibraltar	Pestilence.
1805	North American ports	Yellow fever; from New York 37,000 of the 70,000 inhabitants fled.
1813	Malta	Plague.
1814	Asia Minor, Palestine, Grecian Archipelago	Plague; 30,000 persons died in Smyrna.
1816	Naples	Plague.
1817	India	Great mortality from cholera; a large proportion of soldiers, both Europeans and natives, perished.
1818	Bombay, Ceylon, Siam, Malacca, China, Islands of Mauritius and Bourbon	Cholera.
1819	Tunis	Plague; half the population perished.
1819 1822	Seaports of the United States	Yellow fever; mortality not so great as before.
1821	Persia	Cholera.
1823	The Mediterranean; Aleppo, Antioch, and other places	Cholera.
1828	Gibraltar	Epidemic fever; great mortality.
1830	Russia	Cholera; 8,576 attacked, of whom 4,630 died.
1830	England, Scotland	Cholera; made its first appearance in England at Sunderland.
1831	Russia, Poland, Hamburg (Germany)	Cholera; Russian and Polish armies attacked; of 3,012 taken ill at Warsaw, 1,462 died; at St. Petersburg 7,567 cases were reported, of whom 3,804 died in forty-eight days.
1832	Great Britain, Paris, Canada, Middle Atlantic and Southern States	Cholera; in Great Britain, mortality not over 6,000; in Paris, about 15,000 of the 750,000 inhabitants; in Canada, about 2,000 each in Quebec and Montreal; in New York City, 3,000 of the 6,000 persons attacked.

1848		
1849	England, America	Cholera.
1865	England	Cattle-plague; resembling typhus.
1865	Smyrna, Constan-tinople, Paris, Marseilles, Naples.	Cholera.
1866	Dublin	New disease; many persons died a few hours after seizure.
1878	Southern States; particularly the city of Memphis.	Yellow fever.
1879	Astrakhan.	Plague.
1884		
1885	Europe	Cholera.
1892		

Health and Safety Products

Catalogs

These companies are also mentioned in Chapter 2, *Wilderness Survival*. We mention them again here because they all have a wide range of products, some of which are specifically applicable to retreat purposes.

E. D. Bullard Co.
2680 Bridgeway
Sausalito, CA 94965

Respiratory equipment, including compressed air purifiers; UNI-PAC first aid kits; and color-coded cabinet kits with patented OSHA inspection form. Free catalog.

Marion Health and Safety, Inc.
9233 Ward Parkway
Kansas City, MO 64114

Emergency medical products and first aid kits. "A complete line of products designed especially for use by the occupational health.nurse." Free product catalog.

Scott Health/Safety Products
Scott Aviation
Lancaster, NY 14086

(1) Scott gas masks, replacement parts, and accessories
(2) Twin cartridge respirators
Two free catalogs.

Tri-Med Surgical Co., Inc.
2 South St.
Garden City, NY 11530

All kinds of professional medical products. Free catalog.

Food Preservation

Stored food is definitely one of the essentials for a retreat. If you prepare it yourself, you have the advantage of feeling self-reliant—maybe even smug—and also of knowing what is in it. Garden surplus or inexpensively bought fruit and vegetables in season, even meat and fish, can be preserved by various methods and shelved for future use. For assistance in preserving foods safely and efficiently, we suggest the following publications. (For game preparation instructions, please see Chapter 2, *Wilderness Survival*, under hunting.)

Books and Pamphlets

Safe storage methods for food vary from region to region. You might want to contact your county cooperative extension agent for information on methods and conditions of storing products in your geographic area.

The ABC's of Home Food Dehydration
Barbara Densley. 1975.
Paper.
Horizon Publishers and Distributors
P.O. Box 490, 50 South, 500 West
Bountiful, Utah 84010

Ball Blue Book
Paper, $2.00.
Box 2005
Muncie, IN 47302

Beef Slaughtering, Cutting, Preserving and Cooking on the Farm
U.S. Department of Agriculture
Farmers' Bull. No. 2263. 1977.
Paper, $2.00.
For sale by the Superintendent of Documents
U.S. Government Printing Office
Washington, D.C. 20402

Canning, Freezing, Curing and Smoking of Meat, Fish and Game
Wilbur F. Eastman, Jr.
Hardcover, $11.95; paper, $5.95.
Garden Way Publishing
Charlotte, VT 05445

Home Canning of Fruits and Vegetables
Home Canning of Meat and Poultry
Two pamphlets, 15¢ each.
U.S. Department of Agriculture
For sale by the Superintendent of Documents
U.S. Government Printing Office
Washington, D.C. 20402

How to Salt Fish
$1.25.
VITA. 1966.
3706 Rhode Island Ave.
Mt. Rainier, MD 20822

The Joy of Cooking
Irma S. Rombauer.
Hardcover, $10.95; deluxe, $20.00.
The Bobbs-Merrill Co., Inc.
4300 W. 62nd St.
Indianapolis, IN 46268

A favorite and much relied upon source book.
Rightly so, because the recipes are tested and
easy to follow, sage advice is generously dispensed, and the book contains a store of information not to be found in any other single book.
For food preservation, consult the following
sections: "The Foods We Keep"; "Canning,
Salting, Smoking and Drying"; "Freezing"; "Jellies
and Preserves"; and "Pickles and Relishes."

Just in Case. A Manual of Home Preparedness
Barbara G. Salsbury.
Paper, $5.50.
Bookcraft Publishers
1848 West, 2300 South
Salt Lake City, UT 84120

*Keeping the Harvest: Home Storage of Fruits and
Vegetables*
Nancy Thurber and Gretchen Mead.
Paper, $5.95; Spiral, $6.95; hardcover, $12.95.
Garden Way Publishing
Charlotte, VT 05445

Kerr Home Canning Book
Paper, $1.00.
Kerr Glass Mfg. Co.
Sand Springs, OK 74063

*Lamb Slaughtering, Cutting, Preserving and
Cooking on the Farm*
Farmers' Bul. No. 2264. 1977.
Paper, $1.40.
For sale by the Superintendent of Documents
U.S. Government Printing Office
Washington, D.C. 20402

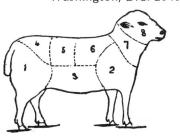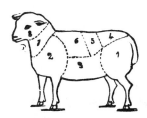

SECTIONS OF SHEEP, OR LAMB.

1. Leg.
2. Shoulder.
3. Breast.
4. Scrag end of neck.
5. Best end of loin.
6. Best end of neck.
7. Chump end of loin.
8. Head.

*Making the Best of the Basics: Family
Preparedness Handbook*
James Talmage Stevens.
Paper, $5.95.
Peton Corp.
P.O. Box 11925
Salt Lake City, UT 84111

Preserving, storing, and using foods; recipes;
instructions for storing fuel and water; yard gardening; soap-making; basic medical supplies; and
other useful information. Attractively presented
and easy to follow, this book appears to be an
excellent buy for the money.

*Root Cellaring: The Simple, No-Processing Way to
Store Fruits and Vegetables*
Hardcover, $11.95.
Mike and Nancy Bubel.
Rodale Press, Inc.
Book Division
33 East Minor St.
Emmaus, PA 18049

Some Aspects of Food Preservation
Pamphlet, 25¢ plus postage.
Ball Co.
Box 2005
Muncie, IN 47302

*Stocking Up: How to Preserve the Foods You
Grow Naturally*
By the editors of *Organic Gardening Magazine*
(rev. ed.).
Hardcover, $13.95; deluxe, $15.95.
Rodale Press, Inc.
Book Division
33 East Minor St.
Emmaus, PA 18049

Stocking Up takes the reader through every step
of food preservation: choosing fruit and vegetable varieties best suited for storing; preserving;
instructions for underground storage; recipes for
the preparation of stored foods; canning foods in
high-altitude areas; how to make soft and hard
cheeses; freezing, canning, curing, smoking, and
storing meat, poultry, and fish. This book probably contains all the information you will need.

Storing Vegetables and Fruits in Basements,
Cellars, Outbuildings and Pits
Home and Garden Bul., No. 119
Pamphlet, 40¢.
For sale by the Superintendent of Documents
U.S. Government Printing Office
Washington, D.C. 20402

Catalogs for Supplies

Barth's of Long Island
Valley Stream, NY 11582

Grain-mill, juicer, yogurt-maker, and seed
sprouter, as well as vitamin and mineral supplements and natural foods.
Free catalog.

B&J Industries
514 State St.
Dept. 9T
Marysville, WA 98270

The Equi-Flow food dehydrator and a full line of
other food preservation items.
Free catalog.

Country Catalog
265 Petaluma Ave.
Dept. 12-K
Sebastapol, CA 95472

". . . Complete sections on food preparation,
books, old-time items, farm needs. Lowest
prices—best savings."
Catalog, $2.95; $2.50 refund with first $20.00
order.

Countryside General Store
Highway 19 East SU
Waterloo, WI 53594

Kitchen and homestead products, books, and
tools for livestock.
Catalog, $1.00.

Cumberland General Store
Route 3, Box 470
Crossville, TN 38555

Canning equipment, tools, old-time farm products
of all kinds.
Catalog, $3.00.

Excalibur Products
6083 Power Inn Rd.
Dept. 190
Sacramento, CA 95824

"We offer you the best quality grain-mill on the
market at the most reasonable price."
Free information.

Garden Way Country Kitchen Catalog
Garden Way Catalog Dept.
90461–1300 Ethan Allen Ave.
Winooski, VT 05404

"The most complete selection anywhere! Dehydrators, pea and bean shellers, jelly strainers,
sausagemakers, etc. More than 500 hard-to-find

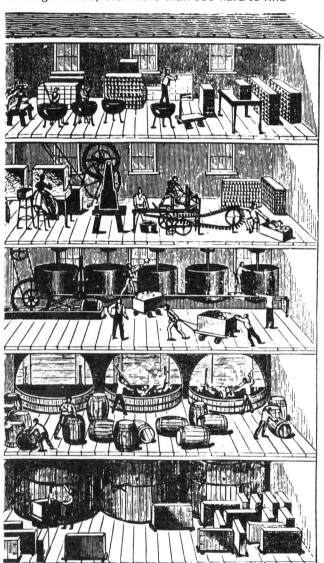

items for home canners and folks who preserve food at home."
Free catalog, 25¢ postage.

Garden Way Press for Cider
Garden Way Research
Dept. 90070
Charlotte, VT 05445

Available in kits.
Free information.

Mother's General Store
Box 506
Flat Rock, NC 28731

Homestead items, cast-iron cookware, food-processing devices.
Catalog, 50¢.

New England Cheese-Making Supply Co.
Ashfield, MA 01330

Cheese-making supplies: rennet, moulds, starter culture, presses, and more.
Catalog, $1.00.

Nutri-Flow, Inc.
5201 SW Westgate Dr.
Portland, OR 97221

Food dehydrators. "Exterior thermo control. One-year warranty."
Free catalog and recipes.

R&R Mill Company
Corona Dept.
Smithfield, UT 84335

Convertible mill—stones for grains, metal plates to grind nuts, and other useful items.
Free catalog.

Reliance Supplies General Catalog
Reliance Products
1900 Olympic Blvd.
Walnut Creek, CA 94596

Bulk food storage containers, home grain mills, food dehydrators, books, as well as fireplace paraphernalia to increase energy efficiency, books, much more. A reputable company, quality merchandise.
Free catalog.

Sears, Roebuck & Co.
925 S. Homan Ave.
Chicago, IL 60607

Suburban, farm, and ranch catalog. Canning and freezing equipment, grain mills, cider presses, more (also in Sears' free general catalog).
Free catalog.

Dehydrated and Freeze-Dried Foods

Catalogs

Dehydrated foods are less expensive; freeze-dried foods may taste a little better and reconstitute more quickly. Both are well-suited to storing because they take up less space than other preserved foods and keep well. Even after they are opened, freeze-dried and dehydrated products will retain their nutritional value and will resist spoilage for months.

Better Foods Foundation, Inc.
200 N. Washington St.
Greencastle, PA 17225

Ready-to-eat cereals, grains, and flours; complete stocks of special diet, health, and protein foods and vitamin and mineral supplements.
Free catalog.

Food Reserves, Inc.
710 S.E. 17th St. Causeway
Fort Lauderdale, FL 33316

"Survival Storage Foods." Complete selection of dehydrated and freeze-dried foods; vitamin and protein supplements.
Free catalog.

International Food Storage Association
5806 114th N.E.
Kirkland, WA 98033
Free information.

Martens Health and Survival Products, Inc.
P.O. Box 51
Moraga, CA 94556

Endorsed by Howard Ruff. Grains, beans, dried and freeze-dried foods. NEST and Mountain House. Vitamins and supplements; water washers, grain mills, and bread mixer.
Free information.

Oregon Freeze-Dry Foods, Inc.
P.O. Box 1048
Albany, OR 97321

Manufacturer of Mountain House and Teakettle brands. Bulk-packed foods for large groups available.
Information, list of dealers on request.

PermaPak
40 East, 2430 South
Salt Lake City, UT 84155.
Free catalog.

Plus Products
Irvine, CA 92714
Free catalog: Better Health Handbook.

Reliance Supplies General Catalog
Reliance Products
1900 Olympic Blvd.
Walnut Creek, CA 94596

Bulk food storage containers, home grain mills, books, food dehydrators, stoves, whole grains, peas and beans, water purifiers, outdoor/emergency equipment, more. Reliance has Howard Ruff's blessing.
Free catalog.

Shaklee
Nutri-Save Co.
Box 1829
Rockford, IL 61110

"Big vitamin savings."
Free price list.

Retreats and Schools

Florida Group Retreat
Through Food Reserves, Inc.
710 Southeast 17th St. Causeway
Fort Lauderdale, FL 33316

"This is the only successful, self-sufficient group retreat in the U.S.: within a tank of gas from anywhere in Florida; direct access to over 150 square miles of lake; excellent recreation and vacation spot, inaccessible to nonparticipants.
Free information.

State Departments of Parks and Recreation
Write or call for current information on campgrounds in your state or in the states in which you are interested. Campgrounds may be used as retreats, but you may have to do a little scouting for the right spot.

USAF Survival and Special Training School
3636th Combat Crew Training Group (Survival)
(ATC)
Fairchild Air Force Base
Washington 99011

Write for unclassified information in your area of
interest. Publications are available on resistance,
survival, and escape and evasion in enemy-
controlled territory, physical and psychological
survival, POW resistance training, survival equipment, and related subjects. Inquiries answered,
referrals made.

Survival Newsletters and Magazines

Doug Clark Survival Letter
P.O. Box 16669
Irvine, CA 92713

Money, politics, food, water, retreats.
$125.00/year.

Earthtone
Publication Development, Inc.
9295 S.W. Electric
Tigard, OR 97223

Features survival articles by Don Stephens. Other
editorial topics: survival gardening, food, health,
family, business opportunities.
Six issues per year, $5.00.

Innovator Reprints
Ringbinder, $36.00.
Stephens Press
P.O. Drawer 1441
Spokane, WA 99210

"Thirteen issues of the now defunct *Innovator*
magazine, selected because their content is still
relevant to today's survivalist. Subjects range
from living on the high seas and emigration to
surviving economic disaster."

Live Free Newsletter
Live Free, Inc.
P.O. Box 743
Harvey, IL 60426

Survival techniques, leadership, and philosophy,
emphasizing dialogue between subscribers.
Four issues, $4.00.

MASSletter
Mutual Association for Security and Survival
P.O. Box 6
Lakehurst, NJ 08733

"Bi-monthly newsletter of interest to people
concerned with the future of society, and survival
of the fittest and wisest. It invites memberships
to join survival groups and congregations now
being formed in the U.S.A."
Write for 1980 prices.

The Middle Class Survival Manual
Survival Publications
500 Esplanade Dr., Suite 1520
Oxnard, CA 93030
Five-issue trial subscription, $7.00.
$40.00 annual subscription; includes two bound
volumes containing 1978 and 1979 issues.
Crash Course for Hard Times, a pamphlet of
survival book reviews, for $2.00.

National Defense Magazine
American Defense Preparedness Association
819 Union First Bldg.
Washington, D.C. 20005
Bimonthly, $22.50/year.

Pride & Joy
Box 19
Niwot, CO 80544

Unorthodox presentation of political opinion and
survival techniques. Defies description.
$26.00/year; sample issue, $1.00.

Ruff Times
Target Publishing Co.
Howard Ruff
Box 2000
San Ramon, CA 94583

Mainly political and economic news and forecasting, but Ruff also has plenty to say about survival and retreat topics.
Send for current prices.

Personal Survival Letter
P.O. Box 598
Rogue River, OR 97537

"Starts where other newsletters leave off!"
Survival, retreating, survival guns, survival rides, other subjects of interest to the survivalist.
Send for 1980 prices.

The Survivor
Kurt Saxon

Saxon has discontinued his highly informative newsletter, but bound copies of back issues are available from Paladin Enterprises, P.O. Box 1307, Boulder, CO 80306.

Retreat Consultation

Joel M. Skousen
President and Chief Architect, Survival Homes, Inc.
Survival Homes Design Division
514 State St.
Hood River, OR 97031
503-386-6553

Building and remodeling for self-sufficiency is Skousen's specialty. Designs and plans for buildings include adequate storage area, protection against vandals and looters, independent heating and electricity, and other survival features.

Don Stephens
Stephens Press
P.O. Drawer 1441
Spokane, WA 99210

Besides tapes and books, Stephens offers personal retreat consultation and other special services. For information packet on underground design services, send $1.00.

Photo by Janet Snow Ritchie

The Ten Safest Areas of the United States in a Nuclear Attack

The following ten areas have less than a 2 percent chance of receiving any fallout from a full-scale Soviet attack on U.S. military and industrial targets.

1. The Pacific coast, roughly from San Francisco, California, to the Canadian border, including a sizable section of central Oregon.
2. The Channel Islands southwest of Los Angeles, California.
3. The southwest corner of Utah.
4. The Durango area of southwest Colorado and northwest New Mexico.
5. The Big Bend region of Texas.
6. Southern Texas below San Antonio.
7. The St. Lawrence River region of upstate New York.
8. The northwestern half of North Carolina.
9. Florida north of Orlando.
10. The area between Ft. Meyer and Ft. Lauderdale, Florida, north of the Everglades.

Survival Guns

Mel Tappan

If you are serious about being prepared to withstand the long-term consequences of a major disaster such as a monetary collapse or nuclear war, and if you prefer a reasonably comfortable postholocaust life-style to squatting in a cave with the remnants of your backpack decaying around you, then you will have to do some hard, unemotional, and fairly extensive planning. In particular, you may have to change your mind about the kind and quantity of firearms that you should assemble to provide food and protection for yourself and those you care for.

Perhaps the most common error made by would-be survivalists grows out of what I call the "backpack mentality." This rather dramatic—if simplistic—approach to survival preparedness consists of putting together a kit of bare basics that could be carried with you as you bolt for the countryside once the disaster has struck or is clearly imminent. That sort of thing may be adequate for dealing with the circumstances growing out of an isolated natural disaster, such as a flood or an earthquake, or to contend with a brief sojourn in the wilderness, but it cannot be regarded as a

Three recommended survival guns: Heckler and Koch 91 heavy assault rifle (top); Remington 870 "Brushmaster" 12-gauge shotgun (middle); Armalite AR-180 light assault rifle (bottom).

Photos by Dr. Bruce D. Clayton

serious response to the problems posed by a catastrophe of the proportions we are considering here.

For one thing, it leads to the "versatility syndrome"—a belief that the more different things a piece of equipment can do, the more nearly perfect it is for survival use. Unfortunately, such thinking demands excessive compromise and choosing items that do not do anything really well. For example, a plethora of so-called "survival knives" are currently on the market. These gadgets usually sport hollow handles to contain emergency supplies but have blades too large for cleaning fish and small game, too straight for gutting or skinning a deer, and too small for chopping firewood or saplings for shelter. These monstrosities are customarily provided with awkward double guards or quillions, valuable only on fighting knives, and the hollow handles so weaken the structural integrity of the knives that they are virtually useless for anything other than starting colorful conversations.

Curiously, this cult of versatility flourishes nowhere more tenaciously than in the area of survival weaponry. Beginning survivalists are prone to confine their selection of survival guns to their individual perceptions of the single, most easily portable firearm that will "do it all." The most common choices that emerge are:

(1) A .22 rifle, because it can be light, accurate, easy to shoot, and the ammunition is relatively cheap and compact. Advocates of this position also assert that a properly placed .22 will kill anything, and they consequently conclude that this is the "ideal" survival arm.

(2) A second—and only slightly less numerous—group prefers the .357 magnum revolver, pointing out the popularity of its ammunition and the broad variety of loads available in both the .357 and .38 special, ranging from hot jacketed soft points to bird shot. Easy portability is again cited as a significant factor, and many consider the .357 optimal for self-defense. The handgun's limited range is usually discounted with the advice that a closer stalk will compensate. Its adherents consider the .357 to be powerful enough to take any game on the North American continent.

(3) Knowledgeable woodsmen frequently limit their choices to a sporting rifle—either bolt action or semiautomatic—in the .30-06 class, usually scoped. Although both guns and ammunition are heavier and bulkier than the previously mentioned alternatives, advocates assert that a .270, .30-06, or .308 will put more meat on the table per ounce of cartridge expended than anything else. The popularity and consequent easy availability of ammunition is also frequently advanced as a priority.

(4) Finally, a few hard cases hold out for black powder arms, observing that one can brew the necessary propellant from charcoal, sulphur, and saltpeter using pebbles, nails, or virtually anything else that comes to hand as projectiles.

These recommendations are so common and they are usually issued with such fervor that some consideration of their merits seems warranted.

One can hardly deny the value of the ubiquitous .22 rimfire in survival planning, but it is only part of the answer. Although a properly placed long rifle bullet will indeed kill any animal that lives, it will not do so reliably or even most of the time, under difficult circumstances. If you are hungry and the only deer you see for a month is running away from you or is outside the .22's quite limited range, that could be important. Further, even though the round is a notorious killer of men, it lacks the ability to stop an attacker before he can harm you unless the brain or solar plexus is hit. In accurate guns, the .22 is a reasonable choice for bringing small game to bag and eliminating close range pests. It is emphatically inadequate for personal defense or hunting animals larger than foxes. The question is not whether the rimfire can be made to perform extraordinary feats under exceptional circumstances, but whether it can be counted on to deliver on demand often enough to keep you alive in a hostile post-holocaust environment. I think not.

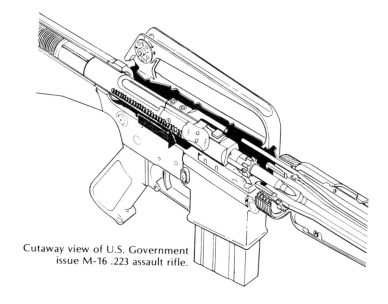

Cutaway view of U.S. Government
issue M-16 .223 assault rifle.

The .357 revolver is a handy tool, having the ability to handle the entire range of .38 special and .357 magnum factory and handloads. I use mine frequently around the ranch, firing thousands of rounds annually through several models, but it would not be my first or even second choice as a survival gun. In fact, it would not even qualify as my first or second choice as a survival *hand*gun.

One of the major problems here is durability. The .357 is a marginal cartridge for either self-defense or deer-sized game when fired from a handgun. It only begins to approach adequate performance in either area when maximum loads with heavy bullets are used, generating pressures in the range of 40,000 C.U.P. Now all revolvers are relatively delicate, finely fitted instruments, and such high pressures greatly hasten the deterioration of their function. Cylinders begin to chatter and the chambers no longer align perfectly with the bore; bolt stops and cylinder hands no longer function precisely; recoil plates set back or become battered; firing pin holes enlarge or burr; and the like. The repairs that most of these ailments occasion require a high level of skill and extremely specialized tools. Unlike a well-designed autopistol, you cannot merely drive out a couple of pins, strip the piece, drop in a spare part, and expect the arm to function. In addition, if you practice double action shooting extensively, as you must if you anticipate using a revolver for defense, wear will be further accelerated and you may soon find your revolver beginning to skip chambers. Finally, if a squib load ever drives a bullet part way into the barrel either during practice or a social confrontation and your firing cadence is fast enough to do you any good, you probably cannot cease fire before touching off another round into your plugged barrel. At best, your gun will probably be destroyed; at worst, the top strap may permanently connect your eyebrows.

An accurate, reliable scoped bolt action sporter in .308 or .30-06 caliber is the most difficult recommendation to criticize as a one-gun survival battery, except on the grounds of self-defense—and even there it may have its place. That place, however, is strictly limited to very long ranges, very few adversaries, or, preferably, both. If you are attacked by several opponents from a distance of say 150 yards or closer, a bolt action rifle is simply not a suitable weapon of defense. The magazine capacity is too limited, and reloading is too slow and clumsy. Nevertheless, these shortcomings could probably be remedied in some rifles by having them altered to accept detachable twenty-round military magazines. Scopes, which get in the way during close combat, could be attached by means of either the Jaeger or Pachmayr mounts so that they could be quickly removed and subsequently replaced without changing zero. The fact remains, however, that the turnbolt design is painfully slow. Even a master rifleman would have trouble firing well-aimed shots with a cadence much faster than one per second, and such things matter acutely when your life is in the balance.

Autoloading sporters in the same power class can be more easily dismissed. None is designed to withstand sustained, rapid fire, and most will change point of impact enough to miss a man-sized target completely at 150 yards after no more than half a dozen or so quick shots. None of the gun manufacturers makes large capacity magazines for these rifles; the aftermarket attempts to provide them customarily result in crude, welded junk; and none of these arms can, to my knowledge, be practically adapted to use military magazines. Finally, if larger game is scarce and you are forced to garner birds and other bite-sized animals for table fare, it is a handloader's nightmare to work up reduced loads for these guns that will not disintegrate the target yet will possess sufficient accuracy for the task while still shooting near enough to the rifle's normal zero that hits can be relied on at close range.

The black powder argument may arouse a dormant pioneer spirit, but it hardly offers a practical solution to the survival dilemma. Advocates of this position seem to forget that *any* centerfire cartridge, rifle, pistol, or shotgun can be reloaded with black powder if nothing better is available. Making the stuff is extremely hazardous even if you know what you are doing, and the kitchen table variety is highly unreliable, lacking the granular uniformity and moisture resistance of the commercial product. Unlike smokeless powder, it is dangerous to store in quantity since it is both unstable and capable of exploding even when unconfined. It would certainly do no harm to keep a flintlock smoothbore around, but acquiring one would be low on my list of priorities.

Now there is really nothing inherently wrong with any of these items in their proper place. In fact, each deserves consideration as a part of a comprehensive survival battery, but no one of them alone is likely to prove adequate to the challenges posed by the survival equation.

All of these selections and many others like them, ranging from crossbows to shotguns, appear to stem from three basic assumptions about the kind of circumstances one is likely to encounter in the aftermath of a preeminent disaster:

(1) Minimal equipment and ease of portability are paramount because one will be constantly on the move, living off the land in some sort of wilderness environment or at least fleeing from one's customary residence and taking refuge in an isolated vacation cabin.

(2) The primary need for arms will be providing wild game for food.

(3) Defense requirements will be casual. One presumes that few other refugees from the disaster will be encountered and that those few will be harmless, unarmed, disorganized, or easily discouraged by any display of armed force, however modest.

These assumptions, individually and collectively, are, I believe, patently naive. The effects of such events as nuclear war or a socioeconomic collapse are both pervasive and long-lasting. No one in the society is apt to be completely untouched by them, and both the social order and its technology are likely to be so disrupted that rebuilding them could easily require a generation or more. The notion of being able to live self-sufficiently as a nomad for such an extended period with no more equipment or supplies than one could carry is unrealistic. Some sort of previously established, well-stocked refuge is called for. Just getting by completely on your own when you are conditioned to having other people provide the

lion's share of what you need to stay alive—food, water, fuel, shelter, clothing, protection, and even entertainment—will be sufficiently trying even with extensive preparations.

A common fantasy exists among inexperienced survivalists that game is both abundant and easy to garner wherever busses do not run and sidewalks do not grow. Those who know better frequently believe that their superior prowess as hunters will make them consistently successful in competing for whatever wild food the country may offer. Both may conclude that hunting will provide all the food they need and that hunting guns should be their sole or most essential arms requirement.

The truth is that game is scarce enough now that most knowledgeable hunters would not care to rely on being able to harvest enough to serve as their primary, long-term food supply. When tens of thousands of frightened, inexperienced city dwellers take to the woods in desperation, the "wilderness" will come to resemble a Palestinian refugee camp, and whatever animals are not slaughtered in the first few days or burned out in the inevitable conflagration that must occur when a few campfires get out of hand, will be very hard to discover. If you do not stock your larder with storable food and plan to grow more, your preparations are inadequate. Foraging to supplement your basic food supply is one thing; relying solely on provender from the wilds is quite another.

Finally, we must consider the degree to which the requirements of personal defense should influence the selection of survival guns. We live in a society where nothing more serious than an overnight power failure can provoke looting and virtually unrestrained violence in our cities. Imagine the implications of nuclear war or monetary collapse—circumstances in which there would be not only a power disruption but also no safe city water, no food in the markets, no fuel at the pumps, little or no means of communication, no police or fire services, no organized medical aid, no sanitation or disease control, and hordes of angry, undisciplined, frightened, violence-prone people in the streets,

Figure 1—Low group. Lines indicate direction for rear sight adjustment

Figure 2 — Correct peep sight. Alignment showing top of front sight at center line and just touching bottom of bull's-eye

Figure 3—Sighted in. Result after sight adjustment indicated on Figure 1

179

Typical assault rifle accessories: A — Variable power scope; B — Quick sighting short scope; C — Brass catcher; D — Bipod; E — rounds; F — Stripper clip and guides; G — Loaded strippers; H — Stripper clip and guide loading magazine; I—Magazine Spacer; J — Assorted magazines; K — Bayonet.

Photo by Dr. Bruce D. Clayton

looting, burning, and attempting to vent their anxiety and hostility on one another. Within days, even the decent people who were unprepared would become a threat in their desperation to feed their families. Soon the survivors would begin to disperse throughout the surrounding countryside in search of food, essential supplies, and plunder. Sporting goods stores, police stations, National Guard Armories, and even some military bases would probably be looted for weapons, and the best of these would be formidable indeed. The more ruthless would doubtless coalesce around strong leaders, realizing that their risks would be lessened and their chances of success increased if they traveled and attacked together.

If you elect to face that prospect armed only with a .22, a .357 revolver, a hunting rifle, or a black powder musket, it is certainly your prerogative to do so, but there are superior alternatives.

Because of the several and not entirely compatible ways in which firearms can serve the survivalist, I have divided my recommendations into two distinct categories: (1) defensive weapons and

(2) working guns. The former have but a single criterion—providing the most efficient possible protection against armed violence—while the latter include the means for securing a wide variety of game for food, eliminating disease-carrying or crop-destroying pests, and providing protection from dangerous animals.

Defense Weapons

Defense weapons need neither the extreme power nor the target grade accuracy that may be occasionally demanded of working guns. They must be functionally reliable in the extreme, however, under the most adverse conditions, capable of both rapid and sustained fire, resistant to abuse, easy to maintain, quick to bring into action, able to stop an opponent instantly with a single torso hit, durable, and easy to strip and repair. Tactically, at least two, preferably three, and optimally four different kinds of arms are required:

(1) A .30 caliber (.308 or .30-06) battle rifle or assault

rifle capable of semiautomatic operation and quick, fumble-free reloading. The .308 (7.62 NATO) is the best choice here, not only because its shorter case and thicker extraction rim suit it well for autoloading actions, but also because it is the standard NATO round and one of the two current U.S. military cartridges. The .30-06 is somewhat more popular commercially and is potentially more flexible for sporting uses, but it is no longer issued by the military and the only reasonably available fighting rifle chambered for it is the Garand, which has some shortcomings for our purposes. It is comparatively awkward and heavy, its capacity is only eight rounds, and it is loaded by means of *en bloc* clips instead of detachable box magazines. Some rather exacting gunsmithing by a well-equipped armorer who knows what he is about can lighten the Garand, shorten the barrel to twenty inches, and adapt it to accept twenty-round M-14 magazines. It also can easily be rechambered to .308 by means of a Navy sleeve. The process is not inexpensive, however, and neither are sound Garands in today's marketplace.

The Springfield Armory M1-A is another possibility, and the early examples of this semiautomatic only commercial copy of the military M-14 were quite good. Recently, however, the G.I. parts previously used in its manufacture have been replaced by investment cast substitutes, and neither functioning nor durability seems enhanced by the change. I have seen several bolts that have failed, and I have reports of several others. Aside from these quality control problems, the major drawback with the M1-A in survival use is the fact that it is designed to function properly only within the narrow and quite mild pressure range of U.S. military ball—a limitation wisely pointed out in the operating manual. The use of ordinary commercial sporting ammunition in the M1-A voids the rifle's warranty.

A Beretta-made BM-59 is one of the finest defensive rifles ever produced, but finding one is a problem. The marketplace abounds with ersatz imitations, some poorly assembled in this country from genuine Beretta parts, some made up from welded Garand receivers and M-14 parts, some with cast receivers, and none with the quality and reliability of the Italian-built product. The genuine article is scarce and expensive, but in my judgment nothing better for the purpose exists.

In terms of price and availability, the Heckler & Koch 91 is currently my first choice. The models

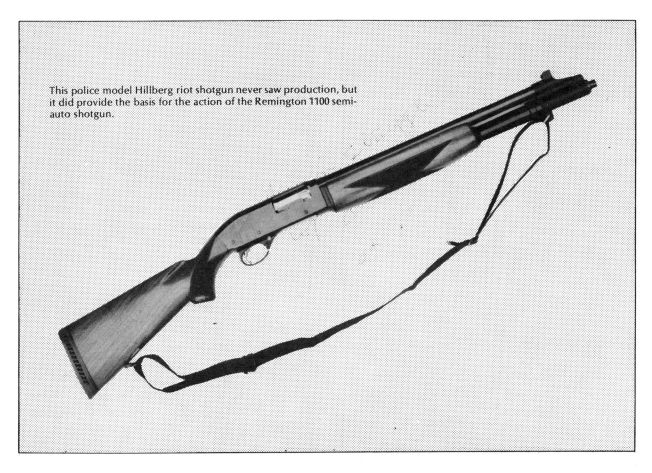

This police model Hillberg riot shotgun never saw production, but it did provide the basis for the action of the Remington 1100 semiauto shotgun.

equipped with the rifled—not polygonal—barrels are also the most nearly trouble-free and reliable firearms I have ever tested. Both the sights and the trigger could stand improvement; the guns are hard on brass, and they are ugly. But they work every time and under adverse conditions that would stop any of their competitors. Further, most of them shoot as accurately as match rifles, they digest military, commercial, and handloads with equal aplomb, they are easy to repair in the field, and a wide range of useful accessories is available for them, including bipods, collapsible stocks, special purpose magazines, and quick detachable scope mounts.

A good .223 (5.56mm) carbine such as the AR-180 or the Ruger Mini-14 would be a useful adjunct to the defense battery, but it should not be regarded as an acceptable substitute for the .30 caliber weapons listed above. It has neither the range, stopping power, nor the ability to penetrate chance barriers that either the .308 or .30-06 has. Its lack of recoil suits it well for the very young, the elderly, or people of exceptionally small stature—and it *is* our issue military round.

(2) Next to the fighting rifle, the most necessary weapon for the survivalist is the defensive pistol. It is not ordinarily considered a weapon of choice, but of convenience. It serves no combat function as well as a shotgun or a rifle can (except in tightly confined quarters such as a car); its purpose is simply to *be there* when you need it. The simple convenience of wearing a holstered pistol tends to insure that it will be at hand even when shoulder weapons are not. If anything, the limitations of the pistol's tactical role make its selection extremely critical. The sidearm is an *in extremis* weapon—it must not fail.

At this writing, the only pistol I can recommend for this purpose without reservation is one of the Colt .45 autopistols based on the Browning 1911 design: the MK IV Government Model, the current Gold Cup, the lightweight Commander, or the combat Commander—all will serve, with suitable modifications.

Space does not permit a detailed argument for this recommendation, but a few telling points can be outlined briefly. Revolvers as a breed are more delicate than the best autopistols, and they are somewhat less likely to function under adverse conditions. This fact is particularly evident when they cannot be maintained in a peak condition of tune by a skilled gunsmith. Cylinder cranes spring and misalignment frequently occurs if you drop them, and ordinary wear tends to make them unreliable in combat. A small kit of spare parts and no tools except a screwdriver and a drift punch will keep a 1911 pistol going indefinitely. Further, revolvers are not well suited to sustained fire. They can be reloaded almost as swiftly with speedloaders as an auto can be with spare magazines, but not as reliably. Also, a few grains of unburned powder under the ejection star of a revolver is all that is needed to put it out of service. Finally, imperfect ammunition is a hazard for either gun, but the most common problems—no powder or a jumped crimp—affect the revolver more severely.

Pistol stopping power has elicited reams of copy, but for our purposes it should suffice to observe that the .45 ACP, although mild enough to be completely controllable in sustained rapid fire, even by trained youngsters, have proven to be more than 90 percent effective in disabling an opponent with one torso hit, in the real world. Anything less hovers around the 50 percent mark or below. If you need convincing, you might find my book *Survival Guns* helpful.

(3) A good hideout or backup pistol is a great comfort, and possibilities here range from the powerful and excellent (but heavy) Detonics .45 through the better two-inch .38s such as the S&W Bodyguard down to the superb, but hard to come by, .22 Walther TPH. The best guideline here is to choose the most powerful weapon that will give you the degree of concealment you need. Do not compromise quality even if you must compromise power or size.

(4) Nothing will offer the same degree of intimidation value, ease of hitting, and near certain stopping power at ranges under forty yards as a twelve-gauge shotgun. Although I would prefer an autoloader, I have found none that equals the reliability and durability of the Remington 870 pump, so that is my current recommendation. Outfitted with a twenty-inch slug barrel mounting rifle sights, fitted with the eight-shot magazine extension and folding stock from Choate Machine Tool Company in Bald Knob, Arkansas, and loaded with #4 buckshot, such an arm would be my choice for night actions or daylight last-ditch defense.

Working Guns

If your budget cannot be rearranged to permit acquiring a comprehensive battery, buy only the defense weapons, since they can be used—albeit somewhat less efficiently—for hunting; the reverse is not true. Next, add at least one quality .22 rifle such as the Ruger 10/22 or the Marlin 39A. Then proceed to acquire the best bolt action sporter and scope you can possibly afford. Unless giant moose graze on your lawn, or grizzlies or polar bears pose

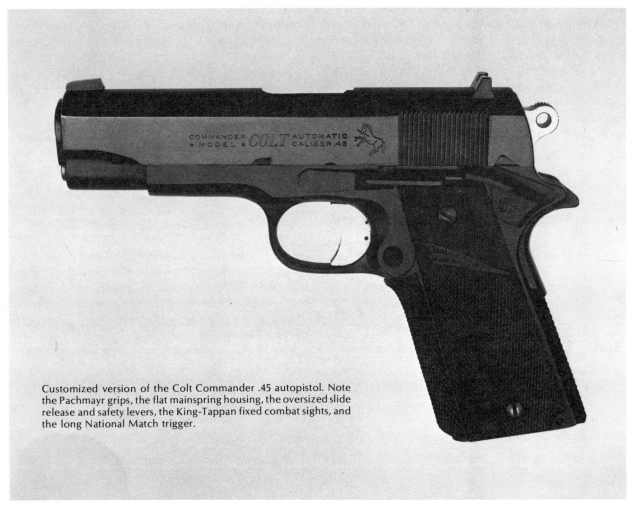

Customized version of the Colt Commander .45 autopistol. Note the Pachmayr grips, the flat mainspring housing, the oversized slide release and safety levers, the King-Tappan fixed combat sights, and the long National Match trigger.

Photo by Dr. Bruce D. Clayton

a daily hazard, the caliber of your hunting rifle should match that of your defense rifle—either .308 or .30-06. If you really need more gun, the .375 H&H magnum would be your best choice, based on ammunition availability, performance, and its ability to handle a wide range of loads—including cast bullets—exceptionally well. The Ruger M-77 and the Interarms Mark X Mauser are the least expensive rifles I can recommend for this service, and the Sako is among the very best.

The addition of a vent ribbed barrel with a variable choke attached will allow your 870 shotgun to serve as both a defense and a working gun. Overall barrel length should be between twenty-two and twenty-six inches. I would suggest stocking high base (not magnum) #6 shot for all hunting purposes.

A working handgun will prove to be a valuable asset for almost any survivalist, and it may be a necessity for some. If you do not hand load (a serious shortcoming when planning for self-sufficiency), I would recommend either the S&W model 25-5 or the Ruger single-action chambered for the

.45 Colt (often referred to incorrectly as the .45 *Long* Colt). Reloaders would be better served by the .44 magnum. You will seldom (if ever) need maximum loads in either caliber since the large, heavy bullets perform well on game the size of deer and black bear when loaded to velocities of only 900–1000 FPS. Such rounds destroy less meat than high-velocity, expanding bullets do, and the lower pressures (around 25-30,000 C.U.P.) greatly increase a revolver's useful life. Effective shot loads at close range are also a possibility, and you can always load the last couple of chambers with maximum performance ammunition should you ever need to stop an obstreperous bull or bear.

These, then, are the basics of a balanced survival battery, although a number of other arms would be quite useful to own. A good little catch-as-catch-can foraging gun such as the Savage 24C combination .22 rifle/twenty-gauge shotgun is almost a necessity. A precision spring piston air rifle such as the Feinwerkbau 124 can keep your larder filled with small game silently and inexpensively, but a few boxes of CCI long .22 CB caps (totally silent from a twenty-two-inch or longer barrel) will serve. In the long run, a quality .22 pistol such as the S&W Kit gun, the Walther PP or PPK, the S&W 41, or the Ruger target models will earn their keep, and a good crossbow such as the Barnett Wildcat is worth its cost. Guns and ammunition will doubtless be among the most sought after trade goods in a post-holocaust world and, for that reason alone, one could hardly have too many.

For most of us, however, the problem is more likely to be not having enough. Do not allow a casual attitude toward survival guns to place you in that perilous category. If financial considerations force you to scrimp on your survival preparations, do it in a less crucial area. You can make do with a poor food storage program if you can supplement it by hunting. You can improvise repairs and construction if you lack the proper tools and materials. You can use electricians tape or rubber bands to hold a bandage in place if you run out of adhesive plaster in your medical kit. You can even skin and butcher a deer with your axe if you must. But defending your life against a determined attack is usually sudden, critical, and competitive. Only the very best tools for that specialized task and the skill to use them can offer the realistic prospect of survival.

PARROTT 10-POUNDER RIFLE (1864).

Mel Tappan is a survival consultant, free-lance writer, lecturer, and survival editor of Guns & Ammo magazine. He devotes full time to evaluating firearms, outdoor and survival equipment, storable food, and communications devices. A native of Texas, Mel Tappan presently lives in Oregon with his wife Nancy. Inquiries regarding consultation by telephone or in person may be directed to him at P.O. Box 598, Rogue River, OR 97537.